THE NEW BUSINESS OF FOOTBALL

The New Business of Football

Accountability and Finance in Football

Stephen Morrow
Heriot-Watt University, Edinburgh

Published by PALGRAVE MACMILLAN
Houndmills, Basingstoke, Hampshire RG21 6XS and
175 Fifth Avenue, New York, N.Y. 10010
Companies and representatives throughout the world

PALGRAVE MACMILLAN is the global academic imprint of the Palgrave
Macmillan division of St. Martin's Press, LLC and of Palgrave Macmillan Ltd.
Macmillan® is a registered trademark in the United States, United Kingdom
and other countries. Palgrave is a registered trademark in the European
Union and other countries.

ISBN 0–333–72308–2

This book is printed on paper suitable for recycling and
made from fully managed and sustained forest sources.

A catalogue record for this book is available from the British Library.

Transferred to digital printing 2002

Printed and bound in Great Britain by
Antony Rowe Ltd, Chippenham and Eastbourne

For Caitlin

Contents

List of Tables and Figures

Tables

Figures

Preface and Acknowledgements

This book is an academic study into *the new business of football*. It is aimed at those who have a background, a knowledge and an interest in Association Football, as well as in business, particularly in the areas of accountancy and finance. It draws on contemporary literature on professional football in the disciplines of accounting, finance and economics and, to a lesser extent, sociology. It will be relevant to anyone who seeks a more rigorous discussion of the issues arising from the business than that which newspapers and other popular media have space for. It is also hoped that the book will interest those who have the responsibility of running today's football clubs, dealing with conflicts which arise out of the incorporation of football and wrestling with the new financial regime in the game.

Thanks are due to all those who have assisted me in writing this book and in my earlier research into accounting issues in football, in particular to those representatives of clubs, banks and fund managers who have willingly met with me on various occasions. My thanks to those clubs in England and Scotland which provided me with copies of their annual reports and provided information requested; to Gerry Boon of Deloitte & Touche for kindly providing me with a copy of the Deloitte & Touche Annual Reviews of Football Finance since its inception; to the Professional Footballers' Association, the Scottish Professional Footballers' Association, the Football Association Premier League, the Scottish Football Association, the Scottish League and UEFA for responding to my requests for information requested and also to those European clubs (Juventus, Ajax, PSV Eindhoven, Strasbourg, Borussia Dortmund, Karlsruher, TSV Munchen, FC Shalke 04, VBV De Graafschap, VfB Stuttgart, Werder Bremen) and to Edwin Gerretson of the KNVB (Dutch FA) for responding to my letters and for sending me information about their respective clubs or associations. Unfortunately the poor response from other European clubs and administrators made it impossible to widen the scope of the book to comment meaningfully on issues relating to the business of football in other European countries.

The book draws on published literature in a number of areas and I am indebted to all those authors referred to in the text. On the subject of literature, thanks are also due to David Rennie for some valuable literature searching carried out in the course of writing his own undergraduate dissertation.

A very special debt is owed to my colleague, Frank McMahon, for taking the time and trouble to read over my earlier drafts, and for providing me with many insightful comments and suggestions. The judgements, mistakes and gaps that remain are, of course, entirely my own.

Finally, much thanks is owed to my wife Jill for her love and support throughout the research and the writing of this book.

STEPHEN MORROW

The author and publishers are grateful to the following companies and organisations for permission to reproduce copyright material:

Extracts from Annual Reviews of Football Finance, Surveys of Football Club Accounts and the report *England's Premier Clubs* are reproduced with the kind permission of Deloitte & Touche, Manchester.

Information on share price returns, trading volume, daily number of trades, average bid and ask prices and return on share price indices is reproduced with the kind permission of Datastream/ICV.

Table 1.1 adapted from Baimbridge, M., Cameron, S. and Dawson, P. (1996), 'Satellite Television and the Demand for Football: A Whole New Ball Game?', *Scottish Journal of Political Economy*. Copyright © Scottish Economic Society.

Extract from Section D, Broadcasting and Finance, Rules of the Football Association Premier League, from the *FA Premier League Handbook 1997–98*, © The FA Premier League Limited 1997.

Table 1.2 © The FA Premier League Limited 1997.

Table 1.4, Figure 2.1 and Table 4.6, 'Stadium Capacities', reproduced with kind permission of Headline Book Publishing Ltd.

Part XIII. Financial Provisions. Article 18, Paragraph 9 of the Regulations of the UEFA Champions League 1998/99, is reproduced with the kind permission of UEFA.

Table 3.1 'Financial Statistics', Office for National Statistics, © Crown Copyright 1998.

Table 3.5 reproduced with kind permission of the London Stock Exchange.

Table 5.1, 'The Traditional Club', reproduced with permission of Barmarick Publications, 'Companies', reproduced with permission of the Accounting Standards Board.

Figure 5.1 adapted from *Tomorrow's Company: The Role of Business in a Changing World*, The Royal Society for the Encouragement of Arts, Manufactures and Commerce, 1995. Reproduced with kind permission of the Royal Society for the Encouragement of Arts, Manufactures and Commerce.

Appendix 2 is reproduced with the kind permission of the Football Association.

Introduction

The Theatre of Dreams

Manchester United celebrated their fourth FA Carling Premiership title in five highly successful years on 11 May 1997. . . .

The success of the team and their attractive style of play throughout the season has further strengthened the popular support for Manchester United and considerably enhanced shareholder value.

(Manchester United plc, Annual Report 1997)

Professional football has existed in the UK for over a century: the Football League was first contested in 1888/89, the Scottish League in 1890/91. Many of the clubs which dominate the game today, clubs like Arsenal, Manchester United, Celtic and Rangers, came into existence in the late 1800s. In the last century football on the field has undergone changes. Basically, however, it remains the same game. Off the field, the picture is very different. Other than bearing the same name and often occupying the same piece of land, there is probably little of today's club that its early supporters or owners would recognise. Perhaps that is hardly surprising. What is surprising, however, is the extent to which much of the change in football off the field has been concentrated in the last decade or less.

It is not easy to escape the changes: Super Leagues like the FA Premier League, The Taylor Report and all-seated stadiums, large scale corporate hospitality and executive boxes, satellite television, football clubs as brands, the rise of merchandising, clubs raising capital and listing on the Stock Exchange, investment trusts dedicated to football, hostile takeovers, football in the court room, the globalisation of the player market, huge financial rewards available for players and directors and so on. Most recent of all is the prospect of the UK's leading club being owned by the company which currently dominates television coverage of football in the UK. Taken together these off field changes have resulted in what can be called *the new business of football*.

Changes in the game are also reflected in changes in its reporting. No longer is football restricted to the back pages of newspapers. *The Financial Times* now has a weekly sports page and journalists specialising in coverage of financial issues in sport. Monthly publications such as *Soccer Analyst* and *Soccer Investor* (both established in 1997) have appeared. *Soccer Analyst* deals with long-term issues affecting football worldwide and carries in-depth articles by experts, academics and professionals in the field, while *Soccer Investor* provides coverage of financial and commercial issues in the football sector. Multinational firms of accountants such as Deloitte & Touche produce regular and extensive surveys and reports on the football industry. Even football magazines such as *Total Football* have a Football Finance page.

This book is offered as a contribution to the background and understanding of *the new business of football*. One vital aspect of this understanding relates to the relationship between football and its coverage. The publicity and comment received by football as a business primarily arises not out of its significance as business, but rather out of football's wider social and historical importance. Football may now be a *new business*, but it is not big business. Profits, turnover and market capitalisation at most clubs are insignificant in comparison to companies in most other business sectors reported by the financial press. More importantly while football is a business it is not *just* a business. As a result any analysis of the football industry which discusses it as just another business will wholly fail to capture the complexity of football. If football was just any old business then the type and extent of coverage it receives would be greatly diminished. Its importance and the extent of its coverage come from the fact that football cannot be reduced simply to economics. Football is the people's game. It has an extraordinary popularity worldwide: large numbers of people attend live matches and play football, larger numbers still are television supporters. People care about and are passionate about football: supporters identify with football clubs, communities identify with football clubs. These factors taken together make any study into the business aspects of football comprehensively fascinating.

The book seeks to advance an understanding of *the new business of football* from a wider academic perspective, but continuing to recognise what distinguishes football from other businesses. It looks at business aspects of football: its income and cost drivers, its capital structure, its accounting policies. It also considers in detail issues of accountability in clubs. In particular, it focuses on conflicts arising out of the incorporation of football and the dichotomy between sport and business, suggesting a contemporary framework for accountability and business behaviour which may help to minimise the extent of these conflicts in the future.

The book considers both England and Scotland. While some aspects of the development of *the new business of football* are more advanced in

England – for example, the creation of the FA Premier League and the central role played by satellite television – a similar pattern of change is emerging in Scotland with a new breakaway Premier League in place for the start of the 1998/99 season accompanied by a lucrative television deal. Although smaller in scale in a business sense, the wider social and political factors which surround football are if anything stronger in Scotland than in England. Indeed, it has been suggested that football is the means by which Scotland and Scots assert themselves and play a role in international affairs (Drucker, in Forsyth, 1992).

For the most part the book will concentrate on the top clubs in the FA Premier League and the Scottish Premier Division. Where individual accounting information is being presented on clubs, this information is in respect of the accounting year ending in 1997 and is in respect of the clubs which made up the top divisions in season 1996/97. One aspect of *the new business of football* which will be discussed in detail is the listing of football companies on the Stock Exchange. Various techniques have been used to list clubs on the market, some of which have resulted in the creation of holding companies with resultant name changes. In Chapter 3, where appropriate, the full name of the company will be provided. Elsewhere for convenience the company will often be referred to by its more familiar club name. A listing of both names is provided in Appendix 1.

1 The New Economics of Football

TELEVISION – FOOTBALL'S ECONOMIC DRIVER

There can be little argument that television, or more especially satellite television, has been the most important contributory factor in the new business era of football. Clubs have benefited directly through much improved television deals. In addition broadcasters have acted as catalysts for change in the structure of the game in both England and in Scotland.

In England commercial television contracts are negotiated on behalf of the Premier League clubs by the FA Premier League. The present four year deal, which runs until the year 2001, is worth £743m to the League over four years; £670m from British Sky Broadcasting (BSkyB) allowing them to broadcast 60 live matches per season, plus £73m from the BBC for the recorded highlight rights. Table 1.1 demonstrates that this compares favourably with previous deals.

The increased importance of television income as a source of football finance is illustrated by the fact that the first deal which provided for televised football in 1965 involved the BBC paying the sum of only £5000 for the right to show televised highlights. Although the extraordinary rise in the size of television deals is partly explained by the increased popularity of football, an equally significant factor is developments in the broadcasting industry (Kuyper, 1997). Until the advent of satellite television, the rights to televise football were shared between the BBC and ITV. The two broadcasters co-operated in their negotiation with the League thus ensuring that the sum offered was only sufficient to make the rights worth selling. The entry of British Satellite Broadcasting (BSB) into the equation in 1988 resulted in a genuine competitive bidding process. The introduction of other pay TV operators in the most recent negotiation resulted in the most competitive bidding process yet, and consequently the largest deal for clubs. Football has benefited from a fundamental reversal in the economics of broadcasting markets (Cowie and Williams, 1997). While in the past programme content had to compete for scarce transmission outlets (i.e. television channels), now large numbers of channels

Table 1.1   Broadcasting history of live televised football 1983–2001

Contract start date	Length of contract	Broadcaster	Live matches per season	Annual rights fee (£m)	£m per live match
1983	2 years	BBC/ITV	10	2.6	0.26
1985	6 months	BBC/ITV	6	1.3	0.22
1986	2 years	BBC/ITV	14	3.1	0.22
1988	4 years	ITV	18	11.0	0.61
1992	5 years	BSkyB	60	42.8	0.71
1997	4 years	BSkyB	60	167.5	2.79

Source: Adapted from Baimbridge et al. (1996), FA Premier League Annual
Report & Accounts 1996/97

compete for (relatively) scarce content. One consequence of this is that economic rents shift from the owners of television channels to the owners of the content, with television companies willing to pay more to the football authorities for the right to broadcast football in this country.

The arrangements for the distribution of television income to clubs in the English Premier League under the present contract are set out in Section D, Rule 8.1 of the Rules of the Football Association Premier League (FAPL, 1997) as follows:

- 50 per cent to be divided equally among the Premier clubs (with an amount equal to half of each Premier League club's share to be paid to clubs relegated in either of the last two seasons).
- 25 per cent to be divided on merit, based on positions in the League table at the end of the relevant season. (In the 1997/98 season the team finishing bottom will receive £159 524 whereas the team finishing top will receive £3 190 480.)
- 25 per cent to be allocated as facility fees to clubs whose matches are broadcast, split between the home and the away club. (In the 1997/98 season a club will receive £247 953 per live televised match. Each team is guaranteed at least three live games.)

Total payments to clubs by the FA Premier League for the season 1996/97 totalled £88.8m, compared to £41.3m for the previous season. This amount included a payment of £50m in respect of the new contract on the basis that it was broadcasting income for the

The New Business of Football

Table 1.2   FA Premier League television payments
1996/97

Position	Club	Television payments (£m)
1	Manchester United	6.3
2	Liverpool	5.8
3	Arsenal	5.7
4	Newcastle United	5.6
...		
18	Coventry City	3.1
19	Sunderland	3.0
20	Nottingham Forest	2.8

Source: FA Premier League Annual Report &
Accounts 1996/97

1996/97 season. Unsurprisingly the top earners were Manchester United who received £6.3m. Table 1.2 sets out the highest and lowest earners.

The deal also provides for so called 'parachute payments' to be made to relegated clubs. Any club which is relegated from the Premier League is entitled to an amount equal to half of the full share of a Premier Division club for two seasons following its relegation in respect of UK and overseas broadcasting monies.[1] For season 1996/97 relegated clubs received a payment of £965 225 each. Under the terms of the new deal the basic award for the 1997/98 season is worth £2.97m per club compared to £1.93m in season 1996/97.

The importance of these payments to clubs can be illustrated by comparing them to clubs' turnover. For season 1996/97 television payments made by the FA Premier League to its 20 clubs was £83.0m, a figure which represents 18.2 per cent of those clubs' turnover. Further television and radio payments are also received by clubs which participate in European competitions and for radio broadcasts. The significance of these payments depends on the club and its involvement in European competition. For example, while approximately half of Manchester United's total income from television of £12.6m in the 1996/97 accounting year came from the FA Premier League deal, at other clubs such as West Ham United the Premier League payment of £3.75m represents practically all of the club's broadcasting turnover

of £3.9m.[2] Blackburn Rovers were the only Premier League club
showing a fall in revenue in 1996/97 of 12 per cent due primarily to
their non involvement in European competitions (Deloitte & Touche,
1998b). Premier League clubs will also benefit from a deal agreed
between the Premier League and the French television group
Canal Plus for the worldwide overseas rights to Premier League
matches. The deal is worth £100m over three years and is expected
to be worth £2m per annum to the top clubs (*Soccer Investor*,
1997a).

In terms of the scale of television income Scotland is markedly
different. Until now Scottish Premier Division clubs' commercial contracts have been negotiated by the Scottish Football Association (SFA)
and the Scottish Football League (SFL). For season 1996/97 the deal
agreed between the SFL and British Sky Broadcasting, the BBC and
Scottish Television totalled only £3.3m. Premier Division teams currently receive 85 per cent of television revenue, with payments being
divided between the home club and away clubs on a 75 per cent/25 per
cent basis for live matches and split evenly between the clubs for
highlights. A separate deal worth £1.3m between the SFA and the
television companies exists for coverage of the Scottish Cup, with payments to clubs being dependent on their progress. Although much
smaller in scale than the English deals, nevertheless the amounts receivable under this deal are a significant improvement on previous
deals. For example, only ten years ago in season 1986/87 the sum
received by the SFL for television rights was only in the region of
£300 000.

However, from the beginning of season 1998/99 the Scottish Premier
Division clubs have voted to break away from the SFL. The breakaway
meant that they were free to negotiate a new television deal in the
summer of 1998 when the existing deal with BSkyB expired. The new
deal, also with BSkyB is worth £45m to the new Scottish Premier
League over four years, a figure substantially higher than previous
deals.[3] The arrangements for the distribution of this income will be
similar to those used in the FA Premier League. The implications of
the breakaway and the role played therein by television are considered
in the following section.

The smaller scale of the Scottish television deal means that the
fees received by Scottish clubs also constitute a much smaller portion
of turnover, compared to their English counterparts. For example,
for the 1996/97 accounting year Celtic's broadcasting and publishing
fees amounted to £2.1m (9.5 per cent of turnover), while television and

radio fees at Aberdeen (one of Scotland's big five clubs) amounted to only £607000 (11 per cent of turnover).

FOOTBALL'S PECULIAR ECONOMICS

The economics literature contains a wealth of studies of professional team sports, especially of baseball in the US and of football in the UK. An excellent starting point when reviewing the UK literature is the monograph by Cairns, Jennet and Sloane (1986) on the Economics of Professional Team Sports published in the *Journal of Economic Studies*. Since this review, numerous papers have been published looking at various aspects of the economics of professional sport. Several of these papers, particularly those looking at aspects of professional football in the UK will be referred to in this chapter and elsewhere in the book.

Professional team sports have been characterised as having peculiar economics (Neale, 1964).[4] The peculiarity centres on the interdependence of the participants, i.e. it has been argued that professional sport organisations are different from other business organisations because the nature of sport means that such organisations must combine together to provide a saleable product. Furthermore, it is argued that the essence of a professional sports league is equal or genuine competition, i.e. that participants in a league require to have sufficient financial backing to allow them to compete with one another on a relatively fair basis. Such competition is important because it leads to uncertainty of outcome, i.e. all other things being equal, spectators prefer closely balanced contests to unevenly balanced contests. It is acceptance of this argument that has encouraged football regulatory bodies to impose various restrictions on competitive behaviour such as transfer systems, redistribution mechanisms and restrictions on cross ownership of clubs, many of which are now being challenged by competition authorities, the courts and the clubs themselves.

The demand for football

One factor which differentiates football from many other forms of entertainment is the fact that every match (or product) is unique and its outcome unpredictable. As such therefore, attendance at any match will be influenced by a variety of factors: the quality of the fixture in terms of the teams involved, the game's significance, the quality of facilities at the stadium and expectations about the outcome of the game and the number of goals scored, which will be dependent on characteristics of the two teams relating to factors such as form, star players and teamwork (Peel and Thomas, 1996). One factor which has traditionally been viewed as a key determinant of attendance demand is uncertainty of outcome.

Uncertainty of outcome can take several forms: uncertainty of outcome in a particular match, in a league over the season, in a league over a number of seasons (Cairns, 1987). In a survey of the extensive literature on estimating the demand by individuals to attend professional team sports in person, Cairns (1990) concluded that while there was no evidence to suggest that spectators value uncertainty of match outcome, there was evidence that they valued uncertainty of seasonal outcome, albeit not uncertainty *per se* but rather the prospect of championship success. Economic analysis of professional sport has drawn heavily upon the notion of uncertainty of outcome, hypothesising that public interest (and thus revenues) will be greater if the results are relatively uncertain (Arnold and Beneviste, 1988).

Influences on demand continues to be one of the most heavily researched areas in the economics of team sports. The majority of papers in this area are concerned with attendances at individual matches for a sample of clubs over a number of seasons. Dobson and Goddard (1992) investigated the demand for standing and seating accommodation in the English Football League. They identified three factors as important determinants of standing attendance: current form and the championship significance of a match (both of which are concerned with uncertainty of outcome) and the geographical distance between the grounds of the two clubs. Of particular importance to attendance in seated accommodation was the club's historical record. Similar results were obtained by Smart and Goddard (1991) in a study of three Scottish League clubs.

Peel and Thomas (1992) in a study of the English Football League found evidence of a U-shaped relationship between attendances and home probability of success: that is that home fans, who make up a large proportion of the attendance at any match, like to see their own team win in a high-scoring game that is not too one-sided. In a study of repeat fixtures within the Scottish League (i.e. each club in Scotland plays the other clubs in its league four times, twice at home and twice away from home), Peel and Thomas (1996) found further evidence of a U-shaped relationship between attendance and home team probability of success with no apparent liking for uncertain outcomes. In this study, perhaps unsurprisingly, they also found that non core attenders were motivated to attend by anticipating a win for their team.

The papers identified above use pooled cross-sectional time series data to isolate the impact on demand of short-term influences such as the current form of the home team and the quality of the opposition. An alternative approach is required for variables such as admission price or final league position that do not change on a weekly basis. Studies of the impact of longer term variables require annual time series data on a season by season basis.

Simmons (1996) analysed the economic determinants of club attendance, finding evidence that for almost all clubs, attendance responds to real ticket prices in the long term, with 'casual' spectators being more price sensitive than season ticket holders. Dobson and Goddard (1996) found that performance, admission prices and goal scoring were short run influences on demand, while performance and the unemployment rate are identified as significant long run determinants of attendance.

It is important to bear in mind that the papers identified in this section deal with time periods in which the economic structure of the game was quite different from that found now. For example, both papers referred to in the previous paragraph use data for periods ending with the 1991/92 season, the last season before the introduction of the FA Premier League. Since then the game has of course undergone changes which are likely to cause different results in studies of the economic determinants of club attendance. For example, one noticeable change has been the movement towards season tickets. Premier League football, coupled in many cases with reduced stadium capacities as a result of redevelopment work and the movement to all seated stadiums has resulted in many clubs having excess demand for tickets for home games and often lengthy season ticket waiting lists.

In financial terms, it is has long been recognised that attendance figures are not an accurate indicator of the financial fortunes of clubs (The Football League, 1983, para. 74). Nevertheless, they remain an important determinant of club revenues as shown in Table 1.3.

Gate receipts, however, lack the growth potential of other income sources, in particular television, both directly, and indirectly through the sponsorship, advertising and merchandising revenues which arise out of increased broadcasting (Cameron, 1997). Deloitte & Touche (1998b) noted that while matchday revenues continued to grow

Table 1.3   Gate receipts and turnover (FA Premier
League)

	Gate receipts (£m)	Gate receipts as a percentage of turnover
1995/96	113.5	32.8%
1994/95	105.0	32.5%
1993/94	83.9	34.7%
1992/93	72.8	34.6%

Source: Deloitte & Touche (1997, 1996), Touche
Ross (1995)

for Premier League clubs in 1996/97, they grew at a much slower rate
(21 per cent) than television income (123 per cent). Consequently
matchday income as a percentage of total income dropped from
47.4 per cent in 1995/96 to 43.4 per cent in 1996/97.

Television and the supply of football

It is not difficult to understand why a sport which has relied on
attendance as its primary income source should have been nervous
about television (Rowe, 1996). The extent to which a relationship exists
between television coverage of football and gate receipts has been
the subject of much comment. Since the advent of televised football the
football regulatory authorities have held the view that too much
television (in particular live broadcasts of matches) represented
a threat for football attendances.[5] Williams (1994) notes that even
in the mid-1980s, the FA was routinely refusing permission for
terrestrial television to carry live television coverage of major foreign
matches, while a similar attitude was being adopted by the SFA,
particularly with regard to coverage of English football (Boyle and
Haynes, 1996).

The associations were assisted in this by Article 14 of UEFA's
statute on televised football, which stated that a football association
in one UEFA country would authorise the broadcast into another
UEFA country only if the association of the 'receiving' country did not
object to the transmission. The introduction of satellite television,
however, made it impossible to enforce Article 14. BSkyB's transmitting signal to the UK emanates from one source, in contrast

to the regional transmission systems used by both the BBC and the ITV network. As a result it became impossible, for example, to exclude Scottish audiences from English Premier League football. The protectionist stance adopted by bodies like the SFA was further weakened when UEFA took the decision to relax its statute on cross border television before the start of the 1994/95 season. The new article (now Article 44 of the UEFA statutes) was designed in order to provide some possibility for the scheduling of matches at times when they will not be interrupted by contemporaneous transmission of televised football, a task recognised by UEFA as being particularly difficult in the present broadcasting environment. The relaxation of the rules on cross-border transmission of televised football also ensured that UEFA could supply the largest European wide television audience to advertisers and sponsors for its three European competitions, which were now to be run on separate nights of the week. In other words, the relaxation of Article 14 was further recognition of the increasing power (and economic influence) of television within football.

In today's BSkyB world of televised football, negative comment is still to be found in the press and elsewhere about the detrimental effect of too much televised football. Cameron (1997) describes it as a 'killing the goose that lays the golden eggs' argument, the suggestion being that too much televised football will spoil the market. He rejects this argument on the grounds that it presupposes irrationality on the part of the broadcaster, noting that there is no reason why increasing the availability of sport on television should contribute to a reduction in its consumption.

Of the large amount of academic literature on the economics of professional sport, little deals with the relationship between broadcasting rights and the primary source of income, gate receipts. In a study of the influence of television on attendance at FA Premier League matches in the 1993/94 season, Baimbridge et al. (1996) found that while the live transmission of Monday evening matches resulted in a significant decline in attendance, live satellite transmission of Sunday matches and those advertised for terrestrial edited highlights failed to reduce match attendance. However, they also concluded that notwithstanding the drop in attendance at the Monday match, the financial terms of the television deal ensured that clubs were in fact better off overall.

Such studies, however, do not present the full picture. They consider only the loss of spectators at the match that is being televised. Of greater significance is the extent to which higher quality television viewing displaces attendance at lower status games. Cowie and Williams (1997) assert that transmission of previous matches, both of a particular club and of other clubs in the League, may have a positive effect on stadium attendance by boosting awareness of the product. They assert that this may also boost sponsorship income, which can be used to finance an improvement in the quality of the event, which in turn leads to higher stadium attendance. In the United States, Zhang et al. (1998) investigated the relationship between broadcasting media and minor league hockey attendance. Their conclusion was that the current broadcasting arrangements (involving home games on cable television, away games on commercial television and radio broadcasts) and the quality of that broadcasting were positively related to the game attendance in providing information for and increasing the interest of spectators.

Even by restricting the discussion to purely economic terms (wider social and political issues are considered in Chapter 5), studies which focus on the determinants of demand and thus implicitly equate spectators with customers, only provide a partial understanding of the importance of spectators within the football industry. In particular insufficient consideration is given to the peculiarities of the product in economic terms. In these terms the customer concept is incomplete because it fails to consider the role played by the supporters in creating the product that they are asked to buy, i.e. the atmosphere. In other words football needs supporters not just as customers but because they form part of a unique joint product.

Television clearly plays an increasingly important role within football as a source of finance. Importantly, given capacity constraints and pricing policies at top clubs it also provides a means of allowing supporters to identify with the soccer market (see Chapter 5). The nature of the product is significant from the point of view of television. Much of the attractiveness of football on television is the atmosphere created by the supporters. Without supporters, football on television would be a notably less attractive product both as a television spectacle and consequently as a source of revenue to clubs. As Rowe (1996, p. 569) notes 'in a complete inversion of the sport-spectator relationship, there might be a future necessity of admitting spectators free to the actual event or even of paying them for their "crowd atmosphere" as if they were extras on a Hollywood film set'.

Regulatory capture

A recognition that television revenues (including related sponsorship and advertising) had the greatest potential for growth as a source of income for football clubs and had the potential to dwarf gate receipts has contributed to the television broadcasters becoming arguably the most important economic force in UK football. A similar situation arose in American sport in the 1960s. This recognition has arguably contributed to a shift in power to the television companies. On the positive side it can be argued that television has acted as a catalyst for change in football. Szymanski and Smith (1997) argue that left to their own devices market forces would not have brought about the restructuring of the football industry, due to the absence of a market for corporate control (see the section on *Corporate control issues* in Chapter 3). In their view only when external forces (in this case a combination of the television companies and the Taylor Report) imposed a co-ordinated strategy on the competing firms was there any prospect for change. On the negative side, it can be argued that such a narrow economic view of football fails to recognise its political and social dimensions (see Chapter 5) and that in fact football has sold out or debased itself through its relationship with television. Evidence of this is found in the everyday concerns of supporters as to the scheduling of matches, last minutes changes of dates and times and the unwillingness or inability of clubs adequately to consider their supporters, to whom they have already sold season tickets.

While there is little argument that a major driving force in the clubs' relationship with the television companies has been money, the role of the regulators in the takeover of football by television is more complex. Unlike individual clubs the objectives of the Football Association (FA) and the Scottish Football Association (SFA) are described in terms of protecting and promoting football at all levels. For example, Object 2 in the SFA's Memorandum of Association is 'to promote, foster, and develop, in all its branches without discrimination against any person for reason of race, religion or politics, the game of Association Football . . .'. For many it is difficult to see how sanctioning new league structures which generate larger amounts of wealth, but which concentrate that wealth in fewer hands is consistent with such objectives, notwithstanding platitudes offered about the new structures being for the good of all the game (see following section).

It can be argued that the decisions by, first, the FA in 1991 and latterly the SFA in 1998 to sanction the breakaway of the top clubs from the respective football leagues in England and Scotland is evidence of regulatory capture. Regulation exists in areas of economic activity, such as the provision of water or electricity or the Lottery, where the nature of the activity or its means of production, distribution or sale and/or the absence of a competitive market structure requires the creation of an external watchdog to guide and monitor the economic activity. Regulatory capture occurs where a regulatory body is effectively captured by the body it is charged with regulating, in other words the activities of the regulatory body are dictated by the wishes of the group it is supposed to be regulating. The regulation of accounting in the UK provides one example of regulatory capture. It can be argued that the body which formerly set accounting standards in the UK, the Accounting Standards Committee, was captured to an extent by large UK companies, the economic grouping whose activities it was supposed to be regulating, thus reducing its effectiveness in that role (for example see Hopwood and Page, 1987).

One analysis of recent events in football is that the bodies charged with regulating the game of football in England and Scotland, namely the FA and the SFA were captured by the major clubs, which resulted in the sanctioning of the break-away league structures. Although the direct capture of the associations was by the clubs, the most important factor in the capture, was television, or more accurately the television companies' money. Despite their stated objectives of promoting football at all its levels, pressure from the top clubs which wanted to benefit from television's millions resulted in the associations giving the top clubs the official approval they wished for their new structures.

Redistribution and competition

Redistribution of wealth is justified within sporting competitions as a way of trying to ensure competitive balance. The importance of redistribution varies both over time and from sport to sport. For example, in professional football in the UK in direct contrast with US professional sports, there has never been a clear intention to equalise the playing strengths of competing clubs. Also, the mechanisms put in place to achieve redistribution vary over time and from sport to sport. In US professional sports direct mechanisms such as the player draft system and salary caps are to be found, in addition to indirect measures such as the equal distribution of television and merchandising revenue (see also Chapter 2). In UK professional football redistribution has taken place primarily through indirect revenue sharing agreements in respect of revenue from sources such as television, the pools companies and gate receipts. In a UK context it has often been argued that the transfer system has also played a part in redistribution.[6] The validity of this claim will be discussed in Chapter 2.

More wealth, less redistribution?

One of the ironies of recent changes in the structure and operation of the league structure in England, and the forthcoming changes in Scotland, is that the time of football's greatest wealth is also the time of least redistribution within the industry. Throughout the 1960s income sharing or cross subsidisation schemes grew in importance as new competitions and joint revenue sources were developed. In the 1980s, however, the dissatisfaction of leading clubs led to a sharp reversal of this trend and to a scaling down of income sharing. The present situation in England and the situation which will exist in Scotland from season 1998/99 onwards reflects the wishes of the largest clubs to receive a greater share of the benefits accruing to their league organisation.

Income sharing arrangements in the Football League were altered in favour of the larger clubs in 1986, in response to a threatened break-away. This resulted in the levy on gate receipts paid by the clubs to the League to cover administrative and other joint expenses being reduced from 4 per cent to 3 per cent. The gate receipts levy disappeared on the creation of the Premier League. Under the 'tri-partite' agreement between the FA and the Football League which allowed the FA to set up the Premier League, the Football League receives £1m per annum from the Premier League and £2m per annum from the FA. In Scotland gate revenue sharing arrangements were altered in 1981 after which clubs were entitled to retain all their home League match gate receipts. The process of redistribution of monies received from the Pools Promoters' Association in respect of *inter alia* the League's copyright in the club's fixtures was also altered. Under the former system pools money was awarded to clubs on the basis of so much per point gained, irrespective of the division of the league in which a club operated. Under the present system each club is awarded a fixed amount plus a merit payment dependent on its position within all the leagues.

Given the smaller financial scale of football in Scotland, monies received from the Pools Promoters' Association has always been a significant source of income to clubs and continues to be so. Its importance can be illustrated by the fact that in season 1995/96 the amount received by the Scottish League for television fees (£3.3m) was in fact less than twice the amount received in respect of fixtures copyright (£1.7m). The former system of distribution of pools money, combined with its crucial importance to the financial health of many Scottish clubs, provided some interesting conflicts for clubs when they realised that they would actually be considerably better off doing well (but not well enough to get promoted) in the old second division, rather than getting promoted and then accumulating a smaller number of points in the higher division. As Crampsey (1986, p. 5) noted 'it could be argued that a club in this situation accepted promotion out of a sense of duty to the spirit of the game rather than as a commercial reward, perhaps indicating that normal business criteria do not always apply in Association Football'. This was an example of the notion of 'running behind' introduced by Rottenberg (1956) where a club tries to be in contention rather than trying to win.

Despite the emphasis of television coverage on the top division, until 1986 television revenue in England was shared equally among all member clubs of the Football League.[7] Under the terms of the 1986 deal with the BBC and ITV arrangements were put in place such that the First Division clubs received 50 per cent, the Second Division 25 per cent, and the Third and Fourth Division 12.5 per cent each of the total television deal. The amounts received by each division continued to be shared equally among the clubs of that division as part of the football industry's redistributive mechanism. These arrangements remained in place until the break-up of the League structure in 1992/93.

The break-away of the top clubs from the Football League resulted in the principle of inter-league redistribution being rejected in favour of the top clubs arranging their own improved deal directly with the television companies. As discussed above, it may be argued that it was the prospects of television money and the removal of any requirement to share that money with lower division clubs which led to the break-away. As such the Premier League and the Football League now negotiate their own deals. The Premier League's rules for redistribution of television monies to member clubs were set out earlier in this chapter. Similar rules are used by the Football League. As can be seen from these rules, there is an element of intra-league redistribution as half of the monies are split evenly among all of the member clubs, irrespective of their number of appearances on television or footballing performance. Furthermore, BSkyB is required to show each club at least three times, resulting in a minimum level of facility fee. The redistribution extends to those clubs which are relegated from the Premier Division for the two seasons following their relegation through the operation of parachute payments.

Club objectives

A commitment to income sharing is unlikely to substantially influence behaviour within professional football leagues in this country again. Primarily, this can be explained by considering the objectives of the participant clubs. In studies into the objectives of clubs carried out in the 1970s and 1980s it was common to describe clubs as utility maximisers, seeking to maximise playing success while remaining solvent (for example see Sloane 1971, 1980; Sutherland and Haworth, 1986 and Arnold and Beneviste, 1987b). This description was in contrast to the idea of conventional companies as profit maximisers. At that time any movements away from income sharing and hence away from uncertainty of outcome may have been considered irrational within the contexts of a self-contained domestic league with (joint) profit maximising objectives (Arnold and Beneviste, 1987b). However, when playing success is the dominant objective (within the solvency constraint) because it provides access to an additional market, i.e. European competitions, then the question of outcome uncertainty within a domestic league structure becomes less important. Clubs wish to do well enough within their domestic competitions in order to qualify for European competitions. The desire to be competitive in Europe lessens any commitment to income sharing domestically because clubs will wish to maximise both the likelihood of reaching European competitions and of being genuine competitors in those competitions.

Changes in the operation of European competitions are indicative of changes in the operation of sport. The replacement of the European Cup with the UEFA Champions League further increases the importance of getting into Europe. Furthermore, the decision to allow

Table 1.4   Record gate receipts

Club	Receipts	Details
Newcastle United	£744 544	v Monaco, UEFA Cup quarter-final, 4 March 1997
Manchester United	£739 841	v Borussia Dortmund, Champions League semi-final 2nd leg, 23 April 1997
Nottingham Forest	£499 099	v Bayern Munich, UEFA Cup quarter final 2nd leg, 19 March 1996

Source: Rothmans (1997)

the eight highest ranking national associations to enter the runner up in their national championship into the Champions League in addition to their champions obviously doubles the chance of clubs from countries such as England, Germany and Italy being able to participate in the competition.[8] Changes made to the European Cup were driven by the desire to maximise revenue. Under the former system, all countries were treated equally: the champions of every national association were invited to take part in the European Cup. From a competitive point of view this was entirely appropriate. From the point of view of maximising revenue it can be argued that it made less sense, allowing in teams from less attractive leagues in countries with smaller television audiences, in preference to teams from more attractive leagues with larger, and hence more lucrative, television audiences.

The Champions League is a highly lucrative competition, expected to be worth about £10m to the 1997/98 winners (Harverson, 1997b). The financial provisions in respect of the Champions League are set out in the Regulations of the UEFA Champions League, Articles 18 and 19. Gate receipts for both qualifying phase matches and Champions League matches are retained by the home club. Large sums are made by clubs participating in European competition through gate receipts. Table 1.4 demonstrates that the three highest record gate receipts identified in the *Rothmans Football Yearbook* per club are all in respect of matches in European competitions. Furthermore, the receipts for the 1997/98 season are likely to have exceeded these amounts for those clubs involved.

Notwithstanding record gate receipts, however, the biggest rewards come through the sale of sponsorship and television rights. These amounts are pooled by UEFA and then distributed according to criteria specified in Article 18, Paragraph 9 of the Regulations of the UEFA Champions League 98/99 as set out below:

The revenue generated by the contracts concluded for UEFA for the 72 group matches, 8 quarter-final matches, 4 semi-final matches and the final of the UEFA Champions League will be allocated as follows

a) 68.5 per cent of the total amount to be paid to the 24 clubs taking part in the UEFA Champions League, i.e.:
- 40 per cent of the total amount to be used for participation bonuses and point bonuses for the 72 group matches
- 15 per cent of the total amount to be paid out as fixed sums for the quarter-finals, the semi-finals and for the final
- 13.5 per cent of the total amount to be paid into a pool to be distributed to the competing teams according to the amount paid by the countries concerned for transmission rights (TV Pool)

b) 21.5 per cent of the total amount to be used as a share for UEFA's member associations (including the TV Pool share to be paid to the associations of the 24 competing teams in the UEFA Champions League) as well as for those teams that are eliminated in the qualifying phases of the UEFA Champions League, and in the rounds preceding and including the second round of the European Cup Winners' Cup and the UEFA Cup; a special bonus will also be paid from this amount to the domestic league champions that are not eligible to compete in the UEFA Champions League; finally, UEFA will be allocated its own share of the proceeds.

c) 10 per cent of the total amount to be used a share for football-related financial measures, in accordance with the decision of the Executive Committee (e.g. youth football, players' training and education).

Within the system an element of redistribution exists. This is to be expected given that one of UEFA's Objectives is 'fostering solidarity within the European footballing community, through the sustained support of financially weaker clubs' (Regulations of the UEFA Champions League 1998/99, Annex V, paragraph 1.2). Indeed in the *Bosman* case (see Chapter 2) the Advocate General specifically identified the Champions League as an example which demonstrated 'that the clubs and associations concerned have acknowledged and accepted in principle the possibility of promoting their own interests and those of football in general by redistributing a proportion of income' (CJEC, 1995a, para. 232). However, the extent to which paragraph 9 of Article 18 and the whole concept of the Champions League can be seen as evidence that 'Sport takes priority over financial interest' (Annex V, para. 1.2) and of the merits of redistribution are at best debatable, given that the competition is now structured around the elite clubs and associations in Europe. It is difficult to see how excluding the champions of leagues run by lesser associations can be interpreted as fostering solidarity within the European footballing community. An alternative explanation for the current format of the Champions League is that it is another example of regulatory capture. In this case, Europe's governing body has effectively been captured by the top clubs which have been driven by the prospects of greater wealth from sponsorship deals and in particular from television revenues. Under the threat of a European Super League outside UEFA's control, it can be argued that the regulator has acquiesced to the wishes of the powerful clubs.[9]

In view of the potential income available from European competitions there is little incentive for the top clubs to redistribute their wealth domestically. This is so because it may diminish, first, their chances of getting into Europe, and secondly, their competitiveness in that marketplace. In addition, top clubs will wish to be well placed should a European Super League actually come about. A further aspect is the ownership framework of top clubs and the objectives of their stakeholders. In the UK, several of the top clubs such as Manchester United, Chelsea and Celtic are now listed on the Stock Exchange. As is discussed in Chapters 3 and 5 this brings additional pressures on clubs. While there is no evidence which suggests that these clubs are being run on a profit maximisation basis, nevertheless the presence of external shareholders who have invested for financial reason means that clubs must endeavour to generate a satisfactory return for these investors. As such, clubs must seek to maximise revenue sources, which can be equated with saying first, ensure the retention of the top division domestic status, and secondly, attempt to ensure European qualification. In conclusion, given the existence of a lucrative market outside the domestic league and the objectives of clubs, the behaviour of clubs in seeking to reduce the extent of redistribution of income is quite rational in economic terms.

Redistribution and television

The redistributive element which is found in deals like that between the Premier League and BSkyB arises due to the fact that television deals continue to be arranged between the broadcaster and the league, not directly with the individual clubs. The economic rationale behind such deals is that clubs cannot sell rights to their own matches because the clubs and the matches are part of a joint product.

Two main factors will influence whether or not these deals will be arranged on a league basis in the future. One factor is likely to be the behaviour of the clubs themselves or, more particularly, the top clubs. It is well recognised that there is greater interest in watching the elite top clubs like Manchester United or Liverpool than watching clubs like Coventry City or Leicester City. To an extent, the existing system already recognises this through the facility fees. In other words, while Manchester United and Liverpool both received in excess of £2m in facility fees for 1996/97 reflecting the fact that their matches were televised live twelve and eleven times respectively, Coventry and Leicester (both televised 4 times) received just over £700000 each. The existence of facility fees is a logical extension of the aim of the top division clubs to do away with redistribution to the lower division clubs.

Until recently, it has been in the best interests of the top clubs to pool all their broadcasting rights and to permit the League to negotiate television deals which both maximise income and benefit the operation of a league. However, changes in television technology have encouraged several top clubs like Manchester United and Rangers to take advantage of their popularity by launching or planning to launch their own satellite television channels. Middlesbrough was the first British club to launch its own television channel, broadcasting after every home match and for one hour per week on Thursday evenings. At present, however, only friendly matches or testimonials can be shown. The likely introduction of Pay-Per-View television in the future may carry risks with it for the smaller Premier League clubs (see also the Conclusion). The increasingly profit-conscious stand of several top clubs may result in these clubs seeing the opportunity to increase their television income at the expense of one of their less popular Premier League 'competitors' as simply a rational economic or business decision. Many club chairmen outside of the Premier League might see this as ironic justice given the way their own clubs were dealt with when the top division clubs were acting collectively.

A second factor concerns the validity of the League arranging television deals on behalf of its member clubs. The existing deal between the Premier League and BSkyB has been referred to the Restrictive Practices Court by the Director General of Fair Trading under the Restrictive Practices Act 1976. This is on the grounds that the five-year deal may be anti-competitive because competitors of BSkyB will have no opportunity to compete for the rights to show Premier League football until 2001. Under review are two provisions. First, whether the Premier League has the right to enter into television and satellite broadcasting contracts on behalf of the Premier League clubs on an exclusive basis. In other words, did the twenty Premier League clubs act as an illegal cartel in negotiating a television contract collectively? Secondly, whether the Premier League has the right to prohibit all televising, recording or transmitting of Premier League matches not so authorised.

In each case the Court will consider whether the rules under review are contrary to the public interest. If it so decides, then it may make an order to restrain the parties from enforcing or giving effect to the rules or from making any other agreement of like effect. Such an order would bring about a transformation in football finance because it would permit clubs to negotiate broadcast rights independently of the Premier League and would thus call into question the operation of league structures such as the Premier League. This case could have as important an impact in the structure and financing of football as the *Bosman* case (see Chapter 2).

Implications of change

Such decisions must be tempered, however, by a recognition of the nature of sport. The requirement for competition, and thus uncertainty of outcome, means that there must exist some off the field co-operative relationships between clubs not found in conventional industries (Alberstat and Johnstone, 1997). Strengthening one or two elite clubs at the expense of the rest may lead to the outcome of matches falling below the optimal level of uncertainty. One significant consequence of the much improved television deals combined with the removal of industry wide redistributive mechanisms is the risk of spiralling inequality of income distribution (Baimbridge et al., 1996). Notwithstanding the existence of the parachute payments, the opportunity cost of not being in the Premier League is severe given that 50 per cent of the television deal is divided equally among the twenty clubs. The opportunity cost is not, of course, simply lost television income. Other sources of income are also likely to be reduced although there may also be possibilities of reducing expenditure.

Szymanski (1998) has attempted to find a systematic way to build all of these issues into an economic model which results in a financial value for divisional status for individual clubs. Under this model, the cost of relegation from the Premier League, for example, to Tottenham Hotspur was estimated at £10.6m; for Bolton Wanderers it was estimated at £1.8m. Opportunity costs are also relevant to the City. Collins Stewart, stockbrokers to Southampton, estimated that relegation to the First Division at the end of season 1996/97 would cut the club's annual revenues by 26 per cent to £7.9m and reduce its profits by 57 per cent to £1.5m (Harverson, 1997a).

As the top clubs become wealthier, they are in a position to acquire the services of more star players. One risk of this scenario is that it could lead to the outcome of matches or competitions falling below the optimal level of uncertainty. Even within the existing structure it would be possible to alter the distribution of income for the benefit of the lesser teams within the League. For example, boosting the equal share television payments under a League organised deal is one logical way of attempting to ensure the optimal league uncertainty of outcome and intra-league income inequality (Baimbridge et al., 1996).

It can be argued that removing collective television deals would exacerbate the inequality of income distribution. Where collective television agreements ensure a substantial redistribution of the income from that deal, then it can be argued that such deals are not against the public interest because they help preserve competitive balance within a league. This was the stance taken in recent cases in the Netherlands and in Spain. In the Netherlands, in a case brought in 1996 by Feyenoord against the KNVB (Dutch FA) over collective television agreements, the Dutch court held that while broadcasting rights are in principle owned by individual clubs, the benefits to the league from having a collective deal which benefited all members individually, outweighed any argument of anti-competitiveness. Likewise in Spain, in 1993 the Spanish Competition Court ruled that it was lawful for the Spanish League to assign broadcasting rights collectively rather than on a club by club basis.

From the broadcasters' point of view, however, this may well seem to be a restrictive practice. Given the movement away from redistribution of income sources such as gate receipts, why should it be the responsibility of television companies to ensure that wealth is redistributed in football and that a competitive, well-balanced league is maintained? Recent changes in Italy are interesting in this regard. In September 1998 the collective approach to the sale of broadcasting rights was abandoned when the country's four biggest clubs (Juventus, AC Milan, Inter Milan and Napoli) entered into a six-year agreement with Canal Plus, owner of the Italian pay TV network, Telepiú, for exclusive coverage of their home league matches. Under this contract, away teams would receive an 18 per cent share of television receipts received by the home club (Betts and Harverson, 1998). If the Restrictive Practices Court was to follow the Italian approach then there will be far reaching implications. The main risk is that any requirement for a competitive marketplace for broadcasting rights may actually undermine the competitive balance of many existing sports leagues (Alberstat and Johnstone, 1997).

The Scottish dimension

As discussed earlier in this chapter, the top Scottish clubs have agreed to break away from the Scottish Football League and a new structure accepted by the SFA is in place for the start of the 1998/99 season. As in England, a major driving force has been the desire to increase the financial rewards available to the top clubs, particularly through improved television deals. The deal negotiated between the break-away clubs and the television companies is worth £45m over four years and is significantly better than the existing deal set out previously. However, for various reasons the value of the deal, both in total and in terms of its worth to individual clubs remains significantly poorer in scale than the deal between the FA Premier League and the television companies.

The Scottish position is complicated by the fact that the economics of sport are even more peculiar in Scottish football than in most other professional sporting leagues. In particular, the importance of competition and uncertainty of outcome within the Scottish League is less prominent given the historical dominance of two clubs, Celtic and Rangers. What has traditionally been important in Scotland has been the intense competition and rivalry between these two clubs alone, a rivalry that has allowed both to prosper financially. While the Louis Schmelling paradox demonstrates that sporting competition is more profitable than sporting monopoly, Jennet (1984) notes that the most profitable activity of all remains economic collusion among sporting competitors. Murray (1984, p. 1) noted that:

Games between Celtic and Rangers are unique in the bitterness of their religious divisions, and this has ensured the financial success of both clubs for most of the century. The title 'Old Firm' was given to these two teams just after the turn of the century, in recognition of the business aspects of their games, a business, it has later been claimed that is based on bigotry.

Scottish football finds itself in a very unusual position whereby the financial and footballing success of these two clubs seems to invalidate conventional economic theory on sporting competition. One important reason for this unique situation arises from wider sociological factors which surround these clubs (see for example Finn, 1991a, 1991b; Moorhouse, 1991; Horne, 1995; Murray, 1998).

Much has been made in recent years of the fact that Scotland's top two clubs receive less from television than 'small' English clubs, despite their stature, supporter bases and television popularity. In terms of maximising income the top two clubs have been held back by the requirement to arrange television deals through the Scottish League. While satellite broadcasters recognise the value of matches involving (and more specifically between) the Old Firm, the fact is these matches are not sold individually but as part of a package consisting of eight other teams whose attractiveness as television products is not likely to significantly extend beyond the Scottish border. Given that the population of Scotland is approximately one tenth of England, if a large English audience is not interested in watching matches such as Kilmarnock versus Dunfermline then the result is that the market value of the television rights for that league will reduce accordingly. While a club such as Wimbledon may not have the stature and profile of one of Scotland's top clubs, as long as television rights continue to be sold for leagues as opposed to individual clubs then its participation in what is perceived as higher quality joint product within a much larger marketplace will ensure that its rewards from television will greatly exceed those of clubs such as Celtic and Rangers.

The problem for the Scottish break away clubs is that nothing in the new structure is likely to alter materially the competitive imbalance in Scottish football or its popularity outwith Scotland, if as seems likely the same ten clubs compete on the same basis as before in a similarly titled league. Some recognition of this problem has come from Scotland's leading two clubs, however, with Rangers and Celtic promising to share a proportion of what they might have expected to earn on their own through television with the other top division clubs, in order to strengthen the quality of the league. This apparent willingness to share is a limited recognition of the importance of competition, albeit similar to what has taken place in England, only within a very limited number of elite clubs. This was described by the Celtic chairman Fergus McCann as giving 'the other eight clubs the confidence that they have the income to back any improvement in quality' (*Soccer Investor*, 1997c). This is important because the introduction of a Super League means that a relationship will exist between the costs that a club will require to incur in order to compete effectively in footballing terms, and the costs which must be incurred by other clubs making up the top flight (Cairns, 1987). While Scotland's top two will continue to be on a different financial level from the other eight clubs, the decision to provide a guarantee of improved cash flows will reduce the problems faced by their competitors through the increase in the long term costs of participation.

What the top Scottish clubs wanted was an opportunity to promote a smaller elite league which would be more attractive to television companies and sponsors, without being constrained by the wishes of another thirty smaller Scottish clubs. As a result the decision to compensate the smaller clubs by £1.7m p.a. can be seen as a rational economic decision: giving away a small amount of pie to the smaller clubs as a token in the knowledge that their sanction of the breakaway would provide both a much larger cake for the elite clubs in the future and a means of escaping from the archaic voting structure which characterised the former league structure and which made it difficult for the larger clubs to initiate changes without the support of the smaller clubs.

REACHING FOR THE SKY

Nothing has emphasised more dramatically the changes in the finance of football and the dominant influence of television companies than the revelation on Monday 7 September 1998 that the directors of Manchester United plc were in discussions with the satellite television company BSkyB about its £575m bid for the football company. Two days later the board of Manchester United plc recommended acceptance of an increased £623.4m offer, making it the largest acquisition of a sports club in the world.

While it was no surprise that the news was greeted with indignation by many supporters, politicians and commentators, equally the bid itself should have come as little surprise to those familiar with recent and ongoing developments in *the new business of football*.

Top level football in the UK and beyond has become inextricably linked with television. Thus the purchase of the most successful club in the UK, Manchester United, by the key company in the broadcasting of the game, BSkyB, was a logical outcome of this tightening link. The attractiveness to BSkyB of owning Manchester United can be explained by referring to some of the issues mentioned earlier in this chapter.

Crucial is the possibility that in the near future clubs will individually be able to negotiate the sale of television rights to their own matches as opposed to collectively on a league basis. At present, BSkyB has exclusive rights to broadcast FA Premier League football until the year 2001. If the Restrictive Practices Court finds that the Premier League has been acting as an illegal cartel (see the section on *Redistribution and television* earlier in this chapter) then BSkyB has an ideal insurance policy in that in addition to its broadcasting expertise it will also own the rights to the UK's most popular and financially lucrative team. On the other hand, should the Court take the view that the sale of collective television rights by the FA Premier League is appropriate, BSkyB, using its established market position and influence, will still be in a strong position to bid for future rights on their expiry in 2001.

Related to the sale of television rights is the question of Pay-Per-View television. Manchester United is the most popular football club in Europe, if not the world. As such BSkyB will be in a strong position to benefit from pay as you view football matches, not just in the UK, but also most importantly, drawing on the club's world-wide audience.

A third factor is the increasing likelihood of a highly lucrative European Super League of which Manchester United would be a key participant. Ownership of Manchester United would thus allow BSkyB to have an influence on both the structure of the league and of the accompanying broadcasting arrangements. Notwithstanding the high price paid for the club, these three factors mean that there is little doubt that the deal makes prosperous business sense for BSkyB.

The extent to which the BSkyB take-over of Manchester United will have an influence on the ownership of other clubs remains to be seen. An immediate response came from the media group Carlton Communications which announced on 10 September 1998 that it had held exploratory talks with Premier League champions, Arsenal. Since then practically every major club has been linked in the press with some potential suitor, usually a media based company.

The BSkyB/Manchester United deal has been referred to the Office of Fair Trading to allow an investigation of the competition issues arising out of any takeover. Given this, it is likely that any future bids will be delayed until the outcome of the referral becomes public. However, notwithstanding the outcome of that referral, for the reasons set out above, any future interest by media companies is likely to be concentrated only on those very few major clubs who have a wide international appeal such as Liverpool, Celtic and Rangers.

2 Rich Man, Poor Man – Players in the New Business of Football

Considerable structural change in the football industry in recent years has not been restricted to the introduction of satellite television and its effects on club revenues. Another essential factor affecting the industry, both its finances and its treatment of employees, has been the landmark ruling in the Court of Justice of the European Communities (CJEC, 1995b) in the case of *Union Royale Belge des Sociétés de Football Association ASBL* v. *Bosman* (hereafter the *Bosman* case). Bosman is now perhaps the most famous Belgian footballer of all time. His fame has resulted, however, not from his abilities on the field, but from persistence and determination to seek justice in a court of law against his former club and the football authorities. This chapter considers the role of players within the business of football and in particular the implications of the Bosman ruling on this role.

THE HISTORICAL ROLE OF PLAYERS

The transfer market

Transfer markets have a long history in professional football, and are to be found in most football leagues operating under the jurisdiction of UEFA (the governing body of football in Europe) or FIFA (the governing body of world football). By contrast in the wider corporate environment, there is only a very limited number of examples of the operation of any kind of transfer market.[1] Interestingly, transfer markets are not common even in most other professional sports. For example, the highly regulated North American sports labour markets do not contain player markets comparable to those found in professional football although other forms of labour market control, such as reserve clause systems under which a team owning a player's contract has exclusive negotiating rights for that player, and player draft systems which control and distribute new player entry, have been used in different sports. In the UK, cricket does not have a transfer market, although such markets are to be found in rugby league and to a lesser extent in rugby union.

Every player in the employment of a league club must be registered both with that League (e.g. the FA Premier League) and the Association to which it is affiliated (e.g. the Football Association). Only players who have signed the appropriate registration form and who have been registered and approved by that league are permitted to play in competitions organised by that league. The historical roots of the transfer system can be traced to a clause inserted in the regulations of the FA in 1885 which required all players to be registered annually with the Association. The clause, designed to protect smaller clubs by preventing players from club-hopping, instead resulted in the registration becoming something to be bought and sold in its own right (Miller, 1993). If a larger club wanted a particular player, then it was required to compensate the smaller club financially, in order that the smaller club could buy a replacement or service its debt (Harding, 1991). In practice, however, it resulted in the creation of a transfer market, with the registration (that is to say the player) becoming something to be bought and sold in its own right.

Until 1963 if a player wished to change club he required his existing club to agree to the transfer. If it agreed, then a transfer was possible if a buyer could be found who was willing to pay a satisfactory fee. If it refused, then he had no option other than to continue to play for his existing club. At the end of the playing season the player would be placed on either the retained list or the transfer list on the club's terms, the only proviso being that the terms be no lower than the agreed minimum wages and conditions. The operation of this early transfer system, referred to as the 'retain and transfer' system, effectively meant that the club holding a player's registration held a monopoly over him, in that any transfer required the approval of both regulatory bodies and most importantly of all the consent of the club holding the player's registration.

In a case brought by the Newcastle United player George Eastham,[2] with the support of the players' union, the Professional Footballers' Association (PFA), the 'retain and transfer' system was successfully challenged when the High Court ruled in 1963 that the system was an unreasonable restraint of trade.[3] The Eastham case resulted in a new contractual system being devised. This designated an initial contract period, usually one or two years, and an option period (equal to the initial period). If the option was not exercised then the player was free to sign for another club. The option allowed the club to renew the contract on terms no less favourable than the initial terms. If the player rejected the offer then either party could invoke the disputes procedure. In most cases this resulted in an independent tribunal consisting of representatives of both sides and an independent chairman setting the level of transfer fee for the player. In essence, therefore, the system continued to allow clubs to retain a player even after the contract had expired and to claim a fee for that player. As a result the transfer system continued to be challenged by the PFA.

In 1977 the system was further modified by the introduction of so called 'freedom of contract'. The basic difference here was that having fulfilled his contractual obligations, a player was free to make the best deal he could with any club offering terms. The club holding the registration was entitled to a compensation fee only if it offered to extend the player's previous agreement on no less favourable terms. The transfer fee was agreed between the two clubs or, in default, by a Compensation Tribunal where two clubs from the same league were involved, or a Commission of the International Football League Board where two separate football leagues were involved. Under this system retention in theory only existed while the contract was in force, during which time the club was able to retain a player unless and until they receive the fee it wanted. At the end of the contract the player was free to move to another club while the two clubs negotiated a fee or until the matter was settled by arbitration.

In Scotland the situation was more restrictive. The basic principle was similar to that in England, that is where a club wished to re-engage a player then the terms of re-engagement offered must be no less favourable in all monetary respects than the terms of the previous contract. In those circumstances the club was entitled to a compensation fee in respect of the loss of the player's registration. The situation differed, however, where a player did not accept the club's offer of re-engagement and indicated his desire to leave the club. In those circumstances, after the expiry date of the contract, without affecting its right to a compensation fee, the club could do one of three things as set out in Rule 60(A)(7) of the Rules of the Scottish Football League (SFL, 1997).

First, it could enter into a new contract with the player, with the provision that his registration could be transferred to another club at any time during the currency of the contract for a fee determined in accordance with League Rules; secondly, it could enter into monthly contracts under the financial terms of the previous contract; or thirdly, it could continue to pay the player the basic wage payable under the contract which had just expired for a period of 31 days. In this third case, the League Rules state that where the player has refused offers of employment from any other club or 'because there are other relevant circumstances, the club may retain its entitlement to a compensation fee . . . without being obliged to continue paying the basic wage from the expiry of the 31 day period'. In the event of the club ceasing to pay the player at the expiry of the 31 days, then the club may enter into monthly contract(s) with that player 'on such terms and conditions as the club and the player may mutually agree'. Such monthly contracts do not affect the club's continuing right to a compensation fee and on the expiry of any such contract 'the club shall not be bound to pay the player for any further period of 31 days or any other period beyond the date of such expiry or to offer to enter into any further contract with the player'.[4]

Applying these provisions to the letter thus allowed clubs in certain circumstances to treat players effectively as modern day slaves. The best known example of a player with a Scottish club being the victim of these rules was Chris Honor. Honor had a two-year contract with Airdrie which expired in 1993, after which he signed monthly contracts for a further year. At the end of that period, without breaking the rules of the Scottish League, the club was able to stop paying the player while retaining his registration and preventing him for playing for another club unless it received a transfer fee. The player is currently challenging the retention system in court. If he is successful then any player will be free to move when his contract expires, irrespective of age (see also the section on *The new system* later in this chapter).

As mentioned previously one objective behind the creation of the transfer system was to prevent players club-hopping. From the clubs' point of view, the transfer system has been an important mechanism in helping them to build teams that will achieve footballing success. In other words, players are bought and sold by a manager with the intention of increasing playing strength and improving a team's performance and thus achieving football success. However, to the players the merits of the system are less obvious. Early writings on the economics of football suggested that it was appropriate to adopt a unitary perspective of an organisation when discussing football clubs, with all relevant participants in the clubs being assumed to share the same objective of playing success (for example, see Sloane, 1971). This was rejected by Stewart (1986, p. 25), noting that 'the assumption of commonly held objectives belies the existence of the retain and transfer system, which, operating explicitly to restrict players' labour market mobility, was devised in recognition of the fact that, in its absence, a player would behave in a manner consistent with the pursuit of his own and not his employers' objectives'. Nevertheless, in so far as it was the system which existed in the marketplace and despite dissatisfaction with the system, players and their representatives have utilised that system to their best advantage in their search for higher earnings, increased job satisfaction or whatever. However, it would be quite wrong to equate their ability to use the system in many cases to good advantage with any acceptance of its principles.

Salaries

In England a maximum wage for all players was imposed in 1901 (Vamplew, 1982). Although no maximum wage existed in Scotland, in practice actual wages paid by the top clubs was governed by the rate being paid in England. It was not uncommon for Scottish clubs to offer to pay a few pounds more than the going rate in England in an attempt to persuade players to stay north of the border (Crampsey, 1986).

The maximum wage rate was set at £4 per week until the First World War. When finally abolished in 1961, after a campaign led by the PFA, it was set at £22 per week during the season and £18 per week in the close season. Its abolition had an immediate impact, with wages spiralling and a substantial reduction in the number of professionals employed by the 92 league clubs. The average earnings of a first team player in Division 1 rose from £1173 in 1960 to £2680 in 1964, while between seasons 1960/61 and 1966/67 the number of professionals employed by the 92 league clubs fell by 20 per cent from 3022 to 2395 (Sloane, 1969). By way of comparison, between 1948 and 1960 the average wage bill of clubs rose by only about 6 per cent per annum (Szymanski, 1997). The period from 1946/47 (the end of the Second World War) through to the abolition of the maximum wage in 1961 saw a period of very high attendances both in England and Scotland (see Figure 2.1). Attendance at Football League games reached a post-war record of 41.3m (an average match attendance of over 23 000 across four divisions) in season 1949/49. By comparison, attendance at Premier League and Football League games in season 1996/97 was 22.8m, an average match attendance of 11 190 (Rothmans, 1997). In Scotland, a similar trend was observed to emerge (Jennet, 1984). Aggregate League Championship and League Cup attendance fell from 6.4

Figure 2.1   Average Football League attendance 1946/47 to 1960/61

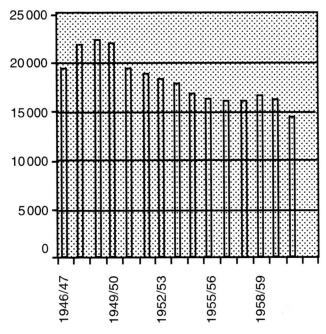

Source: Rothmans (1997)

million in 1956/57 to 4.5 million by 1971/72 (Cairns, 1987). By season 1996/97 attendance at League and Coca-Cola Cup matches was 4.1m.

During this period there is little doubt that players were being exploited vis-*à*-vis the wages they were receiving from clubs compared to the revenue they were generating for those clubs through gate receipts. For example, according to Jimmy Hill, then Chairman of the PFA, the average footballer in the days of the maximum wage had a salary that put him in the same income bracket as a bus driver or a commercial clerk, and the top players, of whom he guessed there were around three or four hundred were on only 30 per cent more than this (Corry et al., 1993). The implications of the *Bosman* ruling on wage rates will be discussed later in this chapter.

The level of players' salaries has also been influenced by transfer market restrictions which introduce an element of monopsonistic exploitation by clubs into the market place. In other words, a club acts as a monopoly buyer of a player's services. Until the decision in the

Bosman case, when a player signed for a particular club, to a certain extent he was tied to that particular club, through the retention element of the transfer system (see the section on *The transfer market* earlier in this chapter). Consequently, each club and its players could be regarded as being in a single labour market, separate from other clubs.[5] As a result monopsony may take effect as soon as a player signs for a particular club. It is only modified to some extent by the fact that another club can offer to buy that player through the transfer market, in which circumstances his salary would be expected to rise.

BOSMAN – FOOTBALL'S COST DRIVER?

The *Bosman* case

Jean-Marc Bosman, a Belgian national, was formerly a professional football player with Royal Club Liégois under a contract which ran until 30 June 1990. Prior to its expiry, the club offered Bosman a new contract which included a reduction in total salary of approximately 75 per cent. This would have placed him on the minimum salary permitted by the URBSFA, the governing body of football in Belgium. Bosman refused the terms of the contract and was placed on the transfer list. His fee was set at 11.7m Belgian Francs (approximately £200 000) in accordance with URBSFA rules.

No club expressed particular interest and Bosman himself eventually contacted the French club Dunkerque. Royal Club Liégois, concerned about the financial solvency of Dunkerque, refused to instruct URBSFA to issue the transfer certificate. As a result the transfer could not proceed. When, in accordance with the rules of the URBSFA, Royal Club Liégois suspended Bosman, the player found himself in football wasteland. He sued the club and the URBSFA and obtained interim injunctions which, in theory, permitted him to play for other clubs. Subsequently Bosman was able to obtain employment with, among others, a Belgian Third Division club, amid suspicion, following his decision to challenge the lawfulness in EC law of football transfer fees for out-of-contract players and restrictions on the number of foreign players which can be selected in a team, that he had been 'boycotted by all European clubs which could have taken him in' (CJEC, 1995a, para. 47). Bosman's case underwent a protracted journey through the Belgian legal system, eventually reaching the Appeal Court in Liege where he sought compensation from Royal Club Liégois,

URBSFA and UEFA, together with a declaration that URBSFA and UEFA rules on transfer fees were inapplicable to him. The Appeal Court referred the matter to the European Court for a preliminary ruling.

The preliminary legal opinion from the Advocate General of the Court of Justice of the European Communities (CJEC, 1995a) found in the player's favour viewing the restrictions as a breach of European law. That opinion was subsequently endorsed by the Court of Justice of the European Communities (CJEC, 1995b) which found that the provision that out-of-contract players could only move between two clubs if compensation was paid to the selling clubs was incompatible with Article 48 of the EC Treaty. Furthermore the restriction on the number of foreign European Union nationals who were permitted to play in competitions organised by national and international sporting associations was also found to be incompatible with Article 48. (For a more detailed consideration of the legal aspects of the case see for example Griffith-Jones, 1997, pp. 126–133, or Morris, Morrow and Spink, 1996.)

It is worth noting that Bosman's case would not have arisen had he been an English national. When his contract with Royal Club Liégois expired, under the rules of the transfer system then applicable in England, if the club had been unwilling or unable to offer him a new contract on no less favourable terms then he would have been entitled to a free transfer. For reasons discussed earlier in this chapter, strict application of the Scottish system, however, could also have been likely to result in a court case.

Uncertainty of outcome and redistribution?

Thomas (1996) notes that labour market restrictions (such as transfer markets) are usually explained in terms of attempting to achieve equalised playing strengths in accordance with the *uncertainty of outcome* hypothesis. One argument put to the Court in the *Bosman* case was that the peculiarities of football economics and in particular of labour markets within professional sport justified the existence of the transfer system. The argument put by the URBSFA (the Belgian Football Association), UEFA and the French and Italian governments was that the transfer system played a part in redistributing wealth among football clubs, thus leading to greater uncertainty of outcome (see Chapter 1). This argument conjures up the romantic notion that the survival and sustainability of smaller clubs is dependent on the cascade of funds from the top clubs.

While the Court accepted as legitimate the aim of maintaining a financial and competitive balance between clubs by preserving a degree of equality and uncertainty of results, particularly given the social importance of football in the community, it rejected the adequacy of the transfer rules as a means of achieving that aim (CJEC, 1995b, paras. 106, 107). Its view rested on various factors. One was the relationship between transfer fees and compensation for training and development, an issue which will be considered later in this chapter.

In the context of uncertainty of outcome and redistribution of wealth, however, the Court was of the opinion that the transfer rules did not prevent the top clubs from securing the services of the top players nor did it prevent the availability of financial resources from being a decisive factor in professional sport. This point was also raised by the Advocate General who noted that the existence of a transfer system usually resulted in smaller clubs being forced to sell their best players thereby further weakening those clubs from a sporting point of view (CJEC, 1995a, para. 224). Although they would be compensated financially they would not be in position to acquire the top players.

As an alternative to the transfer market, the Court concurred with the earlier suggestion of the Advocate General, that measures such as collective wage agreements (see section on *Implications for salaries* later in this chapter) and/or redistribution of club revenue from gate receipts and broadcasting fees represented suitable means of promoting the desired aim of financial and competitive balance. Importantly, these measures would ensure that the aim is achieved without impeding the principle of the freedom of movement (CJEC, 1995b, para. 110; CJEC, 1995a, paras. 226–234). However, as discussed in the section *Redistribution and competition* in Chapter 1, the creation of super leagues like the Premier League has seen clubs move away from the principle of the redistribution of income.

An important reason why the Court took that view, was that despite assertions from UEFA and others involved in the case, in its opinion there was a lack of evidence presented to demonstrate how the transfer market contributed to an equalisation of playing and financial strength and how smaller clubs would be put in serious financial difficulties if the market was abolished.

Some information on the extent which transfer fees play in the redistribution of income between clubs is available for English clubs in the Deloitte & Touche Annual Reviews of Football Finance, and for Scottish clubs from a study carried out by Moorhouse (1994b). Table

Table 2.1   Net transfer fees (payable)/receivable – by division

	1995/96 (£m)	1994/95 (£m)	1993/94 (£m)	1992/93 (£m)
Premier League (net outflow)	(25.2)	(9.5)	(13.0)	(6.0)
Football League				
Division 1	18.3	8.8	6.0	2.0
Division 2	4.0	(0.3)	5.9	3.2
Division 3	2.9	1.0	1.1	0.8
Total funds received	25.2	9.5	13.0	6.0

Source: Deloitte & Touche (1997, 1996), The Football Trust, The Football
League

2.1 sets out the amounts receivable or payable by each of England's professional divisions for the period 1992–1996, while Table 2.2 sets out the transfer flows between divisions.

Table 2.1 demonstrates that in this four-year period the Premier League has been in a net deficit position as regards transfer fees, while for by far the most part the three Football League divisions have been in positions of net surplus. However, in absolute terms the amounts receivable by the lower league divisions are very small. The net inflow to Division 3 from transfers in 1995/96 was only £2.9m compared to the total spend by Premier Division clubs of £94.2m. Furthermore, Table 2.2 shows that for 1995/96 the net benefit to Division 3 clubs from transfer trading with the Premier League clubs was only £1.3m with a further £0.9m coming from transfer trading with Division 1 clubs. Likewise, for the same period the net benefit to Division 2 clubs from transfer trading with Premier League clubs was only £0.9m with a more substantial £3.8m coming from trading with Division 1 clubs.

These tables suggest that there is apparently very little evidence of the transfer market acting as an effective means of redistributing wealth to lower divisions. The information therein, however, is not disaggregated to the level of individual clubs. For example, a club like Crewe Alexandria is commonly identified as one which specialises in buying and selling young talented players. However, the extent to which a particular club chooses to specialise in developing young talent for onward sale, and its success or otherwise in that policy, is basically a strategic decision taken by the management of that club. As such, it could be argued that consideration of the extent to which the transfer system functions as an effective redistributive mechanism must take

Table 2.2   Flow of transfer fees in 1995/96

	Payments by				
	Premier League (£m)	Division 1 (£m)	Division 2 (£m)	Division 3 (£m)	Total received (£m)
Fees paid to					
Premier League	55.8	12.2	0.8	0.2	69.0
Division 1	35.2	15.9	2.7	0.9	54.7
Division 2	1.7	6.5	1.7	0.3	10.2
Division 3	1.5	1.8	1.0	1.4	5.7
Total paid	94.2	36.4	6.2	2.8	139.6

Source: Deloitte & Touche (1997), The Football Trust, The Football League

place at the level of the league and not individual clubs. In other words, what is at issue is the extent to which the transfer system contributes to inter-league redistribution.

The financial effects of the transfer system on Scottish clubs over the period 1982–1991 was investigated in detail by Moorhouse (1994b) at an individual club level. As such this study provided information on those Scottish clubs, similar to Crewe Alexandria in England. He concluded that the transfer system played very little part in the redistribution of wealth from the rich clubs to the smaller ones. There was evidence of some clubs specialising in developing and then selling off talent (notably Greenock Morton and Clydebank) but that this was not a widespread pattern, and indeed there were several clubs for which removal of the transfer market would increase their financial security. Clubs such as Airdrie, Kilmarnock and Dunfermline in fact made significant net losses from the transfer market over this period. However it is possible that these losses were offset either in total or part by other financial benefits received by the club, e.g. if the club's transfer policy helped it to achieve promotion this would hopefully have led to increased gate receipts, improved sponsorship deals, television revenues and the like. The study also demonstrated that both Celtic and Rangers were net spenders in the transfer market over the period, while it was what were described as the midrank clubs such as Aberdeen, Dundee and Motherwell which made net profits over the period. In a study of average surpluses or deficits on transfer spending within 39 English clubs over the period 1989–1995,

Simmons (1997) found that many well-established Premier League clubs incurred sizeable net transfer deficits (e.g. Blackburn Rovers – £4.2m, Liverpool – £3.4m, Newcastle United – £2.4m), while several lower division clubs generated transfer surpluses (e.g. Luton Town – £1.3m, Southend United – £0.9m and Swindon Town – £0.7m). More interestingly, when the period was extended back to 1973/74 he found that only nine of the 39 clubs switched from average net deficit to surplus or vice versa.

On the basis of the available evidence rather than merely assertion, it can be argued that small clubs will not necessarily go out of business as a result simply of the removal of the transfer system. What evidence exists suggests that transfer activity seems to involve the larger clubs, with little evidence to indicate any filter down effect to smaller clubs. The smallest clubs for the most part do not seem to rely to any great extent on the transfer market for survival. Smaller clubs will neverthe-less be deprived of occasional one-off windfalls from the sale of a player. This need not necessarily be entirely negative however. Clubs which have in the past relied on the uncertain income which flows from transfers will in future be obliged to ensure that they operate at a level which is sustainable in terms of ongoing operational income. Interest-ingly, this issue of budgeting difficulties caused by the unreliability of transfer fees was specifically referred to by the Advocate General in the *Bosman* case (CJEC, 1995a, para. 233).

Implications for salaries

Not surprisingly, one consequence of the *Bosman* case has been that clubs have incurred significant increases in their wage costs (see Table 2.3). The level of salaries in sport is much commented and reported upon.[6] For financial reporting purposes, however, clubs are not re-quired separately to disclose players' wages and salaries within their accounts. Therefore published figures include not only playing staff and management but also all the other staff employed by clubs, such as catering staff, marketing staff and accounting staff. As a result any discussion on the effect of the Bosman ruling on players' salaries is necessarily very restricted.

Table 2.3 sets out changes in clubs' wages and salaries over the last four years, comparing these to turnover.

Interestingly, this table shows for the Premier League that although wages and salaries have been growing year on year, following the substantial rise in turnover in 1996/97, wages and salaries now consti-

Table 2.3   Wages and salary costs (related to turnover)

	1996/97 (£m)	1995/96 (£m)	1994/95 (£m)	1993/94 (£m)
Premier League				
Total wages and salaries	213 384	172 683	144 505	116 685
% increase year on year		23.6%	19.5%	23.8%
Turnover	455 471	346 224	322 858	241 479
% increase year on year		31.5%	7.2%	33.7%
Wages/Turnover	46.7%	50.0%	44.8%	48.3%
Scottish Premier [no. of clubs]				
Total wages and salaries	39 693 [10]	28 940 [7][1]	22 017 [8][2]	21 631 [10]
Turnover	81 792	64 118	49 581	48 797
Wages/Turnover	48.5%	45.1%	44.4%	44.3%

[1] Falkirk, Partick Thistle and Raith Rovers did not provide information on wages and salary costs.
[2] Falkirk, and Partick Thistle did not provide information on wages and salary costs.
Source: Deloitte & Touche (1997, 1996), Touche Ross (1995), Club accounts

tute a smaller percentage of turnover than they did in 1993/94. Wages and salaries also constitute a smaller portion of revenue than was the case in earlier time periods. In the period 1974–1989 Szymanski (1993) found that spending on players represented on average about 64 per cent of revenue.[7] Notwithstanding these comparative figures, over the period 1993–1997 it is important to note that the absolute amount of wages and salaries has almost doubled. In Scotland, it is more difficult to draw an overall conclusion for the Premier Division. As several smaller clubs do not disclose information on wages and salary costs, it is therefore impracticable to provide year on year figures. However, over the four-year period there seems to have been a fairly steady relationship between wages and turnover, where the percentage of turnover being represented by wages shows a gradual increase over this period. Similar to England, the absolute amount of wages and salaries has increased substantially over the period 1993–1997.

Such aggregated divisional figures, of course, do not provide the full picture for individual clubs. Big clubs have higher wager bills, but their revenue earning capability mean that these wages often constitute a smaller portion of their revenues. Table 2.4 shows the relationship

Table 2.4   Wages and salaries costs by club – 1996/97

Club	Wages and salaries (£000)	Turnover (£000)	Wages and salaries/ turnover (%)	Gate receipts (y.e. 1997) (£000s)	Wages and salaries/gate receipts (%)
Premier League					
Arsenal	15 279	27 158	56%	10 632	144%
Aston Villa	10 070	22 079	46%	7 346	137%
Blackburn Rovers	14 337	14 302	100%	5 304	270%
Chelsea	14 873	23 729	63%	NA	NA
Coventry City	8 396	12 265	68%	4 850	173%
Derby County	6 407	10 737	60%	4 425	145%
Everton	10 933	18 882	58%	NA	NA
Leeds United	12 312	21 785	57%	6 562	188%
Leicester City	8 914	17 320	51%	6 511	137%
Liverpool	15 030	39 153	38%	NA	NA
Manchester United	22 552	87 939	26%	30 111	75%
Middlesbrough	11 332	22 502	50%	NA	NA
Newcastle United	17 487	41 134	43%	25 505	69%
Nottingham Forest	8 034	14 435	56%	6 812	118%
Sheffield Wednesday	7 571	14 335	53%	6 223	122%
Southampton	4 776	9 238	52%	NA	NA
Sunderland	5 703	13 415	43%	NA	NA
Tottenham Hotspur	12 057	27 874	43%	13 641	88%
West Ham United	8 298	15 256	54%	7 015	118%
Wimbledon	6 018	10 549	57%	NA	NA
Scottish Premier					
Aberdeen	3 812	5 569	68%	2 189	174%
Celtic	8 668	22 189	39%	10 626	82%
Dundee United	2 224	4 878	46%	NA	NA
Dunfermline Athletic	1 532	2 059	74%	NA	NA
Heart of Midlothian	2 835	4 922	58%	2 882	98%
Hibernian	2 520	3 776	67%	2 039	124%
Kilmarnock	1 772	3 446	51%	NA	NA
Motherwell	1 397	1 649	85%	NA	NA
Raith Rovers	1 257	2 841	44%	984	128%
Rangers	13 676	31 664	43%	NA	NA

Source: Club accounts, Deloitte & Touche (1998b)

between wages and salaries and income sources for individual clubs for the 1996/97 season.

As expected there are large differences in the wage bills of individual clubs. Equally important are large differences in the revenue earning potential of clubs. The categorisation of clubs is for the most part predictable. In the majority of cases, the big wage spenders are also the big earners and therefore wages represent a modest percentage of turnover (e.g. Manchester United, Liverpool, Newcastle United and Rangers). Likewise the small spenders with smaller revenue sources and where wages represent a larger percentage of turnover are also equally predictable (e.g. Southampton, Wimbledon and the majority of Scottish clubs). As always, however there are exceptions, most noticeably Blackburn Rovers which has a very high wage bill but an average revenue base. However, in view of the way in which that club has been run in recent years, its capital structure and its attempt to regain its past status as a big name in English football, this figure cannot be seen as surprising. Table 2.4 also demonstrates that wage bills at several top clubs are in excess of their gate receipts, highlighting once again that although gate receipts remain an important source of revenue for clubs, for most clubs it is now only one of several vital sources of income (see Chapter 1).

As mentioned at the start of this section, clubs are not required to break down wages costs into playing staff and others, therefore the figures in Tables 2.3 and 2.4 include all football club employees. Deloitte & Touche (1997) have estimated that two thirds of total wages and salaries costs for football clubs is made up by players' wages costs. The only top division club which does provide a separate breakdown of wages and salaries between playing staff and other staff is Celtic. For seasons 1996/97 and 1995/96 approximately 62 per cent of its wages and salaries costs is in respect of players, managerial and training staff. Deloitte & Touche (1998b) note that the wage bill within the Premier League increased by 31 per cent for accounting years ended in 1997. Given that the average increase for non-football staff is likely to be around 5 per cent, they estimate that average players' wages grew at a rate of at least 35 per cent in 1996/97 (25 per cent – 1995/96) to an amount of £135m for the Premier League. Over the life of the Premier League (since 1992) they estimate that players' wages have increased at 25.7 per cent compound annual growth, compared to 22.7 per cent compound annual growth in turnover.

Growth factors

As we have seen in the previous section, there is evidence of growth in clubs' wages and salaries bills, and in particular in respect of player costs. Increases in players' salaries has absorbed much of the additional wealth that has come into football (see the section on *Television – football's economic driver* in Chapter 1). The main driving force in the increase in players' salaries is likely to have been the *Bosman* decision, although other factors, particularly the role of agents in the bargaining process may also have contributed.

Hitherto transfer market restrictions have played a part in constraining players' salaries. *Bosman* has allowed players reaching the end of their contracts to negotiate improved contractual terms in the knowledge that a club from a country outside the UK will not require to pay a transfer fee as compensation to their original club. Much of the salary growth has arisen out of the arrival of top European players in the Premier League, and to a lesser extent in the Scottish Premier Division. The abolition of the domestic transfer system for players over 24 years old in the summer of 1998 means that this upward pressure may continue. As a result funds which previously flowed between the top clubs in the form of transfer fees have been captured by the players.

Another significant inflationary factor is the desire of top clubs to tie up players on longer term contracts to protect themselves against the *Bosman* ruling. In expectation of the abolition of the domestic transfer system, clubs have moved to lock their top players, particularly younger top players, into longer term contracts.

This has three major effects. First, the club's investment is protected over a longer period (i.e. if another club wishes to acquire one of its players a compensating transfer fee will still be payable during that contract period). Secondly, the club is probably forced to offer improved contractual terms in order to persuade the player to sign up for a long term contract. Thirdly, although wages and salaries will rise at the time of signing the long term contracts, such contracts will possibly keep down future pay rises. Several clubs have attempted to follow this strategy.

The largest year on year increase in a club's wage bill for 1996/97 was Manchester United which saw a 70 per cent rise. A large proportion of this increase related to securing its young players on long term contracts. Italy and the Netherlands were the first countries to abolish domestic transfer markets, while still retaining transfer fees in respect of players coming into and out of the country. One consequence has been a movement to longer contracts. Simmons (1997) notes that typical contract lengths have risen from between two to three years to between five and ten years. (The failure of clubs to use long term contracts pre-*Bosman* is discussed in the section *Efficiency of borrowing* in Chapter 3.)

The capture of wealth by the players can be explained by considering the economic fundamentals of the industry. Szymanski (1997) describes the English football leagues as having *player market efficiency*, i.e. that all the predictable factors which affect player performance are captured by the wage bill, and that furthermore the wage bill is a highly efficient predictor of performance.[8] As a result it is expected that clubs with the greatest revenue earning potential will attract the best players and will bid up wages through competition among themselves. Furthermore there are no formal barriers to entry into football leagues in the UK (unlike the closed league structure found in US professional sport).[9] This means that clubs with lower revenue earning potential will compete to hire players to the point where profits are the minimum feasible for survival. This can be seen by considering the wage bills of clubs like Nottingham Forest seeking to regain Premier League status. Although its revenue earning potential is greater than many other First Division clubs (through for example the receipt of television parachute payments), its desire to regain Premier League status and the resultant income means that it will be prepared to increase its wage bill to the position where profits are the minimum feasible for survival.[10] These factors taken together mean that it is very largely to be expected that football's new income will be captured by the players.

Not all players will be recipients of this new wealth. In fact it is likely that that there will be a more unequal distribution of wealth among players. This will be caused by two factors: first, top players will be able to demand higher salaries and favourable contracts as a consequence of the competition among clubs for their services discussed earlier, and secondly, the increasing number of foreign imports will reduce the opportunities for many players to gain employment with the top earning clubs. In addition, this may contribute to an excess supply of domestic players, which will exact downward pressure on lower level salaries (Simmons, 1997).

Such a widening of the distribution of salaries is a consequence of the abolition of the transfer system and the removal of restrictions on the movement of players. In a study of salary costs at a Scottish Premier Division club pre-*Bosman*, Morrow (1996a) found very little evidence of inequality of income distribution. A Lorenz curve can be used to study the characteristics of salary distribution, with inequality in the income distribution showing as a bulge in the curve. The degree of inequality can then be measured by calculating what is known as a Gini coefficient. The coefficient can take any value between 0 and 1, the larger the coefficient, the more unequal being the salary distribution. The Gini coefficient for the Premier Division club was calculated at only 0.250, implying that salaries were reasonably equally distributed. By way of comparison, in a study of US professional baseball in 1990, a sport in which there is free agency for players, Quirk and Fort (1992) calculated a coefficient of 0.508. The lack of differentiation in the salary structure in the Premier Division club was also in marked contrast to the differentiation in expected realisable or sales values provided by the club's chairman and manager in respect of the same players.

Unsurprisingly many club directors are unhappy with the current growth in salary levels.[11] However, in view of the economic structure of the market discussed above, and particularly given the correlation between club performance and wage bill they have little option other than to pay the going rate. Some might see it a justice for the exploitative treatment of players by clubs in earlier days. However, it is also important that players do not become perceived as exploiting the supporters through exorbitant salary levels and demands (see Chapter 5). Already there is some evidence of dissatisfaction in this regard. The most recent FA Premier League fan survey found that 42.4 per cent of supporters thought that player salaries were 'way too high', compared to 39.1 per cent who thought that were high but recognised the short career of players, 10.8 per cent who thought they were reasonable in comparison with other sports and only 7.7 per cent who thought that most players deserved their earnings (SNCCFR, 1997). The survey, however, also found that it was not usually the fans of clubs with the highest wage bills who complained most strongly, but rather supporters of clubs which are least able to compete with spending on salaries made by clubs which are to the fore. Nevertheless, this level of dissatisfaction can only grow if clubs continue to pass on the costs of salaries to supporters, as witnessed by the decision taken by seventeen out of twenty Premier League clubs to increase their season ticket prices above the rate of inflation for season 1998/99.

The future

It is not possible to predict future movements in wage levels with any certainty. Nevertheless, in the short term there seems little to indicate anything other than further increases as more clubs attempt to lock players into longer term contracts and more players attempt to capitalise on their post-*Bosman* freedom, particularly with changes in domestic freedom of contract.

Looking to the longer term, various factors may have an influence. For example, ultimately it is possible that changes in the operation of the labour market for players will lead to genuine freedom of contract or free agency, akin to that enjoyed by employees in most other occupations. Were this to happen, then experience in the United States suggests that that further upward pressure is likely to be exerted on wage levels, particularly for top or star performers.

Another possibility is regulation in the player salary market. One form of regulation would be the introduction of some system of salary capping. Salary caps are found in American football and baseball and are to be introduced in rugby league in both England and Australia in 1998. They operate by imposing an upper limit on wage expenditure, the aim being to ensure leagues remain competitive, that is that there is uncertainty of outcome. A salary cap does not restrict payment to individual players, but instead imposes an upper limit on the total that a club can spend on player salaries.

There are two kinds of salary cap: *hard salary caps* which impose an absolute limit on payments to players and *soft salary caps* which contain exceptions or loopholes. For example, the soft salary cap which operates in the National Basketball Association (NBA) in the United States allows teams unlimited money to re-sign their own stars. The NBA's annual salary cap is set at 51.8 per cent of the league's 'defined gross revenues', with each team in the league being capped at the same level. While the Australian rugby league salary cap will be calculated in a similar way, in Britain all 31 Rugby League clubs will have a different salary cap figure, defined as 50 per cent of a club's 'salary cap relevant income' for 1998 (Sadler, 1998).

The salary cap is calculated from projections submitted to the Rugby Football League by the individual clubs for income sources such as television rights fees, gate receipts and sponsorship. Relevant income also includes donations which may prove to be a loophole in the operation of the salary cap. Similar to the position found in football, club incomes vary widely in rugby league with clubs like Wigan and Bradford Bulls being rugby league's equivalent of Manchester United. It is noticeable under this capping model, therefore, that top earning clubs will still be able to gain from their financial strength unlike the NBA model.

Whether a salary capping model could be used in football in the UK is debatable. One problem is that football is much more international in nature than other sports in which salary caps are operational. The *Bosman* case was concerned, after all, with the free movement of workers within the European Union. Therefore a salary cap unilaterally applied in, say England or Scotland, would only place clubs from these countries at a disadvantage when bidding for players playing in other leagues. Furthermore although the salary cap may contribute towards ensuring competitive balance within say the Premier League, as was discussed in Chapter 1, in football the European competitive dimension is now increasingly important. Consequently, a domestic salary cap in professional football would serve only to place English or Scottish clubs at a competitive sporting disadvantage to their European competitors.

Notwithstanding the European dimension, as was discussed in Chapter 1, football's direction is very clearly moving from cross-subsidisation and financial redistribution. As such it is difficult to see a salary capping model, even a modified salary cap like that found in rugby league in Britain, being acceptable to the modern football company.

A further problem would be its acceptance by players. While very far removed from the concept of a maximum wage, it is difficult to see why players who have fought for many years and through more than one court case for improved treatment by clubs, should be expected to relinquish any share of the financial rewards which they are now receiving. Any attempt to introduce a salary cap without the consent of the players would almost certainly rightly result in another *Bosman*-type challenge being made in the courts.

Failure to regulate the salary market, however, may well mean that the fight to control wages will have to be left to market forces to resolve. As mentioned previously there is already evidence of club chairmen talking about the need for financial discipline and prudence. This arises out of the fact that many of these clubs are now judged on financial terms as well as footballing terms. The difficulty for clubs, as will be discussed in more detail in Chapter 5, is finding the correct balance between these footballing and financial objectives. This is particularly difficult in the area of players' salaries given the previously identified correlation between wage levels and on field success.

Perhaps one other opportunity for wages control lies with the supporters. In Chapter 5, a framework will be put forward which aims to encourage clubs to recognise the importance of all of its stakeholders when carrying out business. The framework is concerned with the importance of companies maintaining confidence in their operations and in their business conduct. If this confidence is lacking then companies run the risk of exposing themselves to sanctions. One example of companies losing this confidence was shareholder dissatisfaction with increases in top executives' remuneration at British Gas.[12] In this regard, it could be argued that the greatest pressure for wage restraint may actually come from supporters, who as previously mentioned are already beginning to show some signs of disapproval of player salaries. Given their continued financial importance to clubs, both directly through gate receipts and sales of merchandise and indirectly through their importance to television as part of the atmosphere and hence the product, it may well be in the best interests of players and their representatives to respond to legitimate concerns supporters may have about spiralling wages.

Implications for the transfer market

The end of the transfer market?

Table 2.5 sets out the transfer expenditure within England for recent seasons.

The table shows that the total level of real spending on transfers within the football league has continued to rise in recent years. It should be noted, however, that the decision in the *Bosman* case was not announced until December 1995. Nevertheless it is expected that the decision will have an impact on the market for players in a number of ways in due course.

In terms of expenditure in the transfer market, one impact of the *Bosman* decision for English clubs is that a large amount of transfer activity has been with clubs outside England, in particular overseas clubs. For season 1995/96 Deloitte & Touche (1997) calculated that £93

Table 2.5   Transfer fees paid (between English clubs)

	1995/96 (£m)	1994/95 (£m)	1993/94 (£m)	1992/93 (£m)	1991/92 (£m)
Premier League	94.2	84.0	66.9	50.8	46.4
% increase year on year		12%	26%	32%	10%
All leagues	139.6	109.9	91.8	73.2	74.9
% increase year on year		27%	20%	25%	(2%)

Source: Deloitte & Touche (1997, 1996), Touche Ross (1995, 1994, 1993), The Football League

million flowed out of the English game as a net result of transfer between English and overseas clubs, while by 1996/97 more than 5 per cent of the players in the Football League were foreign nationals (Simmons, 1997). Of course one important aspect of the transfer market for football players is that it can become a truly international market in that language is not a major barrier.[13]

It seems unlikely that transfer markets will disappear entirely. A new domestic transfer system has been introduced in the UK in the summer of 1998. Under the new system any player aged 24 or more, who is out of contract on or after 1 July 1998 (or 16 May 1998 where the transfer was between Scottish clubs), is free to transfer his registration to another club without that club requiring to pay a transfer fee to the club which previously held his registration. (The new system will be considered in more detail in the next section.) This is significant as the transfer system contributes to what Simmons (1997) describes as the *matching system* within football. What this means is that the operation of the transfer system makes it easier for clubs to change to try to achieve success, i.e. to buy and sell players in the hope of finding the right blend of players and management which will contribute to sporting success, leading also to financial success.

The fact that players will be free to move for no fee at the end of their contracts means that some reduction in inter-club transfer fees might be expected as that information is reflected in buying clubs' behaviour. Most likely, a player's realisable value will converge towards zero as the end of his contract approaches. In financial markets, such reactions are not uncommon. For example, in the fixed interest government securities markets, the phrase 'the pull to redemption' refers to the fact that redeemable securities will converge toward their nominal value as the date of redemption approaches. One consequence of this will be that where a club believes that a player will not wish to remain with the club after the end of his contract or where the club does not wish him to remain, we may expect to see clubs attempting to move that player on some time in advance of the expiry of his contract.

Longer term contracts seem to be inevitable at the top end of the market. As a result, negotiation will revolve around conflicting objectives, with players often seeking to retain the benefits of mobility, while clubs will seek security in their investment. In this contract negotiation there will be risks to both sides. The purchase of Alan Shearer by Newcastle United for a then world record fee of £15m probably reflects the risks for both parties more clearly than most transactions, involving as it has an exceptionally high initial investment, unprecedented publicity and consequent commercial benefits for the club, managerial turnover, outstanding footballing form, serious injury, the possibility of relegation and several high profile on-field incidents involving the player!

Monitoring

Another factor which may influence the level of activity and the size of fees is City interest in the transfer market. In financial terms, investing in a player is a form of capital expenditure. In accounting terms, as will be discussed in detail in Chapter 4, that investment now requires to be shown as an asset on the club's balance sheet. One institutional investor interviewed in connection with this book said that discussions between himself and club management on the subject of players were always in the context of ROI (return on investment), a commonly used ratio for assessing the success of capital expenditure in financial terms. In his view the intangible nature of the investment in players did not mean it should be treated any differently from other investments, believing that it was not dissimilar to investments made in industries such as music or recording, drugs companies or software companies.

As will be discussed in Chapters 4 and 5, several merchant banks have taken an interest in assessing the capital expenditure on players by clubs. In this regard a model developed by Dr Bill Gerrard at Leeds University has been prominent (see Dobson and Gerrard, 1997). The model identifies three factors – player characteristics, selling club features (such as divisional status) and buying club characteristics (such as divisional status and current league performance) – as explaining 80 per cent of the variation in transfer fees. One study carried out by a merchant bank and heavily reported in the financial press suggested that about £14m of shareholder value was wiped off Tottenham Hotspur through poor player purchases.[14] The report concludes that 'player capital expenditure for a quoted football club is a cardinal issue': which should leave no one in doubt about how the City views attempting to buy success through the transfer market.

Compensation for training and development

In the *Bosman* case UEFA argued that the purpose of the transfer fee was to provide compensation for clubs which had invested in the recruitment and training of players (CJEC, 1995a, para. 235). This argument and the linkage asserted by UEFA between transfer fees and the survival of smaller clubs was rejected by the Advocate General who noted that the majority of transfer activity was in respect of established players and as a result it was difficult to see such fees as providing compensation for training and development (CJEC, 1995a, para. 237). The Court was even more dismissive of the argument that transfer fees acted as a means of compensation for training and development, noting that transfer fees were 'by nature contingent and uncertain and are in any event unrelated to the actual costs borne by clubs of training both future professional players and those who will never play profession-ally' (CJEC, 1995b, para. 109). Nevertheless, the Advocate General was of the opinion that it would be desirable to maintain or develop a system that protected those clubs which had invested in youth policies, but that this compensation should relate to the expenditure incurred by the club (CJEC, 1995a, para. 239).

The case for compensation

The argument for compensation rests on the recognition that football-ers' skills are industry specific not firm specific (Stewart, 1986). Without some form of compensation to clubs for skills training then the nature of the footballers' task means that there is a risk that other clubs can poach promising young players. Thus there may be little incentive for clubs to engage in training (Simmons, 1997). However, the risk of poaching within an industry where the skills of the employees are primarily industry specific rather than firm specific is not restricted to football. For example, professional accounting firms invest large sums in training professional accountants but are still faced by high staff turnover and poaching by other firms. At present, under-investment by football clubs in training is partially mitigated by state funding of youth training. But the prospect of obtaining a transfer fee provides an impor-tant incentive for clubs to engage in training, i.e. in purely financial terms the absence of a transfer market among clubs may act as a discouragement to investor clubs if no return is available to them for personal discovery and development.

The case against compensation

Logical as much of the preceding discussion is, there are counter argu-ments about the appropriateness of maintaining any kind of transfer system which is designed to compensate clubs for their investment in training young players. We have already touched on one question, namely that of why football clubs should be treated any differently in terms of compensation from other companies that carry out training and development. Arguably the only thing which differentiates football clubs from other organisations is that there has always been some compensatory mechanisms in place in football. Leaving aside such circular reasoning, it is commonly asserted that football clubs will reduce their investment in training and development if no compensatory fee exists. Little evidence presently exists to back up this assertion. More fundamentally, it can be asked why *any* organisation should be compensated for training its workforce? In other words, in many occupations ongoing training is commonplace and indeed it could be argued that there is often an expectation that training should take place. If, on the other hand, there is evidence of development taking place or of added value being provided then arguably there is more validity for a compensation scheme to exist.

In this regard it is interesting to consider whether clubs can distinguish between training and development. As will be discussed in Chapter 4 very little information is currently provided by clubs in their annual reports on the extent to which they invest in training and development, other than in terms of physical assets such as facilities. In a study carried out into accounting for football players at a Scottish Premier Division club, Morrow (1996a) found that the club was unable to provide financial information on the historical costs incurred in respect of training and development of its players in total. If clubs believe that compensation for investment in training is appropriate, then, as a minimum, it is reasonable to expect them to be in a position to quantify that investment. Indeed, far from simply accumulating costs it might be expected that clubs are able to assess the effectiveness of that training, using ROI type calculations as discussed earlier with regard to player purchases. There remains a suspicion that decisions taken by many clubs on questions of training and development are taken on the basis of custom and practice. Some evidence of established custom being challenged has been provided with the decision by the breakaway clubs in Scotland to replace the Reserve League with an under-21 league.

Various other questions emerge in considering this area. For example, is it possible to develop older players as well as younger players? To what extent is a player's ability improved by coaching and to what extent is it natural artistic ability? Should a club be rewarded for training a player who is blessed with inherent ability? How much of a player's improvement is down to the quality of a club's coaching? More intriguingly, what about the reverse situation, i.e. what about a player who believes his ability has been harmed by a club's training and managerial approach?[15] Why should clubs be compensated for poor training?

Some answers have been provided to these questions and others as a result of a survey carried out on behalf of Scottish Football's Independent Review Commission to establish the views of professional footballers in Scotland (Moorhouse, 1997). The report details the findings of a statistically reliable sample of 203 professional players in Scotland, supplemented by the results from a separate consultation with 18 members of the Scottish international squad.[16]

Some of its findings are as follows:

- 78 per cent of the international squad and 80 per cent of professional players in Scotland, believed that managerial tactics and bad coaching are having too marked an effect on the game;
- substantial minorities both in the international squad and of professional players in Scotland have a negative view of the training and development that they received at their first club. For example, only 56 per cent of the international squad and 61 per cent of professional players in Scotland agreed that 'clubs took a great deal of trouble to coach and develop the young players', while only 45 per cent of international players and 49 per cent of professional players agreed that 'people in charge of young professionals were good coaches who knew how to bring on players of that age'. It is also worth remembering that this survey is by definition a survey of those players who have achieved success within the present system of youth development.
- 89 per cent of the international squad and 97 per cent of professional players in Scotland thought that coaching was at least as important as (56 per cent, 85 per cent), or more important than (33 per cent, 12 per cent), natural ability.

It is obviously difficult to reduce a detailed report down to a few paragraphs. Nevertheless, it is clear that there are concerns with both the coaching available to professional players and the lack of good coaching and training facilities available to young Scots. It is also clear that players are not against coaching, but that they insist that it must be high quality.

The question of who should carry out the training is related to this issue. At present, in the UK, unlike most of continental Europe, no formal qualifications are required to act as a coach or trainer. Several top clubs, however, have taken the view that foreign coaches will contribute to a successful improvement in playing quality, with notable success. For the first time in both cases, in season 1997/98 the manager/ head coach of the winners of the top division in England and Scotland were from outside the British Isles. Returning to the survey, only 15 players (of whom seven were very recent professionals) thought that the general level of coaching in Scotland was as good as it is anywhere else in Europe, a view, unsurprisingly, not held by any member of the international squad. The question of who should carry out training of players, particularly young players, can also be considered from the point of view of the clubs. As mentioned previously, it is often asserted that the transfer system compensates those small clubs which invest time and money in developing young players. It might be reasonable to ask why the large football clubs are not carrying out this training and investment themselves. In one of the most damning findings of the survey, only 16 per cent of professional players and 11 per cent of the international squad believed that most clubs are geared up to play a much bigger role in youngsters' training. Why should clubs with large resources and infrastructure be so ineffective at training and developing young players that they have to rely on small inadequately funded clubs to develop players for them? Although the study considered only Scotland, there is little doubt that the same problems exist in England as witnessed by recent moves to overhaul clubs' youth development schemes.

The new system

Notwithstanding the above findings, a new transfer system was introduced in England from 1 July 1998 and in Scotland from 16 May 1998. Following the decision taken in the *Bosman* case, transfer fees are no longer payable in respect of the transfer of any player from one British club to another, where that player is aged 24 or over and where he is out of contract on or after 30 June 1998 (16 May 1998 in the case of a transfer between Scottish clubs). For players who have come to the end of their contract before the age of 24 then compensation will be payable. Where two clubs are unable to agree a fee for such a player then a tribunal is required to decide on the appropriate level of compensation. That compensation will be dependent on a number of factors: the expense of training and development, a player's first team appearances, his international appearances, efforts made by his club to retain his services, efforts made by other clubs to acquire his services and so on.

The system is recognised by the football associations, the football leagues and the players' unions as something of a half-way house, designed to reflect the principle of player mobility while still encouraging clubs to invest in training and development. In England it is designed to encourage clubs to continue to have Youth Training Schemes, now to be entitled Football Scholarship Programmes for players aged 16 to 19 years old and to attain Academy Status where they are prepared to have coaching, education and development programmes from the ages of 16 to 21 years old.

So far the operation of the new system has seen several players move between British clubs during the summer of 1998 for no fee. How well the new system will operate with regard to encouraging the development of young players, or indeed how long it will survive before being challenged by a player or a club or whoever, is at this stage an interesting but unanswerable question.

3 The Capital Structure of Football Clubs

INTRODUCTION

The phrase *capital structure* refers to the way in which a company is funded for the medium to long term. In practice the distinction between short term financing and long term financing has become blurred, as financial innovations and changing presentation methods have allowed enterprises more freedom to obtain financing over different future time periods. As a general rule we can use the following definitions:

- *'short term'* – less than three years, but usually less than one year;
- *'medium term'* – three to ten years; and
- *'long term'* – over ten years.

Two primary sources of funds are, however, available across all time periods – internal (profits from the operations of the enterprise) and external (creditors and investors). Table 3.1 demonstrates the continuing importance of internal funds as a source of funds for business enterprises in the UK. Variations exist across the different groupings of companies which make up the aggregate data shown in Table 3.1, particularly in respect of small companies. The lack of availability of equity and debt to small companies, identified as the Macmillan Gap in the 1930s, remains a problem today. However, the Alternative Investment Market (AIM) has made it easier for smaller and growing companies to gain access to equity funds (AIM is discussed in the section *Which market?* later in the chapter).

Medium term finance is typically raised from banks as a term loan. The enterprise will frequently use this form of finance either for assets of corresponding lives or to provide a working capital base (i.e. to maintain day to day operations). An alternative to bank funding for *medium term* financing is the use of credit, either through hire purchase or leasing. *Long term* financing is generally used for major fixed assets such as buildings, plant and machinery or to takeover other companies. For *long term* financing, an enterprise may use banks and

Table 3.1 Sources of capital funds of industrial and commercial companies

	1985 (%)	1987 (%)	1989 (%)	1991 (%)	1993 (%)	1995 (%)	1997 (%)
Internal	70	51	33	49	65	53	48
Capital transfers, import/ other credits	1	0	1	1	1	2	1
Borrowing	18	22	41	4	−10	16	9
Capital issues: Ordinary shares	8	19	2	14	18	12	14
Other[1]	3	8	23	32	26	17	28
Total (£m)	46 185	71 415	105 429	67 035	77 643	106 711	136 443

[1] Includes debentures, preference shares, other capital issues and other overseas investment.
Source: Financial Statistics, Tables 8.2 and 10.6B, various dates, Office for National Statistics

other financial institutions or it may issue company securities, such as ordinary shares, preference shares and loan capital.

Ordinary shares (or equity shares) form the major part of a normal company's share capital. Equity share capital provides a permanent source of finance to an issuing company, i.e. unlike, for example, bank loans, equity shares do not require to be repaid in the future. They have no right to any dividend: although the profits belong to the ordinary shareholders, the company's directors may decide to withhold any distribution of these, wholly or partly, to the shareholders, in order to provide internally generated funds, say, to buy new players or make ground improvements in the case of a football club. Generally, however, where there is a reasonably steady record of profits some dividends will be paid to ordinary shareholders. Ordinary shares thus form the risk capital of the company, and the holders are its proprietors. Ordinary shares usually carry voting rights, allowing the holders to exercise ultimate control over the firm, although some companies have non-voting ordinary shares as well as voting ones.

Preference shares usually entitle the shareholder to a fixed annual dividend out of profits after tax payable in priority to the ordinary dividend. Dividends on preference shares are only payable if the company has adequate distributable profits, but are normally cumulative – i.e. the liability for unpaid dividends must be carried forward to future years and paid out, before any ordinary dividends, to preference shareholders when profits are being made.

Loan capital (or bonds) includes debentures and unsecured loan stock. Interest is payable on bonds regardless of whether the company makes a profit. Most loan stocks are redeemable (i.e. will be repaid at a future date). A debenture is a document which evidences the fact that the owner has lent money to the business for a specified period usually at a fixed rate of interest. Debentures are normally secured on some or all of the assets of the business, e.g. the ground. Should the interest or capital appear to be in jeopardy, the lenders or debenture holders may require the company to sell the asset which secures the debenture in order to repay them.

For various reasons, which will be considered in turn, the capital structure of football clubs have often had little in common with the pattern found for other companies. The majority of football clubs are small companies: historically they have been undercapitalised, restricted in their rights to pay dividends, had little or no retained profit, and relied heavily on borrowings as a source of funding, often bank funding in the form of overdraft facilities and thus short term in nature. Partly, this is owing to regulations on ownership and financial behaviour imposed on clubs by the football authorities, such as the FA and the SFA (see sections on *The football sector in perspective* and *Ownership framework in football clubs* later in this chapter). Other factors such as the nature of the product and of the industry, as well as the characteristics of the owners of clubs, have also contributed to the capital structure found in clubs.

EQUITY FINANCE

Share issues are an important source of finance in the UK company sector. Despite the recent inflow of investment capital into football clubs, Table 3.2 shows that many of the top clubs in Britain remain undercapitalised. A club can be described as undercapitalised when it has a disproportionately low level of equity funding compared to its asset base.

Table 3.2   Assets compared with equity funding, FA Premier League and Scottish Premier Division clubs (1997 accounting year ends)

Company	Total assets less current liabilities	Called up share capital	Equity funding	Asset value per £ of equity funding
	£000s	£000s	£000s	£
Premier League clubs				
Arsenal	23 969	56	293	81.80
Aston Villa	26 882	572	15 722	1.71
Blackburn Rovers	37 079	40 000	40 000	0.93
Chelsea (Chelsea Village)	64 948	1561	36 209	1.79
Coventry City	(6 765)	14	14	(483.21)
Derby County	7 292	1 173	1 435	5.08
Everton	10 183	35	25 003	0.41
Leeds United (Caspian)	15 869	2 849	36 534	0.43
Leicester City	3 422	346	346	9.89
Liverpool	24 455	157	11 475	2.13
Manchester United	101 986	6 494	25 110	4.06
Middlesbrough	(6 022)	1 056	1 056	(5.70)
Newcastle United	54 907	7 162	55 082	1.00
Nottingham Forest	10 179	10 100	17 500	0.58
Sheffield Wednesday	30 495	17 184	17 773	1.71
Southampton	9 041	1 359	2 200	4.11
Sunderland	18 641	82	10 835	1.72
Tottenham Hotspur	50 544	5 035	16 154	3.12
West Ham United	19 644	54	4 446	4.41
Wimbledon	964	160	160	6.03
Scottish Premier Clubs				
Aberdeen	5 707	2 383	3 171	1.80
Celtic	36 312	11 390	28 751	1.26
Dundee United	8 219	1.3	1.3	6 322.31
Dunfermline Athletic	(1 229)	45	825	(1.49)
Heart of Midlothian	6 766	1 012	6 424	1.05
Hibernian	217	500	500	0.43
Kilmarnock	6 478	1 377	1 978	3.28
Motherwell	1 805	269	466	3.87
Raith Rovers	2 813	70	70	40.19
Rangers	82 398	4 614	44 293	1.86

Notes

Equity funding = called up share capital plus share premium

Asset value per £ of equity funding = $\dfrac{\text{Total assets less current liabilities}}{\text{Equity funding}}$

Source: Company accounts

Table 3.2 demonstrates a marked imbalance for some clubs between their asset base and their equity funding. In particular, it highlights a distinction between clubs which have maintained a traditional football club capital structure and those which have altered their structure to allow the inflow of investment capital. Those clubs which have been listed on the stock market have significantly increased their level of equity funding by means of share issues and reorganisations (for example, Aston Villa, Chelsea, Newcastle United, Celtic and Heart of Midlothian). Consequently, for the most part, these clubs now report low asset values per £ of equity funding. Furthermore, clubs such as Everton, Sheffield Wednesday and Hibernian, which while not opting for a Stock Exchange listing, have also recently altered their share structure to allow new shares to be issued, thus substantially increasing the financial resources available to the club.

Other clubs, however, notably Arsenal and Dundee United, have resisted pressure to alter their capital structure and to raise capital through share issues. Consequently, these clubs have a very low level of equity funding in proportion to their asset base, as evidenced by the very high reported level of assets per £ of equity funding. Often these clubs continue to be controlled by their directors (see Tables 3.9 and 3.11). One difficulty for such clubs has been a continuing requirement to find alternative sources of capital to remain competitive and to make the necessary improvements in both infrastructure and personnel. Those clubs reporting negative asset values per £ of equity funding tend to have unusual capital structures. These will be discussed in the section *Ownership framework in football clubs* later in this chapter.

ROLE OF THE STOCK EXCHANGE

The Stock Exchange exists to provide attractive and well regulated financial markets. Such markets allow companies and other organisations (e.g. governments) to raise finance cost effectively, have their shares publicly traded and provide a means for investors to buy and sell shares efficiently and with access to the fullest possible information. Stock Exchanges act as both primary and secondary markets.[1]

The primary market

The activities associated with companies raising capital by becoming publicly quoted, or by following their initial offering with subsequent issues of shares, all come under the umbrella name of the 'Primary Market'. A company issues a security such as a share, usually at a predetermined price, and through the Stock Exchange the investor can subscribe to a new issue. The Stock Exchange in the UK has long played a prominent role in providing capital to UK companies; much more so than in continental Europe where there are smaller numbers of quoted companies and ownership of quoted companies is often concentrated in the hands of a small number of investors (Franks and Mayer, 1994). The importance of the Stock Exchange as a means of providing long-term capital was initially recognised by a football club in 1983, when Tottenham Hotspur became the first British club to make a public issue of shares, raising £3.3m by an offer for sale. The offer was highly successful, being oversubscribed by four times. But it was not a method of raising finance that gained popularity with other clubs in the industry until the 1990s.

The reluctance of professional sport to use the Stock Exchange as a means of raising funds has not been confined to the UK. Stock Exchanges in the USA are the largest and most sophisticated of all. But, although professional sport has long been big business there, the first publicly floated issue was the Boston Celtics basketball team in 1986. Ten years elapsed before the second took place, the Florida Panthers ice hockey team in 1996.

The attractions of the Stock Exchange as a means of raising capital are the same for football clubs as for other companies: the highly sophisticated London Stock Exchange is a large, liquid, accessible source of new capital.[2] Throughout the late 1980s and early 1990s clubs at all levels of the game have found themselves in the position of requiring access to large sums of capital, most notably in order to comply with the stadium safety requirements of the Taylor Report (Home Office, 1990).[3]

In addition to providing new sources of finance to fund stadium improvements, clubs have put forward various other reasons for seeking a stock market listing. These include the strengthening of playing squads, development of commercial operations, investment in youth training programmes, improvement of trading facilities, widening share ownership, widening supporter share ownership, providing increased liquidity to shareholders, reduction of borrowings and the provision of additional working capital. A further very helpful factor is that listing enables existing club owners to dilute their own personal exposure to the business and, importantly, makes it easier for them to liquidate all or part of their holding in the future. Indeed, several directors have benefited substantially through reorganisations and flotations (see the section *Paper prophets?* later in this chapter).

Which market?

Shares in twenty-one British clubs are now listed in London either on the Stock Exchange Official List or the Alternative Investment Market (AIM), while a further three clubs' shares are traded under the OFEX facility (see Table 3.3).

Each market is different in status, cost of joining and the compliance burden of being listed.

The London Stock Exchange's main market, also known as the Official List, is the UK's national share marketplace. The great majority of UK companies are listed and traded there. At the end of 1996

Table 3.3   Listed football clubs

Official List	AIM	OFEX
Aston Villa	Birmingham City	Arsenal
Burnden Leisure	Charlton Athletic	Manchester City
(Bolton Wanderers)	Chelsea Village	Rangers
Celtic[1]	Loftus Road (QPR)	
Leeds Sporting[2] (Leeds United)	Nottingham Forest	
Heart of Midlothian	Preston North End	
Leicester City	West Bromwich Albion	
Manchester United		
Millwall		
Newcastle United		
Sheffield United		
Silver Shield (Swansea)		
Southampton Leisure		
Sunderland		
Tottenham Hotspur		

[1] Celtic shares were listed on AIM until September 1998.
[2] Formerly Caspian plc.
Source: Datastream

there were 2171 listed UK companies on the main market, with a combined market capitalisation of £1012 billion. The Exchange also operates the world's largest market for trading international securities with over 530 international companies listed in London. As such it is the most prestigious listing available, which may help explain its popularity with football clubs.

Launched in June 1995, AIM is the Exchange's market for smaller, young and fast growing companies which are not ready or which do not wish to join the Official List. It has also attracted a number of family owned businesses. AIM now has over 260 companies, including for example Deep Sea Leisure, owners of one of Scotland's top tourist attractions Deep Sea World, and Dobbies Garden Centres, which runs garden centres throughout the North of England and Scotland. It has a total market value of nearly £6 billion and is operated and regulated by the Stock Exchange. It is designed to combine wide accessibility with an orderly well-disciplined market and is the quickest and least costly way of going public. By the end of 1996 over £1 billion had been raised by companies on AIM, either on admission or through further issues of shares.

OFEX is an unregulated trading facility for share dealing in unquoted companies, operated by J.P. Jenkins Ltd in association with Newstrack Limited. There is a code of best practice for OFEX companies and a listing panel of an accountant, a banker, a solicitor and a fund manager who review each application to join the market. However, the market is unregulated and there is no guarantee of liquidity in the shares. The OFEX facility information in the *Financial Times* states that shares traded on OFEX should be considered high risk investments. OFEX can be used as a stepping stone to AIM and 14 companies have taken this route to date.

To be quoted on the Stock Exchange, a company must satisfy, both at entry and subsequently, an extensive set of requirements on disclosure, as set out in the Stock Exchange Listing Rules (commonly referred to as the Yellow Book). The Yellow Book contains rules governing admission to listing, continuing obligations of issuers, enforcement of those obligations and suspension and cancellation of listing.

Chapter 3 of the Yellow Book deals with the initial 'Conditions for Listing'. These conditions include: a requirement to be able to provide unqualified audited accounts for the last three years[4] (3.3); that the directors of the applicant have collectively appropriate expertise and experience for the management of its business (3.8); that the securities to be listed are freely transferable (3.15); that the expected market value of shares to be listed must be at least £700 000 (3.16); and that at least 25 per cent of the shares must be made available to the public (3.19). Similar rules apply at Stock Exchanges in other countries.

However, many of these exchanges historically have required companies to be able to demonstrate records of profits, presenting a problem to many major European clubs, which have often been run at a substantial loss in recent years.[5] For example, prior to granting a listing the Madrid Stock Exchange requires companies to be able to demonstrate profitability in the last two, or three of the last five years,[6] while until December 1997 the Milan Stock Exchange required a new company to be able to show profits for three consecutive years prior to listing. This rule can now be set aside if the company seeking to list has introduced measures to ensure healthy balance sheets, as the Milan market seeks to attract the large numbers of Italian clubs who are seeking flotations. However, despite the promise of market deregulation, several European clubs have considered listing on the London Stock Exchange to take advantage of both the perceived less arduous listing requirements and the most developed market for football club stocks.

AIM offers the advantages of a public equity market, such as increased public profile and access to new capital and investors, within a simplified market structure. Unlike the Official List, AIM rules place no restrictions on the size of companies which join, length of operating record or the percentage of shares required to be held by the public. The costs of listing vary for different companies, but in broad terms the cost of listing (including fees) for the Official List will be in excess of £500 000 compared to approximately £250 000 for AIM and approximately £100 000 for OFEX. Given the apparent fit between the nature and objectives of AIM and the modern football club and the lower listing costs, it is perhaps a little surprising that only seven clubs have chosen to come to the market via AIM.

Companies applying for a listing must provide a complete picture of their business, in the form of an admission document or listing particulars, including information on such things as trading history, management and business prospects. This document provides investors with information to make an informed decision on a share issue.

The rigour of Stock Exchange disclosure requirements for football clubs is perhaps best illustrated at Newcastle United. In January 1997, the forthcoming share flotation apparently obliged the club to carry out a switch of managers in mid-season, (which was unlikely to be the best football option), because of the requirement under Stock Exchange rules to inform potential investors in the club of any material changes that may affect the company.[7] The continuing obligations imposed by the Listing Rules are illustrated by the fact that major decisions taken by clubs, such as purchasing players or sacking a manager, are now first announced through a statement to the Stock Exchange.

Raising capital

The amount raised to date by companies floating on either the Official List or AIM totals £167 million. In addition a further £9.4 million was raised by Celtic in a public offer in January 1995, with the shares subsequently being listed on AIM in September 1995. Table 3.4 sets out the amounts raised by each club and the methods of listing.

Although the sums being raised are large in the context of the football industry, for the most part they are small in the context of new issues on the Stock Exchange overall. Table 3.5 sets out the average amounts raised by UK companies listing on the main market and AIM for the first time.

Comparison of Tables 3.4 and 3.5 demonstrates that only the share issue made by Newcastle United in 1997 generated proceeds for the club close to the average proceeds raised by new issues that year on the main market. However, the proceeds of issues made by clubs through AIM were generally larger than the average proceeds raised by new issues on that market.

Methods of issuing shares

The different methods by which securities may be brought to listing are set out in the Yellow Book. The two most common methods are the Offer for Sale/Subscription and the Placing, both of which have been used extensively by football clubs.

In an Offer for Sale the company sells its shares to an Issuing House, usually a merchant bank which specialises in such work, which then offers them to the general public. Where a company is floated on the Stock Exchange some existing shareholders may wish to sell some of their present holdings. In that event the Issuing House may agree to purchase these shares from the existing shareholders and then offer these existing shares and the new issue shares to the public at the same price. An offer for sale can thus provide a way for the existing shareholders to realise part of their investment.

Table 3.4 Methods of listing and proceeds of offer

	Float Date	Method	% placed on offer	Net proceeds to company (£m)
Official List				
Aston Villa	May 1997	Placing/Offer	16%	15.2
Burnden Leisure	April 1997	Reverse takeover	100%	0.0
Heart of Midlothian	May 1997	Placing	39%	5.1
Caspian	August 1996	Takeover and Placing/Offer	60%	17.1
Manchester United	June 1991	Placing/Offer	38%	6.7
Millwall	October 1989	Placing/Offer	38%	4.8
Newcastle United	April 1997	Offer	28%	50.4
Sheffield United	January 1997	Takeover and Placing/Offer	42%	1.4
Silver Shield[1]	August 1997	Takeover	nil	nil
Southampton Leisure	January 1997	Reverse takeover	100%	nil
Sunderland	December 1996	Placing/Offer	26%	10.7
Tottenham Hotspur	October 1983	Offer for Sale	41%	3.3
AIM				
Birmingham City	March 1997	Placing	30%	7.5
Celtic	September 1995	Admission from Rule 4.2(a)[2]	0%	nil
Charlton Athletic	March 1997	Placing/Offer	35%	5.5
Chelsea Village	March 1996	Introduction	0%	nil
Loftus Road	October 1996	Placing/Offer	44%	12.0
Nottingham Forest	October 1997	Offer for Subscription	11%	3.0
Preston North End	October 1995	Placing/Offer	86%	6.7
West Bromwich Albion	January 1997	Placing	100%	20.5

[1] Silver Shield purchased an 80% interest in Swansea City Football Club, including the assignment of certain debt for £475 000. The consideration was funded by a vendor placing of ordinary shares in Silver Shield which raised £450 000.
[2] The January 1995 share offer was by an Offer for Subscription and Placing. The company moved from AIM to the Official List in September 1998.
Source: Deloitte & Touche *Annual Review of Football Finance 1997*, various share offer prospectuses

Table 3.5   Money raised by new listed UK companies

	No. of companies	Money raised (£m)	Average proceeds (£m)
Main market			
1991	97	2439.5	25.1
1992	82	2937.0	35.8
1993	179	5604.2	31.3
1994	256	11519.3	45.0
1995	189	2961.7	15.7
1996	228	7286.2	31.9
1997	135	7100.3	52.6
AIM			
1995	123	69.5	0.6
1996	145	514.1	3.5
1997	107	344.4	3.2

Source: The London Stock Exchange Fact File 1997, 1998

Placing involves the sale of shares by the company to the Issuing House, which in turn places the shares with its clients, usually institutions such as pension funds and life assurance companies. The public is not invited to subscribe. The advantage of a placing to clubs is that it reduces the risk of undersubscription of the sale, as the issuing house will seek to ensure that all the company's shares are placed. As can be seen from Table 3.4, it has been common for football clubs to bring their securities to Stock Exchange listing by means of a combined Offer for Sale and Placing.

An Introduction is a popular method of bringing securities to listing on the Stock Exchange. Under this method, securities already in issue may be introduced to listing where they are already of such an amount and sufficiently widely held that their marketability when listed can be assumed. An Introduction is a means of getting existing shares listed and available to the public and therefore provides no new capital for the company. Chelsea Village is the only football company to have come to the market by this route. An Introduction allows the shares to benefit from the exchange operating as a secondary market as opposed to a primary market, i.e. the listing provides a wider market for the shares. One benefit of this should be a narrower spread of share prices. Share prices are a function of both supply and demand. A market maker (someone who deals in shares) quotes two prices: a buying price (bid price) and a selling price (ask price). Where demand for a share is low (for example, if the shares are not widely held or traded) then a large spread is likely between the market maker's bid and ask prices. This spread reflects the market maker's risk in trading in less popular shares. (Secondary market issues are covered in detail later in this chapter.)

Shares dealt in under Rule 4.2 (a) of the London Stock Exchange are not listed on the Stock Exchange or traded on AIM. Companies must seek the permission of the Stock Exchange for shares to be dealt in under this Rule. It was originally established to enable member firms of the Stock Exchange to deal occasionally in suspended or unlisted securities 'on-Exchange' as the rules of the London Stock Exchange prohibited them from dealing 'off-Exchange'. Prior to being admitted to the Alternative Investment Market, shares in Celtic were traded under Rule 4.2 (a). Shares in Arsenal, Manchester City and Rangers continue to be traded on a matched bargain basis through the OFEX market under this Rule. The Rule is a useful way to provide a market to satisfy the trading requirements of individuals (often supporters) who hold a small number of shares in a club, where the club is controlled by one or a few individuals, usually directors (see section on the *Ownership framework in football clubs* later in this chapter).

Takeovers are a device whereby one company, the bidder, seeks to acquire the whole of the equity share capital of the target company. This may be done with the approval of the board of directors of the target company where the takeover is seen to be advantageous to the interests of the target company. This is the situation which has occurred at Manchester United where the Board of Directors have recommended acceptance of BSkyB's takeover offer (see section on *Reaching for the Sky* in Chapter 1). In other cases the takeover bid may be regarded as hostile and the directors will seek to frustrate it. A reverse takeover occurs when a smaller listed company seeks to take over a larger unlisted company, as has taken place at Bolton Wanderers, Southampton and Leicester City. Technically, a transaction will be a reverse takeover if an offeror or bidding company needs to increase its existing issued voting equity share capital by more than 100 per cent.

New issues – determinants of success

Although the share issue by Tottenham Hotspur in 1983 was oversubscribed by four times, prior to the recent wave of successful flotations, other attempts by football clubs to raise capital through share issues have not been unqualified successes. This was so even when the clubs involved were major names. For example, when Manchester United was floated in 1991 less than half the shares on offer were taken up, while Newcastle United's attempt to raise £8m through a subscription offer in 1990, managed to raise only £300 000. By contrast, more recent flotations have been well received by the market with issues by Birmingham City, Celtic, Loftus Road and Newcastle United (in 1997) all having being oversubscribed.

Various factors help explain the attractiveness of the more recent share issues compared to earlier issues. An obvious factor is that investors, in particular city investors, have been more enthusiastic about investing in what is perceived as the 'new business of football', characterised by significantly improved television deals and exposure, improved sponsorship and an improved public image. Consequently it is perceived to be a business with good future prospects and this ultimately determines the attractiveness of any investment. The City is also a place for sentiment and trends and there is little doubt that the 1990s saw football (and to a lesser extent other professional sports)[8] become fashionable and catch the imagination of the City.

Another important factor has been the kind of shares issued. The financial asset that has been offered to investors in recent share issues has been for the most part an ordinary equity share. This carries an unlimited right to dividends, provides ownership rights to the shareholder and is comparable in all material respects to other equity shares traded on the Stock Exchange. In other words owning a Marks & Spencer share is comparable to owning a Sheffield United share, other than the obvious difference as regard the nature of each business. The equivalence between football clubs and other companies is not restricted to the nature of share capital. Many clubs have adopted the concept of the customer, familiar in most other companies (such as Marks & Spencer), to reduce the relationship of the football fan to a purely economic one. It can be argued that this concept has transformed the relationship between fan and clubs, facilitating and legitimating the transformation of clubs into businesses and justifying the increase in admission prices (King, 1997). The only rights which are then available to customers of football clubs are those available to customers of Marks & Spencer, namely the economic rights of nonpurchase. (The appropriateness of the concept of the customer to football clubs will be discussed in detail in Chapter 5.)

Previously, however, it was not uncommon for clubs to seek capital through a share issue, but without providing the rights that normally accompanied such investment. The most common approach was to issue shares with restricted voting rights, and which did not, thereafter, provide ownership rights to the shareholder. One such recent example was the Offer for Subscription by Heart of Midlothian in 1994. Under the terms of this offer, investors were invited to subscribe for what were described as 'Club Shares' at 125p per share. These shares provided various rights to holders, such as the right to attend and speak at general meetings, the right to put forward a candidate for election to the Board as well as various other rights and privileges dependent on the level of subscription such as preferential rights to buy a season ticket. However, importantly such club shares did not carry the right to vote at shareholder meetings, except in respect of the appointment, removal or re-election of the directors put on the company board to represent them.[9]

The issue of dual class shares meant that dominant shareholders' control would remain unaffected and that they would largely be free to ignore small shareholders' wishes. Furthermore, given that the payment of dividends was (and indeed remains) an uncommon occurrence in most clubs, it was inconceivable that such issues would have attracted professional investors. Many clubs had an arrogant attitude that assumed that the loyalty of fans and their sense of identity with their club would ensure the success of such issues. In many cases such arrogance was misplaced as issues were undersubscribed. These share issues can be seen as clubs trying to take advantage of the complex social and political relationship which exists between fans and clubs to try and pass off a security which does not hold up to scrutiny under conventional investment analysis. Interestingly, this approach is in stark contrast to the unwillingness of clubs to consider the social and political dimensions involved in being a supporter, instead describing supporters as customers and thus reducing the relationship to a purely economic one (see the section *From fan to consumer?* in Chapter 5). The decision to treat prospective investors as equals within the club, at least from a finance or economic perspective, is welcome, if overdue.[10]

The football sector in perspective

Despite the extraordinary publicity, hype and media attention that has accompanied football's rush to the Stock Exchange and despite the growth of investor interest over a relatively short period of time, in corporate terms football clubs are still very much non-league in stature.[11] Tables 3.6 and 3.7 show the league table based on market capitalisation (and also turnover) for companies listed under the Leisure and Hotels sector on the main market (the sector under which football clubs are listed) and on AIM towards the end of 1997.

While the largest AIM listed football club, Chelsea Village, was also the second largest AIM listed company at that date, this ranking is not repeated for the main market, where the capitalisation of the largest club, Manchester United, is dwarfed by other companies listed in the same market sector.

League tables 3.6 and 3.7 can be partly explained by differences in the corporate structure of football clubs compared to other companies and in the rules which govern their operations.

The majority of large companies are in fact groups of companies or conglomerates. Often these groups have grown as a result of horizontal

Table 3.6   Market capitalisation: Official List, Leisure and Hotels Sector

Position		Market capitalisation (£m)	Turnover (£m)
All companies			
1	Granada	8090	4091
2	Ladbroke	3161	3816
3	Rank Group	2540	2012
4	Air Tours	1740	2174
Football clubs only			
1	Manchester United	411.8	87.9
2	Newcastle United	137.5	41.1
3	Aston Villa	83.0	22.1
4	Tottenham Hotspur	76.0	27.9
5	Caspian	67.0	22.8
6	Burnden Leisure	33.9	5.4[1]
7	Sheffield United	24.9	8.9
8	Sunderland	23.6	13.4
9=	Leicester City	20.7	17.3
9=	Southampton Leisure	20.7	6.3[2]
11	Millwall Holdings	13.3	NA

[1] Turnover of Burnden Leisure for the 14 months to 30 June 1997. This included £1m in respect of the acquisition of Bolton Wanderers. Turnover for Bolton for the year ended 30 June 1997 was £7.6m.
[2] Turnover of Southampton Leisure for the 14 months to 31 May 1997. This included £4m in respect of the acquisition of Southampton Football Club Limited. Turnover for Southampton Football Club for the year ended 31 May 1997 was £9.4m.
Source: The Financial Times, 22 December 1997, Company accounts

takeovers (i.e. acquisitions of companies in the same line of business). In some cases the two companies involved, although operating in the same line of business, may have different geographical marketplaces. A recent example is the acquisition of Courage by Scottish & Newcastle in August 1995. While both companies were major players in the brewing industry, their market strengths were complimentary, in that while Scottish & Newcastle was strong in Scotland and the North of England, Courage's main market place was London and the South of England.

By contrast, football clubs are independent local companies. The independence of clubs is required under the rules of the football authorities, i.e. rules exist which restrict the extent to which any person or persons can own shares in more than one club at the same time. FA Premier League Rules (FAPL, 1997) stipulate that no person or associate of that person can hold more than ten per cent of the issued share capital of another club and that no person can be involved in the management or administration of more than one club without the prior approval of the Premier League (Rule 4). Similar associations between clubs (as opposed to their officials) also requires prior approval of the Premier League (Rule 3). Likewise, in Scotland dual interests in clubs requires the prior consent of the Scottish League (SFL, 1997, Rule 88).

Table 3.7   Market capitalisation: Alternative Investment Market

Position		Market capitalisation (£m)	Turnover (£m)
All companies			
1	Ramco Energy	257.5	8.2
2	Chelsea Village	181.4	23.7
3	Southern Newspapers	178.4	105.4
4	Freepages	162.4	10.8
Football clubs only			
1	Chelsea Village	181.4	23.7
2	Celtic	75.0	22.2
3	Birmingham City	18.2	7.6
4	Loftus Road	12.6	7.5
5	Charlton Athletic	11.8	4.3
6	West Bromwich Albion	10.6	6.1
7	Preston North End	9.0	3.8

Source: The Financial Times, 22 December 1997, company accounts

These rules exist to ensure fair competition and to remove any risk of factors other than those connected with the playing of a football match influencing the outcome of matches. In financial terms, however, they limit the potential for growth by clubs.[12] One recent development has been multi-club ownership within Europe, as opposed to within one country. The most prominent example is ENIC (the English National Investment Company), a sports and entertainment group which has controlling interests in the Italian club Vicenza , the Greek club AEK Athens, the Czech club Slavia Prague and the Swiss club FC Basel, as well as a minority holding in Rangers. Implications arising out of such developments are discussed in the Conclusion.

Nevertheless, it is important to remember that while football itself may remain a very small business, the benefits it brings to other industries that associate with it are vast, particularly through increased television exposure.

OWNERSHIP FRAMEWORK IN FOOTBALL CLUBS

Historically, many British football clubs were private companies owned by small groups of local businessmen and a few hundred small shareholders, most of them fans. Restrictions on dividends and directors' fees conserved money within the industry but made it harder for clubs to attract capable directors and to issue further shares.[13] Such restrictions still remain in place in England. FA Rules require that member club companies include, within their articles of association, provisions restricting the dividends payable on shares. At present, up to 15 per cent p.a. (cumulative for up to three years) of the amount paid up on the shares can be distributed by way of dividend.[14]

The objectives of football clubs is an area which has been much discussed in the literature (see the section on *Club objectives* in Chapter 1). The traditional picture presented is of clubs seeking to maximise playing success while remaining solvent. As such it was argued that shares in football clubs normally provided only psychic income, in the form of influence or power, for their owners (Arnold and Webb, 1986). It has been generally considered that the expected return on investments made by the director/owners of football clubs is not primarily in financial terms, but in less tangible utility returns. This helps explain why a study carried out in 1982 (FIR, 1982) found that in half the 92 English Football League clubs, more than 40 per cent of voting shares were held by directors. A similar Scottish study found that more than 40 per cent of voting shares were held by directors in five of the country's then eight top clubs (Morrow, 1987).

Many club directors feared external involvement because it diluted their control of the club. Even where external finance in the form of share capital was raised, it was not uncommon for directors to dilute the voting structure of non-board members by the simple issue of new voting shares to those whom the directors decided should have them (FIR, 1982). The characteristics of football clubs' financing policies were the result of an active and logical (if in many cases undesirable) policy of internal capital restriction, designed to maintain the power and control of the club within the directors' hands. Such policies have constrained the ability of clubs to attain a sound financial footing and have resulted in many companies being markedly undercapitalised (see Table 3.2). Thus clubs have often been forced to rely on other sources of funding, particularly bank funding, resulting in a financing mismatch with long term projects being funded by short term financing (see section on *Efficiency of borrowing* later in this chapter).

McMaster (1997), however, contends that such a relationship prevails today, observing that recent high profile investments in large clubs which have been made primarily for financial gain are isolated incidents. Such investments reflect the increasing division between successful and unsuccessful clubs, thus suggesting that for the most part commercial criteria are secondary. This view is not universally accepted. King (1997) uses the term 'new directors' to describe the progressive entrepreneurial capitalists who have become involved in the game in the 1980s and 1990s who almost universally believe that football is a business and that clubs therefore must seek to maximise profits.

The current ownership position (1997) is not directly comparable with the earlier identified statistics for some football clubs have altered their capital structure, usually prior to flotation on the Stock Exchange. Such changes have been engineered to allow clubs to circumvent Football Association rules preventing shareholders or directors from exploiting clubs to make money. In particular, Rule 34 of the FA Handbook restricts the cash that directors and shareholders may take out of clubs in the form of dividends or salaries or by selling grounds. One popular route clubs have followed to Stock Exchange flotation, has seen the football club turned into a subsidiary of a new holding company. Shares in the holding company are then listed on the Stock Exchange, and it is argued that FA rules do not apply to the new holding company. This route was followed by, for example, Newcastle United and Nottingham Forest. Other clubs have come to the market after being taken over by existing companies, for example Leeds United was taken over by Caspian.

The nature of the relationship between investors and clubs can be examined by considering the current ownership framework of clubs. Tables 3.8–3.11 set out the ownership framework for clubs in the English Premier League and the Scottish Premier Division, while Table 3.12 deals with those clubs outside the top two divisions which are listed. For the purpose of these tables, a listed club is any club listed on either the Stock Exchange main market or AIM. For listed companies, where appropriate, the directors' shareholdings and other substantial interests relate to shares in the holding company.

An ownership classification

Table 3.13 uses the detailed information provided in Tables 3.8–3.12 to set out a classification of ownership for UK clubs at their 1997 accounting year ends. This classification provides a basis for investigation into the investment motives of director/owners and other investor/owners.

Concentrated ownership exists where one or few individuals or institutions own a large percentage of the shares in a company. Diversified ownership exists where ownership of a company's shares is more widely held, usually as a result of a share issue. Diversified ownership often results in a company being owned by the City. However, only three football clubs have a high proportion of shares owned by institutional investors: Manchester United (60 per cent owned by institutions), Caspian, now Leeds Sporting (56 per cent owned by institutions) and Tottenham Hotspur (45 per cent owned by institutions). However, although a share issue will result in more widely diversified ownership of a football club, it need not result in the change of control. Many football club flotations have resulted in significant increases in the number of shareholders and the percentage of shares held by those other than directors, but still ensuring that overall control of the company remains in the hands of one or a few original shareholders. For example at Tottenham Hotspur, Alan Sugar owns 41 per cent of the shares.

It is worth noting that although any holding in excess of 50 per cent provides the holder with control of a company in a strict or legal sense, in practice effective control is often exercised with much smaller percentage shareholdings. This happens because the remainder of shareholders (minority shareholders) often own relatively few shares

Table 3.8   Ownership framework in listed Premier League clubs
(1997 year ends)

Name of company	Directors' shareholdings	Other substantial interests (over 3% of issued share capital)
Aston Villa plc	35.0%	None disclosed
Caspian Group plc (renamed Leeds Sporting plc)	3.5%	SBC Warburg (13.1%) Schroder Investment Management Ltd (10.8%) Jupiter Asset Management (8.4%) Phildrew Nominees Limited (5.4%) Twenty-nine Gracechurch Street Nominees Limited (3.7%) Midland Bank Trust Co. (3.5%)
Chelsea Village plc	20.7%	Swan Management Ltd (32.3%) N.Y. Nominees (25.8%) Havering Ltd (4.7%)
Leicester City plc	42.5%[1]	None disclosed
Manchester United plc	17.0%	Marathon Asset Management (5.6%) Abu Dhabi Investment Authority (3.8%)
Newcastle United plc	65.7%[2]	Leonard Hatton (3.6%)
Nottingham Forest plc	55.1%	Singer and Friedlander plc (11.7%) Singer and Friedlander Fund (5.9%)
Southampton Leisure Holdings plc	18.0%	R.H. Everett (13.5%) Mercury Asset Management (7.7%) J.L.C. Corbett (7.6%) I.L. Gordon (3.1%)
Sunderland plc	50.8%	P. Reid (4.9%) J.A. Featherstone (3.2%)
Tottenham Hotspur plc	40.9%	The Equitable Life Assurance Society (4.1%)

[1] Includes both special shares and ordinary shares.
[2] D.S. Hall has a beneficial interest in 82 797 610 (57.8%) ordinary shares in the company. These shares include 81 776 870 (57.1%) ordinary shares owned by Cameron Hall Developments Ltd, a company connected with D.S. Hall. Cameron Hall Developments Ltd is described as the ultimate parent company in the company's financial statements.
Source: Company accounts

Table 3.9   Ownership framework in unlisted Premier League clubs
(1997 year ends)

Name of company	Directors' shareholdings
The Arsenal Football Club plc	87.5%
Blackburn Rovers Football and Athletic plc	The ultimate parent company of the club is Rosedale (JW) Investments Limited, a company controlled by Mr Jack Walker, who is not a director of the club.
Coventry City Football Club (Holdings) Ltd.	0.9%. However, the List of Past and Present Members indicates that at 13 June 1997 (accounting year end 31 May 1997) two Guernsey based companies (Craigavon Ltd and Sphere Trustees) owned 31% each of the shares in the club. In addition, a further 10% (5668 shares) were owned at that date by a director, Mr Derek Higgs, whose year-end holding was 100 shares.
DCFC Limited (Derby County Football Club)	93% controlled by directors or companies and/or pension schemes in which they are interested. 91% was owned by Derbyshire Enterprises, a company wholly owned by the DCFC Chairman Mr Lionel Pickering. A share swap took place after the year end. The principal shareholders in the new holding company, Derby County Limited, are Derbyshire Enterprises (69%) and Electra Fleming (25%).
The Everton Football Club Company Ltd	82.1%
The Liverpool Football Club & Athletic Grounds plc	59.6%
Middlesbrough Football & Athletic Company (1986) Limited	The Chairman of the club, Mr S. Gibson, is the ultimate controlling party by virtue of his 75% holding in the shares of The Gibson O'Neill Company Limited, which in turn holds 75% of the shares in the club. Gibson O'Neill is the ultimate parent company. None of the directors have a direct shareholding in the company. The remaining 25% of shares are owned by ICI Ltd.
Sheffield Wednesday plc	5.7% of ordinary shares. Convertible preference shares (18.4 m) were issued

Table 3.9   *Continued*

Name of company	Directors' shareholdings
	in May 1997, of which 90% were subscribed for by Charterhouse Tilney Securities Ltd for £17m. This represents 34% of the diluted ordinary share capital of the company (i.e. after conversion).
West Ham United plc	63.5%
The Wimbledon Football Club Limited	0.3%. At the year end, the club Chairman Mr Sam Hamman had a controlling interest in the ultimate parent company, Blantyre Ventures Limited. Since the year end, 80% of this holding was sold for £30m.

Source: Company accounts, information available at Companies House

Table 3.10   Ownership framework in listed Scottish Premier Division clubs (1997 year ends)

Name of company	Directors' shareholdings	Other substantial interests (over 3% of issued share capital)
Celtic plc	55.4%	None disclosed
Heart of Midlothian plc	45.4%	The Governor and Company of the Bank of Scotland (7.1%) London Uberior Dunedin Nominees (6.0%) Chase Nominees (3.5%) Magwest Nominees Limited (4.3%) Phildrew Nominees Limited (4.3%) Willbro Nominees Limited (4.4%)

Source: Company accounts

Table 3.11   Ownership framework in unlisted Scottish Premier Division clubs (1997 year ends)

Name of company	Directors' shareholdings
Aberdeen Football Club plc	29.5%
Dundee United Football Company Ltd	32.2%
Dunfermline Athletic Football Club Ltd	11.1%. Woodrows of Dunfermline own 79.6% of the issued share capital of the company and are the ultimate holding company. The club chairman, Mr Charles R. Woodrow and a director, Mr Andrew T. Gillies are both directors and shareholders in the holding company.
The Hibernian Football Club Ltd	0.12%. HFC Holdings Limited is described as the ultimate holding company in the financial statements. This company is 90% controlled by Sir Tom Farmer, the remaining 10% of shares being held by Mr R.M. Petrie, the Managing Director of Hibernian Football Club Ltd.
The Kilmarnock Football Club Ltd	76.0%
The Motherwell Football & Athletic Club Ltd	21.6%. In August 1998 Mr John Boyle acquired 51% of the shares in Motherwell for £2.5m, giving him a total stake of 76%.
Raith Rovers Football Club Ltb	The company's ultimate parent undertaking is Raith Rovers FC Holdings Limited, which controls 51% of the voting share capital of the club. This company is 82% controlled by Mr Alan Kelly, a director of both Raith Rovers FC Holdings Ltd and Raith Rovers Football Club Ltd and Chairman of Kelly Copiers.
The Rangers Football Club plc	61.0%. The club Chairman, Mr David Murray, owns 44 500 ordinary shares (0.1%) in the club personally. In addition, he has a controlling interest in the share capital of the ultimate holding company, Murray International Holdings, through which he has a further beneficial interest in 27 964 067 ordinary shares (60.6%). A further 25% of the shares are owned by the English National Investment Company.

Source: Company accounts, information available at Companies House

Table 3.12　Ownership framework in other listed clubs (1997 year ends)

Name of company	Directors' shareholdings	Other substantial interests (over 3% of issued share capital)
Birmingham City Football Club plc	58.9%[1]	Jack Wiseman (6.6%)
Burnden Leisure plc	29.6%	Gordons (Bolton) Ltd (16.1%)
Charlton Athletic plc	62.0%	Glyn Mills Nominees (Lombard) Limited (3.4%) David Hughes (2.9%)
Loftus Road plc	25.6%[2]	Mercury Asset Management (9.9%) Trustees of Wasps Football Club (9.8%) James Arbib (6.3%) Jupiter Asset Management (6.2%) St James Place Unit Trust Group (4.3%) Invesco Asset Management (3.1%)
Preston North End plc	1.3%[3]	Baxi Partnership Limited (40.7%) Guild Ventures Limited (11.7%) Scotcom Nominees Limited (9.9%) Vidacos Nominees Limited (6.6%) MSS Nominees Limited (5.1%) Fairmount Trustees (3.1%)
Sheffield United plc	16.0%	Mr B. Proctor and family (4.3%) Fidelity Investment Services Limited (4.2%) Schroder Investment Management Limited (3.6%)
Silver Shield plc	45.4%	Meespierson ICS Nominees Limited (4.5%)
West Bromwich Albion plc	4.9%	Mr G. Waldron (9.3%) Waterhead Ltd (3.4%) Mrs D. Waldron (3.2%)

[1]　Shares held by Mr D. Sullivan, Mr D. Gold and Mr R. Gold through their holdings in Sport Newspapers.

[2]　The chairman Mr Chris Wright is interested in a further 2 000 000 shares (5.0%) as trustee of Culture Vulture Pension Fund of which he is also a potential beneficiary.

[3]　The Chairman of Preston North End plc, Mr B. M. Gray, is a director of Baxi Partnership Limited.

Source: Company accounts

Table 3.13   Classification of football companies by ownership type

Concentrated ownership		Diversified ownership – concentrated control		Diversified ownership
Dominant owner	Family/ director control	Dominant owner	Family/ director control	
Blackburn Rovers	Arsenal	Aston Villa	Leicester City	Caspian
Derby County	West Ham United	Newcastle United	Nottingham Forest	Manchester United
Everton	Dundee United*	Sheffield Wednesday	Aberdeen	Sheffield United
Liverpool	Motherwell*	Sunderland	Heart of Midlothian	Southampton Leisure
Wimbledon		Tottenham Hotspur	Burnden Leisure	West Bromwich Albion
Dunfermline Athletic		Celtic	Charlton Athletic	
Hibernian		Birmingham City	Silver Shield	
Kilmarnock		Loftus Road		
Raith Rovers		Preston North End		
Rangers				
Middlesbrough				

*   This classification reflects the very small number of shares in issue at each of these clubs: 13 004 in the case of Dundee United; 266 996 in the case of Motherwell.

Note: Lack of publicly available information on the nature of the substantial shareholdings in Chelsea Village and Coventry City Football Club (Holdings) Ltd makes classification of these companies impracticable. In general terms, it should also be borne in mind that any classification of this nature is, of course, subjective

Table 3.14   Ordinary shareholdings in Scottish & Newcastle plc at
27 April 1997

Shares of 20p each	Shareholdings		Total shares held	
	Number	%	Number (millions)	%
Up to 2 500	36 111	84.66	26.3	4.26
2 501 to 10 000	4 539	10.64	20.3	3.29
10 001 to 50 000	1 064	2.49	24.2	3.91
50 001 to 200 000	511	1.20	53.5	8.67
200 001 to 500 000	230	0.54	72.7	11.77
500 001 to 1 000 000	89	0.21	63.9	10.35
Over 1 000 000	110	0.26	356.6	57.75
	42 654	100.00	617.5	100.00

Source: Scottish & Newcastle Annual Report and Accounts 1997

individually and in practice are not able to act in concert. This point can be illustrated by considering the analysis of shareholders for Scottish & Newcastle plc in Table 3.14. While a large number of people own a small number of shares in the company, control of the company is vested in the hands of a few very large shareholders. This ownership pattern is repeated at most major companies.

Several clubs are identified as having a dominant owner or shareholder interest. This occurs where an individual has chosen to make a large personal investment, either directly or indirectly through another company with which he is connected, in a particular club. Given the distinction between ownership and control, dominant owners or shareholders can be found in both concentrated and diversified ownership structures.

Cameron (1994) splits such benefactors into two camps: first, those whose interest was forged in childhood and for whom the recipient of their investment has to be the club they supported in those earlier days, and secondly, those who want an involvement in a viable business venture, having no particular allegiance to a particular club. While this simple split is appealing, more realistically the first camp needs to be subdivided into those benefactors who, notwithstanding their supporter status, still view the club as a business or investment opportunity, and those others for whom normal business or investment criteria are set aside when it comes to football.

The traditional view of football club directors is of those designated in the final category, namely supporter/benefactors. Historically a club such as Liverpool (the Moores family) would be described as having such benefactors. The clearest recent example, however, is that of Jack Walker at Blackburn Rovers. Such individuals have been seen as philanthropists: otherwise level-headed successful businessmen who set aside their normal economic or investment criteria when it came to investing in the club they have always supported. In such cases, the investment decision was driven at least partly by sentiment and emotion, and a desire to bring success to the club. It is important to bear in mind, however, that philanthropic investment of this type does not prevent the investor choosing to run that company as a business. Until the advent of the Stock Exchange in the football industry, the presence on the board of such a philanthropic supporter was often seen as the best way on ensuring that the club was able to compete at the highest level.[15] Stock Exchange involvement has now left some of these investors sitting on potentially very large capital gains.

King (1997) describes those directors who want involvement in a viable business alternative as 'new directors', arguing that they are different from their predecessors and from their European counterparts,[16] because the football club is identified as an investment opportunity in its own right, and therefore it is essential that it is profitable. The majority of new directors, however, can still be described as supporter/benefactor types. While there may be differences in the degree and intensity of their past supporter status,[17] Fergus McCann at Celtic, Alan Sugar at Tottenham and Chris Wright at Loftus Road (QPR) are all examples of the 'businessman first, supporter second' type of owner. An interesting example of a new director who was not originally a supporter is David Murray who has invested substantially in Rangers, through his steel business, Murray International Holdings. Prior to his investment in the club David Murray was not a Rangers supporter, and famously in 1988 tried to buy into his local football club, the Scottish first division team Ayr United. The directors of Ayr, however, turned down his investment. Opportunity later arose at Rangers. It is interesting to note, however, that even successful businessmen who perhaps initially have no emotive link to a club can also end up making decisions on grounds other than financial. A good example of this was David Murray's decision to retain the Danish internationalist Brian Laudrup until the end of his contract in the summer of 1998 because he was dealing with 'the dreams of a football club', a decision which had an opportunity cost to the club of the transfer fee forgone of some £4–£5 million.[18]

Although the profit objective is a distinguishing feature of new directors, this need not necessarily mean short term profits. Newcastle United and Middlesbrough can be identified as clubs where the financial strategy has not prioritised immediate profit. In both cases two strategies are apparent. First, both clubs can be seen to have speculated to accumulate, i.e. both clubs took the decision to invest heavily in players and facilities (with the consequent negative short term profit impact) in order that they were in position to benefit most from improved television contracts and lucrative European competitions. Secondly, it can be argued that the football clubs have been part of a much larger and more integrated strategy of capital accumulation where they have been used as positive symbols of the local regions, designed to attract international capital and investment to the area and to assist in its regeneration (King, 1997). In such cases, one can view the football clubs as short term loss-leaders, designed to lead to longer term benefits for the two regions and in particular for their local businessmen such as Sir John Hall at Newcastle and Steve Gibson at Middlesbrough, and businesses such as ICI at Middlesbrough (see the section on *Clubs in the community* in Chapter 5).

Not all benefactors, however, fit neatly into the classification identified above. One such example is the investment made by the Kwik-Fit owner, Sir Tom Farmer at Hibernian. Prior to his investment in the club in 1991 Hibernian was very close to going out of business. The club was also the target of a hostile takeover bid initiated by the then chairman of city rivals, Heart of Midlothian, Wallace Mercer. Far from being a supporter/benefactor, Sir Tom Farmer has little or no interest in football, despite the fact that his grandfather was one of the founders of Hibernian. Furthermore, there has been little evidence since the investment of the idea of speculating to accumulate, or of Hibernian being part of some grander capital accumulation project. In this case the investment motive seems to have been simpler: namely the preservation of part of the local community of Leith in which Hibernian is based, being that part of the city in which Sir Tom Farmer has his own roots. This is a powerful example of the role that football clubs play within a community[19] (see sections on *Community accountability* and *An inclusive approach to the community* in Chapter 5). Interestingly, although this type of investment is rare at the higher levels of football in the UK, it is much more common at the lower levels where local businessmen regularly bankroll struggling local clubs in an attempt to preserve a football club in the local community, albeit that such investors are more often than not also supporter/benefactors.

Corporate control issues

Recent flotations at clubs such as Aston Villa, Newcastle and Sunderland have seen the reduction in the holdings of dominant owners of the 'supporter benefactor' type discussed above, such as Doug Ellis, Sir John Hall and Bob Murray. One consequence arising out of this is that these individuals are now exposed to financial accountability of a sort with which they were not previously familiar in respect of their football club. The existence of a less concentrated ownership structure may lead to improved accountability on the part of directors of football clubs, as directors are obliged to recognise the rights of other shareholders. A logical extension of such accountability arising out of diversified ownership is the creation of a market for corporate control. One of the most notable features of the London Stock Exchange is the market for corporate control which exists in the form of corporate takeovers. The possibility of takeover is identified as a discipline on the behaviour and performance of UK company directors, leading to improved corporate efficiency. The incidence of hostile takeovers is a peculiarly Anglo-American phenomenon. For example, in 1985 and 1986 there were 80 hostile bids in the UK, and 40 hostile tender offers in the US in 1986. By contrast, Germany has had just three cases of hostile takeover in the post-World War II period (Franks and Mayer, 1996).

It is interesting to consider the extent to which the widening of share ownership is likely to lead to a market for corporate control in UK clubs. Evidence presented in Tables 3.8–3.12 suggests that even where share ownership has been widened, many clubs continue to be controlled by one or a small group of individuals. In such circumstances it is doubtful whether the market for corporate control would operate as an effective disciplinary mechanism. McMaster (1997) suggests that even if a club were to be taken over, many small shareholders would perceive that it would require a substantial shareholder to carry out the takeover, hence increasing the concentration of shares to a greater extent. Future changes in the ownership framework at Celtic will be interesting in this regard. At present, the club is 51 per cent controlled by a majority shareholder, Fergus McCann, with the remaining shares being widely held among approximately 10 500 shareholders. Mr McCann has indicated his desire to sell his stake in the club in the summer of 1999 and that his preference is for his stake to be distributed among Celtic supporters. Given that initiating a deal of this nature may well reduce the proceeds to Mr McCann, compared to a sale to a single or a few buyers, once again this highlights that motives other than purely financial continue to play a part in the football industry. It should also be noted, however, that Mr McCann is still likely to make a very healthy return on his investment.

Notwithstanding the above comments, a second factor is whether football club shareholders dissatisfied with the conduct of a board of directors will actually exercise their heaviest sanction, i.e. selling their shares. Evidence presented later in this chapter indicates a very low level of trading in the shares of many football clubs. Such thin trading almost certainly arises because many football club shareholders are supporter investors who invest out of loyalty to their particular club (or other non-pecuniary motives) rather than following rational investment logic. With this loyalty between the club and its supporter shareholder constituency, it seems unlikely that many shares would be traded in the event of shareholder dissatisfaction, and as such, in practice the directors need not fear the threat of a disciplinary takeover.[20]

Paper prophets?

Received wisdom used to suggest that the only way to make a small fortune out of a football club was to start with a large fortune. In the football industry of today the situation is very different. The directors of several clubs which have recently been floated on the Stock Exchange have found themselves becoming very wealthy, while other owners are now sitting on large paper fortunes as a result of their past investment.

Returns on investment which have been made by some directors, however, have been surrounded by controversy. For example, one relates to the restructuring of Leeds United and its subsequent takeover by the Caspian Group. Like many clubs, Leeds was a private company owned mainly by a small group of local businessmen and a few hundred small shareholders. The directors concluded that the club would only realise its full potential within the changing football industry if it altered its status as a business. They decided that the club should be converted into a publicly quoted company and aim for a Stock Exchange quotation. In August 1995 a financial restructuring took place which resulted in the creation of Leeds United Holdings plc. The restructuring left the club's three directors with almost 98 per cent of the shares, while the stake held by the small shareholders was reduced from 18 per cent to 2.2 per cent. The majority of small shareholders chose to take shares in the new holding company rather than a cash offer of £2 per share. In July 1996, the club was taken over by the media and sports group Caspian in a deal which valued the club at £16.5m, leaving each of the three directors with proceeds from the takeover in excess of £5m. Unsurprisingly, controversy surrounded the deal, both with regard to the profit made by the directors, and the way in which the stake of the original small shareholders in the football club was diluted in the reorganisation.

The events at Leeds United are certainly not unique. At Southampton, the original investment of £14 000 made by the five directors of the club (including the Chairman of the FA at that time, Keith Wiseman) was worth about £6m on paper after the merger of the club with Secure Retirement and the flotation of the Southampton Leisure Holding Group on the Stock Exchange.[21] Similar stories of paper profits exist at other clubs. Doug Ellis paid £500 000 for his shares in Aston Villa. At the most recent accounting year end (31 May 1997) his holding was worth almost £32m having already cashed in £4m. Ken Bates initially bought Chelsea for £1 and an agreement to guarantee its debts. His holding at the last accounting year end (30 June 1997) was now worth over £33m. Sir John Hall and his family initially paid £3m for Newcastle United. At the most recent accounting year end his holding was worth in excess of £100m. At Manchester United, Martin Edwards initial investment was £600 000. At the most recent accounting year end (31 July 1997) his holding was worth over £60m, having already cashed in £33m. The successful acquisition of Manchester United by BSkyB would see Mr Edwards make approximately £85 m.

Controversy has inevitably accompanied the level of such returns, both real and paper. Supporters of many clubs (and indeed small shareholders in the case of a club such as Leeds United) will view the returns made by some directors as totally unjustifiable. It could be argued that in some cases directors have presided over football clubs and companies that were going nowhere, yet they are now benefiting personally from the upsurge of interest in football as a commercial and television proposition rather than through their own efforts. However, at other clubs some would view the gains of directors as more justifiable. Often such investors put money into clubs when no one else would and took substantial risks (such as the guaranteeing of football club debts) at a time when the financial future of football did not look so secure. Many have worked very hard to transform ailing clubs into vibrant organisations with a strong financial situation. As a consequence many supporter investors are also sitting on large paper gains, although such gains may be of little importance to them.

Football is not the first industry to have gone through a boom period which has brought enormous wealth to its investors. The difficulty is that, to many, football is 'the people's game'. As such it makes very large gains for a few difficult to accept for the many. What it reflects is that football is no longer immune from the operation of the free market dominated society. Whether individual major investors should be described as far sighted, greedy, lucky, astute or whatever depends on each individual case and on your perspective.

THE SECONDARY MARKET

In addition to providing a primary market for the issue of new securities, the Stock Exchange also acts as a secondary market, where securities can be traded throughout their lives. Dealing on the secondary market does not raise new finance for the quoted company, but does provide permanent marketability, i.e. it allows the initial investors to sell their investment as and when they choose. Without the secondary market companies would find investors less willing to tie up their money for extended periods, thus making the raising of finance by share issues almost impracticable.

Potential investors are interested not only in the permanent marketability made possible by the secondary market, but also in whether or not their investment is efficiently priced. Efficiency in the context of pricing implies that, at all times, all available information about a company's prospects is fully and rationally reflected in the share price. In other words, that the share price of a company reflects its future expected cash flows.

Valuing football club shares

The share price of a football club should therefore reflect a whole variety of information: some club specific, others industry specific; some certain, others requiring subjective estimation. The more secure a company's future cash flows, the more attractive that investment will be to investors. The top clubs have a secure core earnings base. These are large clubs with loyal supporters, who are therefore in a position to sell every seat in the ground for the foreseeable future. Clubs like Liverpool and Manchester United also have predictable and secure sources of revenue from such as television companies, merchandising and advertising.[22] It is the security of such earnings, which makes investment in this type of club such an attractive option. Smaller clubs will have less secure earnings of this nature and hence carry greater risk.

The share price also reflects expectations about future events. Much of the price gains in football club shares in 1997 (and subsequent downward corrections) reflected changing expectations about revenues that might be available under future Pay-Per-View television deals. Equally, share prices should also reflect expectations specific to clubs, for example, the likelihood of promotion or relegation, or of gaining access to the Champions League.

Returns on the market

Overall, shares in the football sector rose by 774 per cent in the period 1 January 1993 to 31 January 1997, out performing the Stock Market as a whole by a factor of ten. Spectacular performances by shares of many listed clubs, a rush of high-profile flotations and the launch of investment products such as specialist football funds and equity warrants attracted much attention and resulted in football becoming a stock market favourite. 1997, however, saw a significant downward correction to the sector's value. While many in the City were quick to view this as the end of the City's infatuation with the game, others saw it as evidence of respectability and a new maturity in the sector. Table 3.15 sets out the returns on football club shares until the end of 1997 compared to movements in the FT All Share Index and the FT Leisure and Hotel Sector Index (the sector within which clubs are listed on the main market).

Table 3.15 demonstrates clearly the split between share price returns in listed clubs before 1997 and then during 1997. The six clubs with the longest history on the Stock Exchange (up until and including Caspian which listed in August 1996) all show a positive share price return since flotation.[23] Those clubs which listed in late 1996 (Loftus Road and Sunderland) or later, all show negative share price returns since flotation. However, the significant downward correction to the sector is most apparent by considering only the share price return in the calendar year 1997. Here all clubs show a negative or nil return for the year (or that part of the year since flotation). By contrast the return for 1997 on the FT All Share Index for 1997 was 19.7 per cent, while on the FT Leisure and Hotel Index it was 2.4 per cent.

When considering returns on shares, it is more illuminating to compare these with movements in the market generally. Table 3.15 sets out the comparative movement in the FT All Share Index and the Leisure and Hotel Index for individual clubs over the period since flotation. Of the six clubs identified as having a positive share price return since flotation, three of those clubs (Manchester United, Celtic and Chelsea Village) have significantly outperformed the return on the FT All

Table 3.15   Return on football club shares (period to 31 December 1997)

Company	Float date	Share price return since float date (%)	Return on FT All Share Index since float date (%)	Return on FT Leisure and Hotel Index since float date (%)	Share price return during 1997 (%)
Aston Villa	06/05/97	−34.8	11.3	−0.8	−34.8
Burnden Leisure (Bolton Wanderers)	01/04/97	−48.5	16.6	−1.0	−48.5
Heart of Midlothian	16/05/97	−26.8	8.1	−3.5	−26.8
Caspian (Leeds United)	01/08/96	28.4	30.5	9.2	−48.4
Leicester City	22/04/97	−39.5	14.6	−0.4	−39.5
Manchester United	07/06/91	720.8	100.2	95.7	−5.3
Newcastle United	01/04/97	−30.0	16.6	−1.0	−30.0
Sheffield United	01/01/97	−25.2	19.7	2.4	−25.2
Southampton Leisure	14/01/97	−49.3	18.0	1.6	−49.3
Sunderland	23/12/96	−41.0	20.7	3.5	−54.0
Tottenham Hotspur	12/10/83	288.0	452.4	238.3	−39.5
Birmingham City	06/03/97	−27.0	12.4	−5.7	−27.0
Celtic	28/09/95	274.0	40.2	37.1	−36.4
Charlton Athletic	20/03/97	−35.6	15.9	−2.1	−35.6
Chelsea Village	29/03/96	91.7	30.8	12.7	0
Loftus Road (QPR)	23/10/96	−56.2	22.0	4.9	−62.9
Nottingham Forest	09/10/97	−26.4	−1.7	0.1	−26.4
Preston North End	29/09/95	11.3	39.1	36.5	−24.6
West Bromwich Albion	02/01/97	−48.2	21.2	3.7	−48.2

Source: Datastream

Share index, by a factor of approximately seven in the case of Manchester United and Celtic and three in the case of Chelsea Village. Superior performance is greater still when compared to the sector index.

Of the other three clubs identified as having shown a positive share price return since floatation (Caspian, Tottenham Hotspur and Preston North End), the performance of Caspian is not significantly below that of the FT All Share Index. The underperformance of Tottenham can be best explained by the fact that it has the longest record of listing, since 1983. In the early years of its listing the City showed little enthusiasm for the stock, or indeed for the concept of listed football clubs, with even the sector's red-chip stock, Manchester United, underperforming the market in the early days of its listing. The great surge in City interest and consequent positive share price effect did not take place until the mid-1990s. The performance of Preston North End is perhaps most significant in terms of predicting future movements in football club shares. Despite listing at roughly the same time as Celtic, shares in Preston North End have significantly underperformed those in Celtic, and have underperformed the market as a whole by a factor of about four. Taken together with the results for listed clubs overall, this may demonstrate that a maturity is developing in the sector. In future the market will distinguish between the highest quality football shares and the rest, with that judgement being made on the basis of factors such as quality of earnings, brand loyalty, profile, etc, rather than being driven by market sentiment and media hype.

Movements in share prices

As was discussed previously, the share price of a football club should reflect publicly available information. In an efficient market, new information should be quickly absorbed into share prices. Much of the information that will affect football club share prices is not dissimilar in nature to information that affects share prices is any company. For example, information such as changes in expectations of the likelihood of Pay-Per-View television, or the announcement of new sponsorship deals should be reflected in the share price of, say, Manchester United in much the same way as information on new contracts or new products would be absorbed into the share price of a company like ICI. Of potentially more interest is the relationship between club specific information in the form of match results and share prices which has given a focus of media interest. A City joke at the time of the 1995/96 season climax ran that Manchester United had become the only company to report to shareholders twice a week: during its own games, and once more when Newcastle play.

Events Study Methodology, as first developed by Fama, Fisher, Jensen and Roll (1969), can be used to study the way in which specific information is absorbed into share prices. It involves estimating the impact on share returns of a company-specific event, such as the announcement of a takeover bid. The abnormal return associated with the event is a measure of the gains or losses attributable to that event, and is calculated as the difference between the 'Actual' (observed) return on the share and the return on the share one would have expected had no event taken place. Following the event, the expected return needs to be estimated, the simplest method of estimation being to measure the return on the market, using an index such as the FT All Share Index.

Two different clubs are used to illustrate the effects of match results being absorbed into share prices for parts of season 1996/97. Sunderland was selected because the club was involved in an ultimately unsuccessful fight to avoid relegation from the Premier League, while Manchester United was chosen as an example of a club whose financial results were expected to be less reliant on the outcome of individual match results, owing to a highly diversified income base.

A simple events study was carried out on shares in Sunderland plc for matches played after the club's flotation in December 1996. The abnormal return was calculated for the day after each of the club's matches. The three clubs finishing in league positions 18–20 in the Premier League are automatically relegated to the First Division. The results are presented in Table 3.16.

Table 3.16 demonstrates a very strong correlation between match results and abnormal return in the latter part of the season as the club struggled to avoid relegation, with defeats which dropped the club into the relegation zone being shadowed by large negative abnormal returns. With rewards as they are from continuing Premier League status, it is not surprising that the share price is sensitive to results which will determine whether or nor that status, and the lucrative financial benefits which accompany it, is retained. In the earlier part of the season, where there is less immediate pressure from relegation, there is less apparent correlation. Indeed, on one occasion (the 1–0 victory over Arsenal) there is evidence of negative correlation. However, it should also be noted that the club was in mid-table position for most of the part of the season immediately following the flotation. Hence, there

Table 3.16   Abnormal return on Sunderland plc shares

Date	Event	Post-event league position	Abnormal return
26/12/96	Won 2–0 at home to Derby County	11/20	2.4%
28/12/96	Lost 2–0 away to West Ham United	13/20	−0.5%
01/01/97	Drew 2–2 away at Coventry	11/20	0.8%
11/01/97	Won 1–0 at home to Arsenal	11/20	−3.5%
15/01/97	Lost 2–0 at home to Arsenal	FA Cup	−0.3%
18/01/97	Drew 0–0 at home to Blackburn	12/20	1.9%
29/01/97	Drew 1–1 away at Leicester	11/20	1.4%
01/02/97	Lost 1–0 away at Aston Villa	12/20	0.4%
22/02/97	Lost 1–0 at home to Leeds United	14/20	−2.7%
01/03/97	Lost 1–0 at home to Blackburn Rovers	15/20	−1.9%
05/03/97	Lost 4–0 at home to Tottenham Hotspur	16/20	−0.8%
08/03/97	Won 2–1 at home to Manchester United	15/20	0.4%
12/03/97	Lost 2–1 away at Sheffield Wednesday	15/20	−1.3%
16/03/97	Lost 6–2 away at Chelsea	15/20	−4.4%
22/03/97	Drew 1–1 at home to Nottingham Forest	16/20	−1.4%
05/04/97	Drew 1–1 away at Newcastle	15/20	−0.6%
13/04/97	Lost 2–1 at home to Liverpool	18/20	−4.0%
19/04/97	Won 1–0 away at Middlesbrough	16/20	5.8%
22/04/97	Lost 1–0 at home to Southampton	18/20	−8.4%
03/05/97	Won 3–0 at home to Everton	17/20	No abnormal return
11/05/97	Lost 1–0 away to Wimbledon	18/20	−8.7%

Source: Datastream

Table 3.17   Abnormal return on Manchester United plc shares

Date	Event	Post-event league position and number of points	Number of points clear of team in second place/ (points behind team in first place)	Abnormal return
20/10/96	Lost 5–0 away at Newcastle	5th, 19 points	(5 points behind)	−0.4%
26/10/96	Lost 6–3 away at Southampton	5th, 19 points	(5 points behind)	−3.2%
02/11/96	Lost 2–1 at home to Chelsea	6th, 19 points	(8 points behind)	−2.0%
08/03/97	Lost 2–1 away at Sunderland	1st, 57 points	3 points ahead	−0.5%
05/04/97	Lost 3–2 at home to Derby County	1st, 63 points	3 points ahead	−0.5%

Source: Datastream

would have been little reason for investors to have unduly negative expectations of the prospect of relegation.

Manchester United is recognised as one of the most developed businesses within world football, with highly diversified and secure income sources. A simple events study was carried out by calculating the abnormal return on shares in Manchester United plc for the day after matches lost by the club in the 1996/97 Premier League season. The results are presented in Table 3.17.

As can be seen, each of the defeats was accompanied by a negative abnormal return. However, on three of the five occasions this was very small in scale. It does perhaps demonstrate that even at a club like Manchester United with its diversified and secure income sources, new information in the form of operating results can still have an impact on share prices.

It is also interesting to look at the abnormal return from two other significant events at Manchester United in recent years. The 1–0 victory at Newcastle on 3 April 1996 was seen by many commentators as the 1995/96 title-decider. The market reacted by pushing the share price up 13 pence to £2.80, equivalent to an abnormal return of 4.6 per cent.

While such a return may have been expected, less predictable was the market reaction to the announcement of Eric Cantona's retirement. Although the Manchester United share price dropped six pence to £6.28, surprisingly this was equivalent to an abnormal return of only −0.1 per cent.

One factor that may influence the results of the event studies is the liquidity in the two shares. It is generally stated that equilibrium prices of securities are determined by aggregate demand while trading is determined by changes in the demand of individual investors (Yadav, 1992). One factor that can affect the demand for individual securities is changes in individual expectations in relation to price changes. Such changes often occur with the arrival of information. Trading volume is frequently taken as reflecting the differential impact of information on the expectations of different individual investors. The distinction between price setting being determined by aggregate demand and trading being influenced by changes in the demand of individual investors is, however, likely to be less distinct where low volumes of share trading are regularly reported in particular shares.

This is often the case with football club shares, where for a variety of reasons, large numbers of investors do not actively trade their securities (i.e. they adopt a buy/hold position). A consequence of low trading levels is that those individuals who do trade will play a disproportionate part in price setting in these shares. This could be described in two ways: either that equilibrium prices are set by a small subsection of the investors, or alternatively, that the prices of thinly traded shares are not actually equilibrium prices at all. In this second case, prices will reflect the changing expectations of a small group of investors in a particular share, i.e. an equilibrium price is not reached for shares in which the operation of a market is distorted by the existence of large numbers of irrational shareholders who do not follow normal investment rules.

Trading volumes are presented for listed UK clubs in the next section. The low level of trading in some shares, including those of Sunderland, means that it is important that the results of events studies are interpreted with reference to the fact that any changes in share prices are being determined by a relatively small subsection of the investors in that company.

The absorbing of club specific information into share prices by the market reaction to unpredictable individual match results may be thought inappropriate and to illustrate the risk of investing in football clubs, i.e. that share prices may be hostage to events on the field. However, it could be argued that such regular revaluations are in fact a strength, in that what we are seeing is company valuation reacting to specific operating information which will impact future cash flows. With rewards as great as they are from, for example, continuing Premier League status, it is desirable that the share price is sensitive to results which will determine whether or nor that status, and the lucrative financial benefits which accompany it, are retained. All companies listed on the Stock Exchange vary in risk and hence potentially in return. Where a business is unpredictable and risky this is reflected by share price behaviour in the market. The main difference between football clubs and other companies is in the nature of that risk.

The regular reporting of operating information should be seen as a model of reporting and valuation. Professional football is unusual as an industry in that 'industrial performance' is entirely explicit and is even announced and tabulated in the national press, television and radio. One advantage, therefore, for investors in football clubs as opposed to investors in other industries, is that there is informational equity in respect of one part of football clubs' business. Relevant information in the form of match results which may affect a company's future cash flows are reported on an inclusive approach, available to everyone at the same time, rather than selectively released to privileged professional investors or financial journalists.

Liquidity in football club shares

As mentioned previously, investing in football clubs in the last few years would have generated very high returns in many instances. Coverage of the returns available by investing in many of these listed clubs often includes negative comment on the role played in creating such high returns by 'thin trading' and 'illiquidity in the market'. An illiquid market in a company's shares occurs where there are only a small number of either potential buyers or sellers of those shares, resulting in limited or 'thin' trading. In such circumstances, security prices will exhibit greater variability as the market seeks to match supply and demand.

Trading volumes

Table 3.18 sets out information on the level of trading in shares in a selection of listed clubs, calculated with reference to statistics on trading volume provided on Datastream. The information relates to the period to 31 December 1997. Where available, the average

Table 3.18   Trading volumes (period ending 31 December 1997)

Club	Market	Period beginning	Average daily trading volume (£)	Average percentage of share capital traded on a daily basis (%)	Average number of daily trades
Burnden Leisure	Main	01/05/97	50 176	0.12	21.0
Caspian	Main	02/09/96	371 337	0.42	54.6
Manchester United	Main	01/01/96	1 033 274	0.31	59.4
Newcastle United	Main	01/05/97	173 787	0.10	NA
Sheffield United	Main	03/02/97	56 351	0.21	25.8
Sunderland	Main	01/01/97	53 655	0.13	8.1
Birmingham City	AIM	01/04/97	10 207	0.05	7.6
Celtic	AIM	15/05/97	17 031	0.02	4.5
Charlton	AIM	01/04/97	5 446	0.05	NA
Chelsea Village	AIM	15/04/97	67 581	0.04	NA
Loftus Road	AIM	12/05/97	16 355	0.09	7.4
Preston North End	AIM	14/05/97	1 456	0.01	0.7
West Bromwich Albion	AIM	03/02/97	6 837	0.06	NA

NA: Not available.
Source: Datastream

percentage of share capital traded in a club's shares was calculated for the month after the club was first listed on the main market or the Alternative Investment Market. In several cases, however, trading volume statistics were not available on Datastream until a later date.

What is immediately apparent is that thin trading is not a concern for all clubs. The highest average trading volume is reported by the football

Table 3.19   Trading volumes (period 1 January 1996 to 31 December 1997)

Company	Average daily trading volume (£)	Average percentage of share capital traded on a daily basis (%)	Average number of daily trades
Leisure and Hotel Companies			
Rank	12 071 090	0.35	192.6
Ladbroke	9 509 139	0.37	130.3
Manchester United	1 033 274	0.31	59.4

Source: Datastream

sector's largest company, Manchester United, with an average daily trading volume in excess of £1 million. Table 3.19 demonstrates that in absolute terms this is appreciably less than the average daily trading volume reported for other quoted leisure companies for the same period. This divergence can be explained by differences in the market capitalisation of the organisations. In relative terms (i.e. considering the average percentage of share capital traded on a daily basis) the figures calculated for each of the three companies are not disproportionately out of line.

All the clubs quoted on the main market report figures of 0.10 per cent or greater, albeit for fairly small time periods in some cases. A lower level of trading would be expected on the lower status market for all companies, and this is backed up by the figures reported for AIM listed football clubs, which are substantially lower in all cases.

It is also informative to consider the figures presented in the final column of Table 3.18, *Average number of daily trades*. These are the total number of times shares were traded in the day, as recorded by SEAQ (the London Stock Exchange Automated Quotation system). Trades are only recorded by SEAQ, however, when the size of the trade is between £2500–£100 000, or when that stock is in a bid situation. Although figures are not available for all clubs, Table 3.18 shows very low figures being reported at several clubs. The low number of such trades further emphasises differences which exist in the nature and behaviour of many football club investors compared to those found in more conventional companies (see section on *Ownership framework in football clubs* earlier in this chapter). In particular the absence in many clubs of institutional shareholders who might be expected to have large holdings and to follow an active investment policy is likely to be a major contributory factor to the low number of trades reported (see the section on *Implications of the ownership framework* later in this chapter).

Bid-ask spreads

One way in which thinly traded stocks evidence themselves is by large bid-ask spreads as quoted by market makers. The bid price is the price at which the market maker will offer to buy shares from the shareholder, the ask price is the price at which he or she will sell shares to the shareholder. The difference between the two prices is the return to the market maker. In normal circumstances, heavily traded shares will have a very narrow spread, whereas the spread will be much greater for thinly traded shares where the market maker believes that they may have some difficulty in matching the transaction (see the section on *Methods of issuing shares* earlier in this chapter). Table 3.20 demonstrates the spreads for quoted football clubs for one month in 1997.

No consistent pattern is demonstrated in Table 3.20. At the extremes, there does appear to be a strong relationship between the thinness of trading and the bid-ask spread (e.g. Burnden Leisure and Celtic) compared to a company such as Manchester United which has a low spread and which is actively traded. Anomalies do, of course exist. For example, for Sunderland a very low spread was found in September despite the fact that there was also a very low incidence of trading of substantial blocks of shares.

Thin trading can be caused by various factors, most of which arise simply enough from a lack of buyers or a lack of sellers. In the case of Heart of Midlothian, evidence suggests that thin trading is caused by a lack of demand.[24] What this indicates is perhaps a lack of conviction among the investing public, beyond those with whom the shares were initially placed, in the merits of shares in Heart of Midlothian FC as a financial investment. Heart of Midlothian is one of the smallest clubs listed on the main market, both in terms of market capitalisation and turnover. Although its accounting results are improving, its income base remains heavily reliant on football activities.[25]

Share denominations

The share price of the majority of companies listed on the Stock Exchange is measured in pence. For example, on 26 June 1998 a quick glance at the *Financial Times* indicated that shares in Asda were trading

Table 3.20   Bid-ask spreads, September 1997

Company	Average ask price	Average bid price	Average Spread (%)	Average number of daily trades
Football clubs: Main market				
Aston Villa	850p	832p	2.22	NA
Burnden Leisure	35p	31p	14.37	13.8
Caspian	24p	23p	5.98	24.5
Heart of Midlothian	108p	105p	3.42	NA
Manchester United	657p	649p	1.23	34.9
Sheffield United	61p	57p	7.25	12.3
Southampton Leisure	80p	72p	10.45	NA
Sunderland	338p	330p	2.37	4.3
Tottenham Hotspur	96p	91p	5.19	NA
Leisure and Hotels: Main market				
Granada	828p	825p	0.43	247.8
Rank	357p	353p	1.14	123.8
Ladbroke	263p	260p	1.10	91.4
Football clubs: AIM				
Birmingham City	52p	48p	7.47	9.0
Celtic	£337	£288	17.07	3.6
Chelsea Village	112p	110p	1.99	NA
Loftus Road	46p	42p	8.91	9.3
Preston North End	543p	523p	3.82	0.5
West Bromwich Albion	£184	£144	27.88	NA

NA: Not available.
Source: Datastream

at 205p, shares in Ladbroke at 338½p, shares in British Telecom at 749p, while shares in Scottish & Newcastle were trading at 848½p. The majority of football club shares are also traded at prices in this range. Where shares can be bought and sold for a few pounds then it is perceived to increase the marketability of such shares. Where prices of shares rise beyond these levels it is not uncommon for companies to have stock splits for the purpose of encouraging marketability. A stock split involves subdividing each original share, say into ten new shares. As a result each shareholder now owns ten times as many shares, but their proportionate ownership of the company remains unchanged. Similarly companies can make a bonus issue in which retained profits are converted into ordinary shares which are then distributed to existing shareholders free of charge.

With both splitting and bonus issues the economic effect should logically be zero. However, the fact that the split or the bonus issue reduces the unit price of the shares to what is perceived as a more marketable size often results in a positive share price effect. For example, Manchester United had a three-for-one bonus issue (i.e. for every one share held prior to the issue a shareholder received a further three shares) which resulted in the share price falling from 607.5p on 28 November 1997 to 156p on 1 December 1997. The new price, however, was equivalent to a price of 624p per share prior to the bonus issue.

Two clubs, Celtic and West Bromwich Albion, are very noticeable for having share prices denominated in pounds rather than pence, and consequently a low absolute number of shares in issue. One implication of such a high share price is that it may act as a barrier to potential investors. It may also make it less likely that individual shareholders will be able to make a partial sale of their holdings in the way that they could if their investment was made up of lots of shares as opposed to one or two highly priced shares. For these reasons, the maintenance of such a high absolute share price seems illogical. However, there may be reasons removed from conventional finance and stock market logic that explain why these clubs have not carried out share splits. Most significantly, it may be that the directors of the club believe that it is in the best interest of the club not to be actively traded, if what that involves is shares being bought up by institutions or persons hostile to them. This belief may be based on a desire to ensure that shares in the club remain in the hands of the supporters of the club.[26] Alternatively, it may be interpreted as an unwillingness by directors to expose themselves to the financial accountability that would be demanded by institutional investors.

Implications of the ownership framework

The ownership structure of many football clubs indicates that there remains a lack of demand for shares in football clubs from institutional shareholders like insurance companies or pension funds. Tables 3.8, 3.10 and 3.12 showed that of 21 quoted football clubs, only nine report significant institutional shareholdings (i.e. greater than three per cent of the issued share capital in their 1997 annual reports). This lack of institutional demand is likely to contribute to the thin trading in many stocks, if all other things being equal, a greater institutional interest in the shares of a particular company would lead to increased levels of trading volume in such shares as institutions move into or out of the shares of that company. Evidence of this lack of institutional demand was seen quite clearly in Table 3.18 where several clubs reported a very low incidence of daily trades.

More generally the ownership structure of a company may well contribute to the short supply of shares in that company. Either, or somewhat obtusely, both of the following factors may contribute to the lack of sellers: concentrated control and wide shareholder bases. As discussed previously, although the flotation of many clubs on the Stock Exchange has increased clubs' shareholder base, often it has not widened the control of clubs (see Table 3.13). If the major shareholder(s) have no interest in reducing their holding, then supply is necessarily reduced. When any small shareholdings are then made available for sale on the open market, previously unsatisfied demand leads to excess demand for those shares, with the result that the share price is pushed up. Holmström and Tirole (1993) found that the amount of information contained in the stock price depends on the liquidity of the market, and that concentrated ownership by reducing market liquidity thus reduces the benefits of market monitoring. A further consequence of concentrated ownership is that it artificially increases the paper worth of the major investors in the club. Clearly if sufficient numbers of the major shareholders were to attempt to sell their shares on the open market, it is unlikely that the prices at which limited tranches of shares are being traded would be achievable for significant blocks of shares.

The width of the shareholder base (i.e. where a large percentage of the shares are held by large numbers of individual shareholders) can also play a part in reducing the liquidity of the market. The majority of financial investment takes place in the hope that it will generate a financial return to the investor. An investor in shares is looking for a return in the form of dividends and/or capital gains as a result of upward movement in the share price. In the case of football clubs, however, many individual shareholders are also supporters of the club and therefore have a stronger bond with, and knowledge of the company than would be expected for commercial investors. In such cases many shareholders invest in their club largely for emotional as opposed to financial reasons, and are therefore less likely to sell their investment for financial reasons. The psychic income is more important to the investor than any financial return.[27] The consequence of this type of investment activity is that, as before, when shareholdings are made available for sale on the open market, previously unfulfilled demand leads to excess demand for those shares, with the result being that the share price is pushed up.

Price setting and long-termism

As discussed previously, one consequence of the buy/hold strategy adopted both by dominant shareholders and many individual supporter-investors is that price setting in many football clubs will be determined to a greater extent by a relatively small subsection of the market, i.e. those who are following an active trading policy. In those circumstances one would expect that the normal trading practices of institutional investors would result in their playing a greater role in price setting.

It is important to remember, however, that despite much press comment about football now being controlled by the City, the City's holding in the shares of the 21 clubs listed on either the official list or AIM remain fairly modest (see Tables 3.8, 3.10 and 3.12). In fact, only three clubs (Manchester United, Caspian and Tottenham Hotspur) could be described as being owned by the City (see the section on *An ownership classification* earlier in this chapter). Of particular significance is the fact that there is some evidence that institutions are wary of investing in clubs in which there remains a dominant shareholder after flotation.[28]

Most investment capital derives from long term savings while the majority of fund management clients have long term liabilities in the form of pensions or insurance contracts. However, despite this fundamental long term standpoint, fund managers are often driven by competitive pressure to focus on short term returns – behaviour, which, it is argued, is to the detriment of the long term competitiveness of UK industry.[29] Some evidence on the time horizon for institutional investors in football clubs is available by considering changes in the substantial shareholding of listed clubs over a period of time. Table 3.21 sets out the significant shareholdings (greater than 3 per cent) in the two clubs with the longest history of market listing.

This table demonstrates that several institutions have maintained sizeable holdings in these clubs over a number of years, in particular Marathon Asset Management at Manchester United and Dempsey and Perpetual Funds at Tottenham. The table only tells part of the story in that it reports only significant shareholdings. For example, Marathon originally invested in Manchester United at its flotation in 1991 and has subsequently built up its holding. Furthermore, given the 1996

Table 3.21   Changes in significant holdings at Manchester United and
Tottenham Hotspur, 1991–7

Year	Substantial interests reported (over 3% of issued share capital)	Number of shares	Percentage holding
Manchester United			
1997[1]	Marathon Asset Management Ltd	3 623 750	5.6%
	Abu Dhabi Investment Authority	2 500 000	3.8%
1996[1]	Marathon Asset Management Ltd	3 623 000	5.9%
	Abu Dhabi Investment Authority	2 500 000	4.0%
1995[1]	Marathon Asset Management Ltd	3 620 000	6.0%
	Fidelity International Ltd	3 075 000	5.1%
	Philen Establishment[2]	2 567 195	4.2%
1994	Philen Establishment[2]	863 439	7.1%
	Marathon Asset Management Ltd	660 000	5.4%
	BBC Pension Trust Ltd	565 493	4.7%
1993	Philen Establishment[2]	863 439	7.1%
	BBC Pension Trust Ltd	565 493	4.7%
	Marathon Asset Management Ltd	450 000	3.7%
1992	Phillips & Drew Fund Management Ltd	943 917	7.7%
	Philen Establishment[2]	863 439	7.1%
	BBC Pension Trust Ltd	515 493	4.2%
	G T Management plc	463 400	3.8%
1991	Phillips & Drew Fund Management Ltd	1 323 798	10.9%
	Philen Establishment[2]	863 439	7.1%
	N. Burrows/T. A. Le Sueur and D. de Ste Croix	481 193	4.0%
Tottenham Hotspur			
1997[3]	The Equitable Life Assurance Company	4 158 840	4.13%
1996[4]	Perpetual Group Unit Trust Funds	1 045 243	5.22%
	Fidelity Investments	975 160	4.87%
	General Accident	867 031	4.33%
	Mercury Asset Management	804 957	4.02%
1995	Perpetual Group Unit Trust Funds	1 467 345	9.16%
	Dempsey Opportunities Fund	499 794	3.12%
1994	Perpetual Group Unit Trust Funds	1 467 345	9.16%
	Dempsey Opportunities Fund	600 714	3.75%
1993	Perpetual UK Growth Fund	700 033	4.37%
	Dempsey Opportunities Fund	650 374	4.06%
1992	nil	nil	nil
1991	B. J. Kennedy	400 000	3.90%

[1] Called up share capital was increased by £4 865 361 following a four-for-one bonus issue of 48 653 608 shares on 1 December 1994. On 26 March 1996 options were exercised over 1 125 000 ordinary shares. On 10 December 1996 the company placed 3 million ordinary shares.
[2] The interest of Philen Establishment duplicated the interest of Mr A. M. AlMidani, a director of Manchester United in the years 1991 to 1995 inclusive.
[3] On 11 February 1997 the Company's shares were subdivided on a five for one basis to increase marketability.
[4] On 15 May 1996 the Company increased its share capital to 20 023 816 ordinary shares by a one-for-four Rights Issue of 4 004 763 new ordinary shares of 25 pence each at 280 pence per share.
Source: Company accounts

rights issue at Tottenham, it is possible that an institution such as Dempsey may have maintained its original holding but not taken up its rights, and hence slipped below the three per cent threshold.

The extent to which institutions are collectively engaged in long term investment in the football sector is difficult to gauge from publicly available information. However, what is not at issue is that there is evidence of thin trading in the shares of many listed football clubs. Far from being a negative factor, the existence of such thin trading could be seen as advantageous and as contributing to the possibility of football clubs being put forward as examples for other Stock Exchange listed companies to follow.

While institutions which invest in clubs may be driven by their normal demands for returns, as previously discussed, many shareholders are, of course, fans who do not wish to sell their shares for a quick profit, but to invest for the long term, whether for financial reasons or for other personal reasons. One of the most successful share issues was made by Celtic in January 1995. This raised £9.4 million for the club, creating 10 500 new shareholders in the process. Despite January being generally recognised as a bad month for raising capital the issue was oversubscribed some 1.8 times. One reason for its success was incentives offered to fans in the form of loans from the Co-operative Bank, which helped ensure that it was investors who were looking to the long term who were successful in acquiring shares, rather than those seeking to make a quick profit.[30]

Such long term investment allows a club to make decisions unhindered by short term pressure for financial results. By contrast, in conventional companies short term pressure exists in the form of the market for corporate control (discussed earlier in the chapter), through which the threat of takeovers is an ever present constraint on the behaviour of managers. The downside for football clubs, however, is that although such investors may not be seeking short term financial returns, they along with many other supporters are less likely to take a particularly long term view as regards the achievement of football success.

ROLE OF BANK FUNDING

British clubs have usually relied heavily on their bankers providing loan and overdraft facilities as a source of finance. Borrowings have been used to finance investment in stadium and facilities certainly, but much of it has also been used to fund transfers and players' wages. Table 3.22

Table 3.22   Indebtedness to the banks: all clubs (number of clubs)

	1997 (£m)	1996 (£m)	1995 (£m)	1994 (£m)	1993 (£m)
Premier League	(42.4) [20]	85.0 [20]	39.5 [22]	9.5 [22]	15.6 [22]
Scottish Premier	(31.2) [10]	15.5 [10]	13.5 [10]	2.7 [12]	14.1 [11][1]

[1] No information was available on Airdrie as the club filed modified accounts with Companies House.

Source: Club accounts, Deloitte & Touche (1997, 1996), Touche Ross (1995, 1994)

sets out the overall position of indebtedness to the banks for the top division clubs in recent years.

In the period 1993 to 1996 the banks provided a major level of funding to clubs in the top divisions, and were thus significantly exposed to the football industry. This situation changed notably in 1997, however. Both the Premier League and Scottish Premier Division clubs now report positive net cash balances. Some of these are temporary in nature, others have arisen out of changes in the economics of football more generally.

Temporary distortions are caused by one-off cash injections, which come about primarily as a result of clubs becoming quoted on the Stock Exchange. Aston Villa and Newcastle United are particularly good examples of this. Both raised large sums by going public on the Stock Exchange at the end of their 1997 accounting periods. Aston Villa, early in May 1997, realised £15.2m in this way and, consequently had a very high cash balance of £12.3m at its 31 May year end. Newcastle United raised a staggering £50.4m in April 1997, reflected in its 31 July year end at £31.4m. In both cases, such positions are likely to be temporary because the funds are earmarked for early investment in the business.

Clubs not listed on the Stock Exchange have also benefited from large cash injections. For example, in January 1997 Glasgow Rangers raised £40 million through selling a 25 per cent stake in the club to the Bahamas-based businessman Joe Lewis on behalf of ENIC (the English National Investment Company): this explains its £28.5m May year end cash balance. A restructuring of the share capital at Sheffield Wednesday in April 1997 led to a capital introduction of £17m into the club which explains its £10.3m April year end cash balance (see Table 3.9).

The football industry in England has also benefited in recent years from large increases in the funds flowing in through significantly improved television deals (see the section on *Television – football's economic driver* in Chapter 1). Notwithstanding the fact that expenses, particularly in terms of player salaries, have also seen marked increases (see the section on *Implications for salaries* in Chapter 2), some improvement in the financial position of clubs might have been expected. Table 3.24 shows that 12 clubs report positive net cash balances in excess of £1m. The most prominent of these is Manchester United, currently able to generate cash at a very impressive rate. In 1997 the company produced £33m from operating activities, resulting in an £8m increase in its cash balance since the 1996 year end. This has left Manchester United with an unusual dilemma for a football club – how to use its cash mountain? This pressure on the club demonstrates the conflicts that many clubs, particularly listed clubs, find themselves in today. City pressure is for the cash to be returned to shareholders; pressure from the supporters is for the cash to be invested in the team or to be used, for example, to reduce ticket prices. Such conflicts are discussed in detail in Chapter 5.

Improvements in the cash position of many clubs aside, it must be noted that the figures set out in Table 3.22 do not provide the full picture of the banks' exposure to individual football clubs, as opposed to the sector overall, as this table included clubs with positive cash balances. Table 3.23 sets out the level of the indebtedness of the top clubs to the banks, for those clubs in deficit only.

Table 3.23 unmasks the real position of several clubs. For those in deficit to the banks, the average indebtedness at the 1997 accounting year ends is in excess of £4m per club in the Premier League and is almost £1m per club in the Scottish Premier Division.

Table 3.23 Indebtedness to the banks: clubs in deficit only
(number of clubs)

	1997 (£m)	1996 (£m)	1995 (£m)	1994 (£m)	1993 (£m)
Premier League	45.9 [11]	100.7 [16]	66.1 [14]	33.8 [14]	30.9 [16]
Scottish Premier	4.6 [5]	15.8 [6]	20.9 [7]	9.8 [9]	15.1 [10][1]

[1] No information was available on Airdrie as the club filed modified accounts with Companies House.

Source: Club accounts, Deloitte & Touche (1997, 1996), Touche Ross (1995, 1994)

This position can be considered in greater detail by looking at the position at individual clubs. Table 3.24 uses a bank gearing ratio to compare the indebtedness of top clubs with their net assets prior to deducting obligations to the bank. In other words, it provides a measure of the bank's security in asset terms. The table also shows a commonly calculated measure of income gearing. Unlike equity, bank loans and overdrafts carry with them the immediate requirement to pay interest on those obligations. The interest cover ratio in Table 3.24 measures the ease with which the company can cover its interest payments out of operating profit.[31] The ratios are defined in the Notes to Table 3.24. The information presented in Table 3.24 has been classified according to the club's financial position and its financial relationship with its bank.

Analysis of club positions

One factor which influences the bank gearing ratio is the extent to which clubs are undercapitalised (i.e. have an insufficient level of share capital given the assets of the firm). This issue was discussed earlier in this chapter in the section *Equity finance* (see Table 3.2).

Clubs in a net cash, net assets position

Clubs in this category all report healthy cash balances and have very strong capital structures. For several (Aston Villa, Newcastle United, Nottingham Forest, Sheffield Wednesday and Rangers) the cash position was fortified by injections through share issues during the year (see Tables 3.8–3.11).

Such share issues have redressed undercapitalisation prevalent in many clubs. This is seen in more favourable interest cover ratios demonstrating an increasing ability to cover interest payments, both as regards profits and cash flows.

Nevertheless, there are significant differences between clubs arising in consequence of the changes in the structure caused by large inflows of cash. Three clubs in particular call for comment: Newcastle United, Wimbledon and Nottingham Forest.

For Newcastle United improved cash balances transformed the net liabilities to net assets. For several years the club ran at a loss and substantial accumulated losses were being carried in the balance sheet. The profit of £7.3m for the year ending 31 July 1997, however, began to reduce this. The club also shows a high level of deferred income on its balance sheet (£29.9m), comprising primarily sponsorship, bond,

Table 3.24 Individual club indebtedness and interest cover ratios

	Cash at bank/ (bank loans and overdrafts) (£000)	Bank gearing (%)	Interest cover (No. of times)
Clubs in a net cash, net assets position			
Arsenal	1 491	NA	17.8
Aston Villa	12 347	NA	134.1
Liverpool	4 245	NA	25.5
Manchester United	16 585	NA	37.7
Newcastle United	31 392	NA	5.0
Nottingham Forest	3 272	NA	−[1]
Sheffield Wednesday	10 296	NA	2.3
Tottenham Hotspur	6 828	NA	46.3
Wimbledon	1 823	NA	265.6
Celtic	3 478	NA	75.6
Dundee United	1 983	NA	NA[2]
Rangers	28 561	NA	8.7
Clubs in a net asset position but with obligations to the bank			
Blackburn Rovers	(4 784)	25.9%	−[1]
Caspian	(1 578)	30.5%	1.3
Chelsea	(2 504)	5.0% (7.3%)	3.6
Everton	(4 378)	30.0%	6.2
Southampton	(43)	0.7%	8.4
Sunderland	(3 028)	16.0% (21.3%)	285.0
West Ham United	(667)	6.4%	2.8
Aberdeen	(961)	20.5% (32.0%)	−[1]
Heart of Midlothian	(1 575)	30.6% (40.7%)	0.3
Kilmarnock	(1 493)	31.5%	2.0
Motherwell	(64)	3.7%	−[3]
Raith Rovers	(351)	23.2%	−[1]
Clubs in a net liability position and with obligations to the bank			
Coventry	(13 655)	−[4]	−[1]
Derby County	(1 381)	−[4]	10.2
Leicester City	(4 060)	167.1%	3.9
Middlesbrough	(9 795)	−[4]	2.0
Dunfermline Athletic	(1 753)	−[4]	−[1]
Clubs with net cash but in a net liability position			
Hibernian	268	−[4]	−[1]

Notes

Bank gearing $= \dfrac{\text{Bank loans and overdrafts}}{\text{Net assets before deducting bank loans and overdrafts}}$

The figure in brackets represent the calculation of bank gearing using net assets excluding capitalised players' registrations.

Interest Cover $= \dfrac{\text{Profit before transfer fees and/or amortisation of costs of registration}}{\text{Interest payable on bank loans and overdrafts}}$

[1] Ratio cannot be calculated as the club made a loss before transfer fees.
[2] Ratio is not applicable, as the club had no interest payable for the year.
[3] Ratio cannot be calculated as the club does not disclose its profit/loss before transfer fees.
[4] Ratio cannot be calculated as club is in a net liability position before deducting bank loans and overdrafts.

NA: Not applicable.
Source: Company accounts

executive scheme and season ticket income in advance (see the section on *Gate receipts* in Chapter 4). Hence it requires to be shown as a debt obligation by companies in the balance sheet. Prior to the club's share issue, Newcastle United relied heavily on both bank funding and funding from subsidiary companies. These amounts were paid off using the £50m proceeds from the share issue thus putting the club on to a sounder financial footing. However, because the issue took place in April, the interest cover ratio reflects the interest payments on bank borrowings throughout the year.

For Wimbledon the high cash position reflects operating cash flows generated by the club in 1996 (£1.7m) and 1995 (£1.2m). This can be explained by the fact that in both those years the club were net sellers in the transfer market. In 1996 net transfer fees receivable were £3.1m, compared to £1.6m in 1995. In 1997, however, the club had net transfer fees payable of £1.9m, contributing to a reduction in the club's net cash position on the balance sheet from £2.4m to £1.9m, with the club's inflow from operating activities being only £77 027. Of greater significance to its net asset position, however, is the important fact that Wimbledon is the only Premier League club which does not own its ground and hence has no asset value included in the accounts (see the section on *Accounting for tangible fixed assets* in Chapter 4).

Nottingham Forest is another club which has undergone a capital reconstruction. The club was taken over in March 1997 by Nottingham Forest plc (formerly Bridgford plc). Immediately following acquisition the company subscribed for £16m of ordinary shares in the club. Subsequent to the year end, Nottingham Forest floated on AIM in October 1997 thereby raising further capital. Interest cover ratios could not be calculated for the company because it made an operating loss of £1.5m before transfer fees. A significant part of the operating loss was a 30 per cent increase in staff costs (£8.0m compared to a turnover of £14.4m) in the 1997 accounting year in consequence of the higher wages being paid in the Premier League (see the section on *Implications for salaries* in Chapter 2).

Clubs in a net asset position, but with obligations to the bank

Clubs classified in this section show the traditional football club picture. Broadly two groups emerge. First, there are four clubs (Chelsea, Southampton, West Ham United and Motherwell) which have a very low level of bank borrowings compared to total assets. With the exception of Motherwell, each of these clubs can also comfortably cover their interest payments out of operating profit. In the case of Motherwell, the pre transfer cost operating profit is not disclosed, though, the club reported an operating loss of £80000 after transfer fees.

Secondly, there are a number of clubs whose bank gearing ratio is in the region of 20–30 per cent. This group includes two listed clubs, Caspian (now Leeds Sporting) and Heart of Midlothian. While in absolute terms this is not a dangerously high percentage, in view of the nature of the football industry, and in particular the nature of security of borrowings, it may be a cause for concern (see following section). For those clubs which include players' registrations as assets on the balance sheet (Chelsea, Sunderland, Aberdeen and Heart of Midlothian), the figures have also been calculated excluding this amount from the net assets (see also Chapter 4). Most significantly this results in Aberdeen's bank gearing ratio rising to in excess of 30 per cent, while that of Heart of Midlothian rises to in excess of 40 per cent. Given that Heart of Midlothian has already used a flotation to raise capital and restructure its finances, such a high bank gearing ratio is a cause for concern. The problem is specifically addressed in the notes to its 1997 accounts as follows:

> The company meets its day to day working capital requirements through an overdraft facility which is repayable on demand. The Company expects to operate within the facility agreed. These views are based on the Company's plans and on the results of discussion with the Company's bankers.

Notwithstanding the above comments, it can be noted that the gearing position has markedly improved in recent years: its 1995 accounts showed net liabilities to the bank of £5.3m and net assets of £1.5m including £2.3m in respect of players' registrations.

It should also be noted that several clubs in this grouping (Blackburn Rovers, Aberdeen and Raith Rovers) are unable to cover their interest payments from operating profit before transfer fees. That continues to be a matter of concern.

Clubs with obligations to the bank and in a net liability position

The most straitened financial position is that of Coventry City, which was hugely indebted to the bank at 31 May 1997. Unfortunately, it is difficult to comment meaningfully on the club's position, given that there is little publicly available information about the ownership of the club beyond that set out in Table 3.9.

Since its 1997 year end Derby County has gone through a corporate restructuring (see Table 3.9). Part of this involves a new investment of £10m from funds managed by Electra Fleming, one of the leading equity financiers to private companies in the UK. Other aspects of the restructuring altered its year end position set out in Table 3.24 considerably. At that point loans of £10.47m to the club from its parent company (Derbyshire Enterprises) were shown as liabilities, thus resulting in the club being in a position of net liabilities. As part of the restructuring which took place in September 1997, these loans were converted into equity shares in the new holding company (see the section on *Ownership framework in football clubs* earlier in this chapter). To treat these loans as equity at the year end would have resulted in a bank gearing ratio of 23.1 per cent. However, Derby also includes its players' registrations as assets on the balance sheet. Ignoring new funds provided by the restructuring, excluding this asset would again result in the club being in a position of net liabilities. Despite this fact, the restructuring will notably improve the gearing ratios portrayed at the 1997 year end. It is also reassuring for Derby to be able to cover its interest payments out of operating profits as evidenced by the interest cover ratio of 10.2 shown in Table 3.24.

Leicester City is another club which has been restructured since its 31 July 1997 year end following the reverse takeover by Soccer Investments plc and subsequent listing on the Stock Exchange. The club's net liability position at the year end arose out if its liabilities to its bank. At its year end the company was just able to cover its interest payments by its operating profit. However, following the reverse takeover, new funds of £2m (approximately) through share issues, in addition to almost £10m of cash reserves held by Soccer Investments, has substantially altered the company's exposure to the bank. These funds were to be used for working capital purposes.

The capital structure of Middlesbrough is discussed earlier in this chapter (see Table 3.9). Furthermore, the objectives of its owners, namely its Chairman Steve Gibson and ICI plc are discussed in detail in Chapter 5. It can be argued that these objectives have involved 'speculating to accumulate'. In other words the club has consciously tried to turn itself into a successful Premier League club by investing heavily in the transfer market and by offering lucrative contracts to players, irrespective of short term profit or cash flow considerations. As a result it is not surprising that the club is heavily indebted to the bank. Although the auditors have drawn attention to a fundamental uncertainty about the validity of preparing the accounts on a going concern basis, in view of the dominant ownership of the club by Mr Gibson through his company Gibson O'Neill, it is also not surprising that the auditors have not felt it necessary to qualify the accounts in this respect. The directors' views on the club's position are set out in the accounting policy note to the accounts:

> The company meets its day to day working capital requirements through an overdraft facility which is repayable on demand. The validity of the going concern basis depends upon the company's ability to operate within agreed overdraft facilities. The nature of the company's business is such that a significant number of future cash inflows are dependent upon the football team's success, and as such, the amount of these inflows in uncertain. Despite this uncertainty the directors consider that current financing facilities, taking into account the company's ability to raise additional funds through its principal activity, are sufficient to meet the company's requirements for the foreseeable future. (Middlesbrough Football & Athletic Company (1986) Limited Annual Report 1997)

The gulf between English and Scottish clubs is shown by considering the case of Dunfermline. Dunfermline, like Wimbledon, does not own its own ground. Wimbledon is a club which is often presented as the poor man of top class English football. Any similarity with Dunfermline, however, in terms of financial poverty ends at the lack of a stadium. While Wimbledon has cash balances of £1.8m and a net asset position of £1m, Dunfermline has obligations to the bank of £1.7m and an overall net liability position of £2.8m. Its reported loss for 1997 of £252 563 left it with accumulated retained losses of £3.6m. Although its auditors did not qualify the financial statements they did discuss the appropriateness of preparing the accounts under the going concern convention, with regard to the inherent uncertainty as to the continued support of the company's bankers and creditors. The directors' reassurances on the subject are provided in the notes to the accounts and are specifically referred to by the auditors:

> The validity of this [going concern] assumption depends upon the trading performance of the company and the continued support of the company's bankers and creditors. The directors have arranged deferred repayment terms for the company's bank loan and its major creditors. The Directors have also prepared cash flows and budgets which show that the company is able to meet its obligations as they fall due within the foreseeable future. (Auditors Report to the members of Dunfermline Athletic Football Club Ltd, 1997)

Clubs with net cash, but in a net liability position

The unusual situation of Hibernian stems from the club's relationship with its parent company. Loan facilities are provided through the parent company. The club's net assets do not include its stadium, which is now leased from another group company, but do include the cost of its players' registrations. Although the club reported a small profit in the 1997 accounting year, its accumulated losses amount to £1.3m. Prior to the club being taken over by its present owners, it was very close to going out of business (see the section on *Ownership framework in football clubs* earlier in this chapter).

The role of the banks is difficult to summarise, owing to the vast differences in prosperity of the clubs. Several clubs have reduced reliance on bank funding by restructuring and increasing share capital by new issues. Others, mainly smaller Scottish clubs, remain heavily and indeed dangerously reliant on their bankers.

Particularly, it should be noted, that accounts figures for cash and borrowings present the position at the accounting year-end. The picture thus may be distorted: for instance, accounts at a 31 July year-end may contain receipts from season ticket sales for the forthcoming season. For such as Manchester United and Celtic with 40 000 or more advance season ticket sales, being an average of £300 each, careful and balanced presentation is essential (see also the section on *Gate receipts* in Chapter 4).

Security for borrowing

Assets as security

In theory, loans and overdrafts provided to clubs by the banks are usually secured over some or all of the club's assets. This security may take the form of a standard security over the club's stadium and/or a floating charge over all of the assets of the club. In practice, the actual security provided by such asset backing is questionable for several reasons.

The financial position of many top clubs remains very poor. Table 3.24 shows that six clubs are actually in the position of having net liabilities in excess of their net assets. This position is a great improvement on that which would have been reported in previous years. Nevertheless, these clubs are technically insolvent and are only kept going by the decision of the banks not to call in their security. One reason for this continued bank support is that the lack of asset backing effectively makes this asset security doubtful, as it would not allow the bank to recover its full liability.[32]

It should be borne in mind that Table 3.24 sets out the net asset position of clubs in accounting or book value terms. In the event of liquidation, clearly what is important is not the historical cost of assets or indeed the revalued amount at which they are carried on clubs' balance sheets,[33] but rather the realisable value of a company's assets, i.e. how much can those assets be sold for. The principal tangible asset of most clubs continues to be its stadium, an asset which is highly specialised in nature and for which there is no evidence of an active market. Notwithstanding the significant investment made by many clubs in recent years, the realisable value of many clubs' stadiums is likely to be their redevelopment value, i.e. the value of the security will depend on the extent to which the land upon which the stadium sits is of interest to developers for more lucrative purposes such as building houses or supermarkets. Even then, such values would depend on factors such as location, planning department policy, other facilities and developments in the area, etc. Once again this may call into question the estimated value of the bank's security.

Fortunately, there is little evidence of banks calling in their legal security for loans and overdrafts. This may be explained in part by the factors discussed above, which in substance amount to an acknowledgement by the bank that the club is almost certainly of greater value as a going concern than as a liquidated entity (see following section on *The lending decision*). It may also be explained by the fact that security other than stadium has been available to banks in the form of the club's players.

Players as security

It has been a commonly held view that banks have relied on their ability to require a club to sell a player as their real security (Deloitte & Touche, 1997). In other words the security available to banks has been provided as a consequence of clubs holding the registration of their players (Morrow, 1996b).

The decision in the *Bosman* case, however, has changed the nature of the transfer market for football clubs. After it clubs no longer receive a fee for out-of-contract players who reach the end of their contracts, if they move outside the United Kingdom. Furthermore, changes brought in by the domestic football regulatory authorities mean that from 1 July 1998 in England and from 16 May 1998 in Scotland transfer fees are no longer receivable by clubs when out-of-contract players over the age of 24 move clubs, even within the UK (see section on *The new system* in Chapter 2).

The effects of such changes to the transfer system and the implications for banks' exposure and future lending policies was investigated by Morrow (1997) in discussions with senior representatives of UK banks involved in lending to football clubs. While acknowledging that the *Bosman* decision was one more risk in an already risky business, perhaps surprisingly, the bankers did not feel the decision in the case had significantly altered their level of exposure. This can be explained by the fact that the banks claimed to adopt an income perspective as distinct from an asset or security perspective when considering their exposure to football clubs and future lending decisions, with quality of income stream (i.e. the club's expected future cash flows and ability to service its debts) being identified as the most important factor.

As security is by definition an issue of last resort, decisions such as that in the Bosman case and also negative accounting information of the type identified in Table 3.24 was not considered a source of major concern to the banks. Nevertheless, the importance of transfers was still evident with the acknowledgement by the bankers that where a bank believed it was exposed to a particular club, it would not be uncommon for arrangements to be in place whereby if funds were received by a club which was extensively funded by bank borrowing, then part of these funds would be commandeered by the bank to reduce the club's overdraft.

Directors' guarantees

Common practice was that club directors would personally guarantee the loans provided by banks to the clubs. The increase in size of major clubs has diminished this practice, though, it is still common at many smaller clubs. Such guarantees in practice were something of a double edged sword in the sense that the decision by the directors to guarantee the loans was an encouragement to clubs to take on a hardly sustainable level of debt.

The lending decision

The decision on whether to lend money to football clubs is primarily based on judgements about the quality of a club's income stream. If the bank believes that a club will be able to service its debt in the future, funds will be advanced. While the external observer may view lending money to an organisation whose liabilities already significantly exceed its assets as an act of folly, from the banks' point of view, as long as the interest charges continue to be met it looks more like a profitable business opportunity. In this regard the most relevant information for banks are historical and projected interest cover ratios of the type set out in Table 3.24. The profit maximisation objective of banks may also explain their preference (which is unlikely to be the club's preference) for the provision of short term finance such as overdrafts, as opposed to longer term finance.

Additional to the quality of a club's income stream, Morrow (1997) found that two other factors were identified by the banks as having an influence on the lending decision: first, the bank's relationship with a club's directors (particularly the bank's view of their other business interests and abilities), and secondly, wider social issues such as the perceived importance of a football club to a local community (see the section on *Preserving a community asset – the role of the banks* in Chapter 5).

Efficiency of borrowing

A particular problem for clubs, which rely on bank borrowings and overdrafts as a source of funding, is that such finance is often short term in nature. By contrast, much of the expenditure which clubs have required to incur in recent years is long term, not least stadium improvements. Recognised finance logic suggests that companies should attempt where possible to match the time periods of investment and the corresponding funding.

While the mismatch in terms of the funding of assets such as stadium improvements may be obvious, it is also argued that clubs have been disadvantaged in their dealings with players by the unwillingness of banks to lend long-term (Szymanski, 1997). One of the consequences of the *Bosman* case is an expectation that clubs will write longer contracts in order to retain the possibility of selling a player before the contract expires. Szymanski questions why such contracts did not exist before, given that labour market economics suggests that they would have been attractive to players and cheaper for clubs (on average) in the pre-Bosman world. The financial constraints faced by clubs as a result of the overall financial position of the football industry are put forward as the most likely explanation.

While banks have been willing to provide finance based on short term beliefs about income coming into the club, they have been unwilling to fund long term employment contracts in case the club itself did not have a long term future. An alternative explanation put forward by Szymanski, and one which was discussed earlier is that the lack of long term contracts may be explained by profit maximization behaviour on the part of the banks, i.e. banks can earn greater profits from short term loans at high interest rates than they might earn from more risky long term loans. The irony for clubs, however, is that such long term support may be what is required to boost their chances of survival.

4 Accounting in the Football Industry

The objective of this chapter is to investigate issues arising from the accounting policies and disclosure adopted by football clubs. The chapter considers the nature and purpose of financial statements and their relevance to football clubs, before analysing significant accounting policies adopted by clubs in respect of vital items such as player costs and stadium investment. Weaknesses of the financial reporting model as it relates to football clubs will be discussed. It should be noted, however, that this chapter is *not* intended to be survey of significant accounting policies adopted by football clubs. This task is already carried out thoroughly for English clubs by Deloitte & Touche in its excellent and comprehensive *Annual Reviews of Football Finance*[1] and in a more limited form for Scottish clubs by Price Waterhouse in its *Financial Review of Scottish Football*.[2]

THE OBJECTIVES OF FINANCIAL REPORTING

There are three primary financial statements of relevance to most football clubs: the balance sheet, the profit and loss account and the cash flow statement. Their objective is the provision of information about the financial position, performance and financial adaptability of an enterprise that is useful to a wide range of users for assessing the stewardship of management and for making economic decisions (ASB, 1995).

The balance sheet provides information annually on the overall position at a given date. For football clubs this date is usually at or around the end of the season. It reports economic resources controlled by a company, its financial structure, its liquidity and its financial viability. The profit and loss account provides information on performance over that annual period, with the revenues of the period being matched with the expenses incurred in earning that revenue.[3] Financial adaptability refers to the company's ability to respond to unexpected needs or opportunities. Information on adaptability is provided through the cash flow statement in particular. In addition to the primary statements, the accounts also include supporting notes that amplify and explain the primary financial statements.

Financial statements of football clubs have concentrated historically on a narrow concept of stewardship, mainly the reporting by directors to shareholders on the use of funds entrusted to them. In short the role played by the financial statements was restricted to providing evidence of the existence of the assets of the company and the claim by outsiders (creditors) on the company. The usefulness of even that role was further restricted by conventions (or practices) under which the financial statements of UK companies are prepared, in particular the historical cost and money measurement conventions.

In *historical cost accounting* assets are recorded in the financial statements at the amount paid at the time of acquisition. No account is taken of future changes in the value of those assets. As a result, a balance sheet does not, and does not purport to, provide values for the individual assets and liabilities of the company, nor indeed a value for the company overall. Instead it is simply a statement of the assets and liabilities of the company in terms of their original cost to the company. Most club accounts, and indeed the majority of UK company accounts, are prepared under modified historical cost accounting. In simple terms this allows certain assets such as buildings and property to be revalued. This will be discussed in more detail in a later section of this chapter.

The money measurement convention means that financial statements include only those items which can be objectively measured in terms of money. In the case of football clubs, therefore, it has been common for significant intangible assets such as the skills and services provided by the players to be omitted, while other assets such as grounds and facilities were often included at figures that bore little relation to their present value or worth.

One consequence of this emphasis on demonstrating stewardship to the shareholders was that the financial statements of football clubs were often fairly limited, both in their usefulness to accounts users and also in the extent to which they captured the economic reality of clubs. Such football club financial statements could have been described as a *visible illusion*, in that although the figures were accurate they did not make any functional sense.[4] Many clubs' balance sheets did not resemble conventional company balance sheets because clubs were often in positions of negative equity, i.e. it was common for assets to be significantly less than the liabilities. Interestingly, in the Netherlands, the football regulatory body, the KNVB, requires that all Professional Football Organisations must have positive or at least zero equity (Brummans and Langendijk, 1995). Such a requirement in the UK would have had serious implications for many clubs. For example, even at the 1997 accounting year ends, five top division British clubs remain in negative equity positions. (The implications of negative equity for clubs seeking to use the Stock Exchange as a means of raising capital was considered in Chapter 3.)

It has been argued in the past that the use of *traditional* financial reporting practices hindered full understanding and consideration of the causes and indicators of clubs' financial difficulties (Webb and Broadbent, 1986). A further problem was a lack of comparability between the financial statements of different clubs, given the very different accounting treatments adopted by clubs for items such as transfer fees, grants and sponsorship income. Financial statements in the UK must be prepared in accordance with accounting standards issued by the Accounting Standards Board (Financial Reporting Standards) or its predecessor the Accounting Standards Committee (Statements of Standard Accounting Practice). Often, however, such standards have been of little relevance to football clubs, as they have failed to highlight the economic and financial peculiarities of the football industry. Despite these peculiarities, no specific industry guidance has ever been provided by the accounting regulators, probably reflecting the view that the financial scale of the industry did not merit such attention.

In recent years, however, there has been a significant improvement in both the quantity, and more importantly, the quality of accounting information provided by football clubs. Partly this reflects a widening of the concept of stewardship; an acknowledgement that stakeholder groups other than shareholders have legitimate needs for accounting information to assist them to form judgements about how well the directors have used the resources entrusted to them. (Issues relating to accountability and stakeholders are considered in detail in Chapter 5.) A variety of other factors has also contributed to the improvement – greater involvement of professional advisers in football clubs, greater financial awareness among football club directors, increased public and media interest in the financial affairs of clubs, a culture of best practice, the need to provide adequate information to potential investors and lenders and improved, more relevant financial accounting standards and generally accepted practice. Problems still remain, however, and some of these will be discussed in this chapter.

ACCOUNTING FOR INTANGIBLE FIXED ASSETS

Accounting for players

The accounting treatment of players is an area of much interest in recent years to academics and practitioners. It is pragmatic to think of players as assets. Other than the ground or facilities they are often practically the only resource of value. Robinson (1969) argued that the main difference between investment in humans and investment in property was the fact that the earning power of an individual, unlike that of property, was not a saleable commodity. The transfer system in which players' contracts at all levels of the game are bought and sold is an exception to this rule (see the section on *The transfer market* in Chapter 2). It is not, of course, the player himself who is the asset, but rather his contract. However, as noted in the *Chester Report of the Committee on Football*, this distinction is somewhat technical, since although 'the transaction may be wrapped up in the jargon of registrations, . . . in effect it is payment for a man . . .' (Department of Education and Science, 1968).

Since 1987 major clubs have adopted a variety of accounting treatments to reflect their investment in players, responding to both the opinions of academics and practitioners and also to external influences such as the decision taken in 1995 by the European Court of Justice in the *Bosman* case. Following the publication in December 1997 by the Accounting Standards Board (ASB) of Financial Reporting Standard (FRS) 10 on *Goodwill and Intangible Assets*, the question of how football clubs should record their investment in players is set to be reopened (Morrow, 1998). While FRS 10 will have far reaching consequences for clubs, its requirements should not come as a surprise to clubs, financiers or analysts, given that the standard is substantially unchanged from the exposure draft, FRED 12, issued by the ASB in June 1996 (Morrow, 1997).

The traditional practice of accounting for football players excluded any valuation of players from the balance sheet, whether they were players bought by a club through the transfer market or those developed internally by the club. Following this practice, transfer fees (and associated costs) are simply charged or credited to the profit and loss account in the year in which the transfer takes place (i.e. treated as income or expenses of the period). One consequence of this treatment is that the reported profit or loss can be substantially affected by both the amount of any transfer fee receivable or payable and also by its timing.

The first club to adopt an alternative treatment was Tottenham Hotspur. In its accounts for the year ended 31 May 1989 it adopted an accounting policy that recorded the cost of players' registrations acquired as intangible assets on the balance sheet. Tottenham was followed by Heart of Midlothian the following year, and thereafter a number of clubs decided that the traditional practice did not in fact present a true and fair view of a football club's financial affairs. Prior to the *Bosman* ruling, thirteen English clubs and five Scottish clubs included player values in the balance sheet (1996 accounting year ends). The most common policy was to capitalise only those players acquired on the transfer market as intangible assets on the balance sheet. The acquisition cost less an estimated residual value at the end of a player's contract was then amortised,[5] either over the period of an individual player's contract,[6] or over the period until the player attained the age of 33.[7] Other clubs incorporated a value for their entire squad, whether bought in or homegrown, with players being included either at capitalised value,[8] Directors' valuation,[9] Manager/Directors' valuation[10] or at a valuation made by an independent panel of experienced sports writers at the year end date.[11]

In the case of *Union Royale Belge des Sociétés de Football Association ASBL* v. *Bosman*, the European Court of Justice ruled that clubs could only charge a transfer fee for a player if he was sold during the period of his contract, or if he was sold at the end of his contract to a club within the same EU member state (see section on *The Bosman case* in Chapter 2). This ruling, combined with uncertainty about the likelihood of the domestic transfer system surviving long term after the *Bosman* decision,[12] has had an effect on the accounting treatment adopted by clubs for their players. While some of the eighteen clubs, such as Rangers and Newcastle United, reverted to the traditional method of taking player expenditure and income through the profit and loss account, the majority of clubs opted to continue capitalising those players acquired on the transfer market, but to alter the amortisation of the asset so that the entire cost of acquiring a player's registration was written off over his contract life. This involves using a residual value of zero at the end of a player's contract, rather than a value based either on a player's salary and a

Table 4.1   Accounting policies in respect of player registrations

	Stock exchange status	Basis	1997 (£000)	1996 (£000)
Premier League				
Chelsea	AIM	Cost of registrations	15 797	6 193
Derby County	Not listed	Cost of registrations	7 938	6 038
Sunderland	Main market	Cost of registrations	4 664	1 829
Tottenham Hotspur	Main market	Cost of registrations	22 624	10 215
Scottish Premier				
Aberdeen	Not listed	Cost of registrations	1 676	2 229
Celtic	AIM	Cost of registrations	8 958	8 152
Heart of Midlothian	Main market	Cost of registrations	1 285	1 650
Hibernian	Not listed	Cost of registrations	1 813	296
Other listed clubs				
West Bromwich Albion	AIM	Directors' valuation	7 793	4 160

Source: Company accounts

multiplier based on his age at the end of the contract or some other appropriate estimate.

Table 4.1 sets out those clubs in the top divisions in England and Scotland (and other listed clubs) which continue to adopt an accounting policy of capitalisation in their 1997 financial statements. All other top division and listed clubs adopted the traditional accounting policy in their 1997 financial statements.

Accounting implications of FRS 10

FRS 10, *Goodwill and Intangible Assets*, was introduced by the ASB in December 1997, and must be applied by companies for accounting periods ending on or after 23 December 1998. The question of how companies should account for assets such as goodwill plus a whole variety of intangible assets such as brand names, newspaper mastheads and licences has been the subject of much controversy for several years. The formulation of FRS 10 is the result of eight years work by the ASB.

FRS 10 was primarily introduced to standardise the way in which large multi-nationals such as Grand Metropolitan and Guinness (which have now merged to become Diageo) and Cadbury-Schweppes account for goodwill and brand names arising out of their acquisitions of other companies. As was discussed in Chapter 3, in economic terms football clubs remain small companies. There seems little doubt that the far reaching implications of FRS 10 for football clubs was not a specific intention of the ASB, rather that it has arisen as a by-product of the larger debate surrounding goodwill and intangibles. Nevertheless, the standard is now in place and clubs have little option but to follow its requirements.

Players acquired through the transfer market

The ASB (1995) defines assets as rights, or other access to future economic benefits controlled by an entity as a result of past transactions or events. The future economic benefits of a football club arises primarily through players performing their trade. This enables a club to generate income through gate receipts, merchandising, television and sponsorship. As such, therefore, the logic of including the cost of acquiring a player's registration as an asset is indisputable, given that it is the acquisition of a player's registration which entitles the club to his services.

The broad thrust of FRS 10 is that intangible assets purchased separately from a business should be capitalised at their cost, as long as the intangible assets are identifiable (i.e. capable of being disposed of separately) and controlled by the entity either through legal rights or physical custody. Interestingly, in the definition section of the standard, the ASB provides 'a team of skilled staff' as an example where it is expected that future benefits will flow to the entity, but that the entity does not have sufficient control over the benefits to recognise an intangible asset. However, the unusual nature of a football player's contract with a club means that the club does have control of a player during his contract term, and hence suggests acquired players require recognition as intangible assets (Morrow, 1996a). Nevertheless, for those clubs which may wish to avoid capitalising the cost of players' registrations on the balance sheet the question of control would seem to provide the best opportunity for challenging what appears to be the required treatment of capitalisation under the standard.

In practice, therefore, when a club signs a player, it will be required to capitalise the cost of his registration on the balance sheet, and then to amortise that amount over the length of his contract. These costs will be shown as intangible fixed assets on the balance sheet. In other words, the accounting policy adopted by all clubs other than West Bromwich Albion in Table 4.1 will become the norm.[13]

The standard also requires that intangible assets should be reviewed for impairment at the end of the first full financial year following the acquisition, and in other periods if events or changes in circumstances indicate that the carrying values may not be recoverable. Potentially this could prove quite troublesome for clubs. Not only could impairment occur in the event of a serious injury, it could be argued that factors such as loss of form by a player, or the player losing his first team place perhaps as a result of a new signing, could also constitute impairment and hence require the carrying value of the asset to be written down. However, is should be borne in mind that the requirements on impairment are not intended to be prohibitive. Broadly, if there is no indication of impairment then it should be assumed that there is no impairment. It should also be borne in mind that the impairment provision exists to protect accounts users, by ensuring that assets are never carried at amounts higher than can be recovered from them.

In practice, clubs should already be engaging in a limited form of impairment review prior to the introduction of FRS 10, through considering the extent to which there has been a permanent diminution in the carrying value of their assets. The following examples taken from the Accounting Policies notes to the 1997 annual accounts illustrate the reviews being carried out by clubs.

Players' Contracts

Players' contracts are included in the balance sheet at Directors' valuation. Values are assessed on a regular basis and any permanent diminution in value below original cost is written off in the profit and loss account.

> West Bromwich Albion plc, Annual Report & Accounts y.e.
> 30 June 1997

Intangible Assets

... Permanent diminutions in values below the amortised value, such as through injury or loss of form, are provided for when management become aware that the diminution is permanent.

> Sunderland plc, Annual Report y.e. 31 May 1997

Players' Registrations and Signing on Fees
... Any permanent diminution in the cost of registrations is charged
to the profit and loss account when identified.
Heart of Midlothian plc, Annual Report and Account 1997

The impairment reviews required by clubs post-FRS 10 will require
them to consider the extent to which the carrying value of their players'
registrations are not recoverable. An asset is regarded as impaired if its
recoverable amount (the higher of net realisable value and value in
use) falls below its carrying value. Again several clubs such as Aston
Villa, Chelsea, Coventry City, West Ham United, Celtic and Hibernian
already disclose a valuation of their players on a realisable value (or
selling price) basis in their 1997 annual accounts. Value in use is the
present value of the future cash flows obtainable as a result of an asset's
continued use.

Homegrown players

West Bromwich Albion is the only club which has an accounting policy
which does not distinguish between acquired and homegrown players
(i.e. players who have come up through the ranks). It includes all
players' contracts in the balance sheet at directors' valuation. Such a
policy finds favour in the earlier academic literature (Morrow, 1996a),
and support initially also appears to be offered by FRS 10 which states
that an internally developed intangible asset may be recognised if it has
a readily ascertainable market value. However, although intuitively we
may view football players as being a good example of an asset for which
a market and hence a market value exists, it is clear that this is not the
view of the ASB.

Its view is that an asset only has a readily ascertainable market
value if, first, it belongs to a homogeneous population of assets that are
equivalent in all material respects, and secondly, if an active market,
evidenced by frequent transactions, exists for that population of assets.
It is unlikely that the services provided by football players could be
viewed as homogeneous and thus would fail to meet the ASB test of a
readily ascertainable market value. It would seem more likely that they
would be included within those assets which by their nature are unique,
such as brands. Such assets are described as being similar but not
equivalent in all material respects. Therefore, while there are valid
theoretical reasons for not distinguishing between homegrown and
acquired players, this distinction is necessary to comply with FRS 10.

The requirement for a readily ascertainable market value will also prevent the upward revaluation of the registration of players acquired on the transfer market.

Is FRS 10 the solution to accounting for players?

There is little doubt that the introduction of FRS 10 will improve the quality and consistency of football club financial reporting. Often large sums of money are spent by clubs on acquiring players. From an accounting point of view it has been anomalous that several clubs have chosen to treat these sums as income and expenditure and hence distort the information available on financial performance. One benefit arising out of the requirement that all clubs must capitalise players acquired through the transfer market is that it will improve comparability within the industry. A further benefit is that it will improve the financial position of several clubs as portrayed by their balance sheets, thus increasing the meaningfulness of that statement and making it less of a *visible illusion*.

For example, at the last accounting year end (1997) clubs such as the quoted Leicester City and the unquoted Coventry City, Derby County and Dunfermline Athletic all had balance sheets which showed positions of net liabilities (i.e. net liabilities being greater than net assets). Hibernian is also in a net liability position, but as noted in Table 4.1, the cost of players' registrations are already included as intangible assets. The transitional arrangements of the standard require the cost of all players previously written off through the profit and loss account to be reinstated at cost less amortisation, where part of that player's contract remains unexpired. This provision will result in these clubs being able to present balance sheets more in keeping with those of conventional companies.

Problems, however, still remain. In many ways those of football club accounts are problems arising out of the historical cost accounting system. The most obvious arises from the requirement to distinguish between players acquired through the transfer market and players who are either internally developed or acquired at the end of their contract without payment of a transfer fee under the *Bosman* ruling. In terms of generating future economic benefits for their employer club there is little which distinguishes between these categories of player, although it could be argued that it is often the high profile purchased players who makes the greatest contribution to things like merchandising income. Differentiation arises, however, from the

ASB's requirement that a past transaction or event is necessary for the recognition of an asset.

Where a club has acquired a player through the transfer market then the payment of a transfer fee to acquire his registration can be considered as the past transaction which allows recognition of the asset. Consequently the balance sheets of clubs which acquire players through the transfer market will look healthier than clubs which are not as active in the transfer market. Furthermore, not only will clubs, which concentrate on developing their own players, be unable to include these players on their balance sheets, the costs incurred in training and developing these players will require to be written off or expensed through the profit and loss account, thus reducing reported profits. Greater consistency would be provided if the recognition event was taken to be the point at which the club registers the player with the appropriate league, irrespective of whether a fee was paid to another club to acquire that registration (Morrow, 1996a). If this approach were to adopted, however, a valuation methodology other than historical cost would be required.

Various player valuation models are currently being developed by economists and some of these have been used in practice by city institutions and others to inform the market in players (see the sections on *Monitoring* in Chapter 2 and *Employees* in Chapter 5). Player valuations could be provided using such models for financial reporting purposes. However, although the ASB has accepted the idea of a limited number of internally developed intangibles being included on the balance sheet at their readily ascertainable market value, the inclusion of all players at valuation on club balance sheets would not fit comfortably within the existing financial reporting framework. The inclusion of valuations of this nature would require a radical change such as the adoption of an alternative accounting model.

It is worth remembering, also, that the problems being discussed above are not peculiar to football clubs. The balance sheet is not, and does not claim to be a valuation of any company, irrespective of whether that company is Manchester United or Marks & Spencer. Furthermore, many people-dependent companies in industries such as software, advertising and accountancy are faced with similar problems with regard to the type of information which they can report within their financial statements, or more importantly the type of information which they cannot report. Football is not the only industry where the primary asset are the services of its people. If changing the accounting model is not a viable option, one alternative solution may be further to improve the quality and quantity of disclosure in football club financial statements. This issue will be discussed in the final section of this chapter.

Market implications

Several listed clubs which have not previously capitalised the cost of their players' registrations will now require to do so under provisions set out in FRS 10. Among these clubs is the sector's blue chip stock, Manchester United. As mentioned above, adopting FRS 10 will lead to improved comparability of football club financial statements which will be of benefits to analysts and investors. It seems unlikely, however, that FRS 10 will have a significant effect on the valuation of football clubs, given our knowledge of the efficiency of the stock market and the fact that the changes which clubs such as Manchester United will be required to adopt are purely accounting changes (i.e. with no direct cash flow effect). Furthermore most analysts and investors will be quite aware of the value or otherwise of the playing staff of a particular club and are thus unlikely to have their opinions on valuation in any way altered by a change in accounting policy.

The question of the appropriate taxation treatment may lead, however, to an indirect cash flow effect arising from the change in accounting policy. According to Deloitte & Touche (1998a), leading accountants and advisers to the football industry, tax relief is unlikely to be obtained for the full cost of player registrations in the year of transfer. Furthermore they argue that the transitional arrangements of the standard (i.e. the reinstatement of player registrations which were previously written off) may be treated as a taxable event and hence eliminate brought-forward tax losses. Clearly, such tax implications would have financial consequences for clubs and hence would have an impact on stock exchange valuations. Only confirmation of their intended treatment of players' registrations by the Inland Revenue will clarify this matter.

Brand accounting

While the importance of brands has long been recognised by management and marketing personnel within companies, it was not until the mid-1980s that it came to prominence as an accounting question. At that time several large multinational UK companies, primarily food and drinks companies, such as Guinness and Grand Metropolitan, took the decisions to capitalise brands that they acquired through the acquisition of other companies as assets on their balance sheet. Until the publication of FRS 10 (discussed above) in December 1997 no accounting standard existed on this matter. The required accounting treatment for brands is in line with that discussed above in respect of players' registrations: brands acquired separately or through the acquisition of another company should be capitalised while internally generated brands may not be capitalised as they are described as unique assets and hence have no ascertainable market value.

The question of brands within football is very pertinent. A brand can be thought of as the name by which a product is recognised, known and sold. For a football club the brand is effectively the club or perhaps more accurately the club's name. The value of a brand is dependent on the revenue that it is able to generate for that club. Much of the value of a brand relates to intangible factors such as reputation, image and customer loyalty. As such, many football clubs would consider themselves as having valuable brands, particularly with regard to customer loyalty. While a stout drinker may be persuaded to drink Murphy's rather than Guinness, very few Sunderland fans could be persuaded to watch Newcastle United other than when playing against Sunderland, very few Hibernian fans could be persuaded to buy a Heart of Midlothian replica jersey.

The majority of football club brands are what could be described as local brands, in that their reputation does not extend to any great extent outside their local area. Despite this, the strength of the brand may be exceptional, as is the case for a club such as Newcastle United. The most recent FA Premier League fan survey found that season ticket holders at Newcastle United spend more on merchandising per head than any other club in the UK (SNCCFR, 1997). Table 4.2 sets out information on the highest and lowest spenders.[14]

The club also tops the table in respect of purchases of several items of merchandising. For example, 73 per cent of its season ticket holders bought an adult replica shirt during the season,[15] 62 per cent of its season ticket holders bought adult club clothing during the season while it was the only club where more than half of its season ticket holders (54 per cent) bought merchandised household items during the season (SNCCFR, 1997). Perhaps the most extraordinary indication of the strength of this club's brand is the fact that fewer than one in 20 Newcastle United fans in the sample had resisted the temptation to buy something connected to their own club over the last 12 months (SNCCFR, 1997).

Table 4.2   Average season ticket holder merchandise spend 1996/97

Position	Club	Merchandise spend per head (£)
1	Newcastle United	159
2	Middlesbrough	150
3	Manchester United	126
. . .		
	Average	109
. . .		
19	Nottingham Forest	69
20	Wimbledon	67
21	Southampton	64

Source: SNCCFR, 1997

Other brands, could however be described as international brands, where name recognition, support and consequently merchandising is independent of customers' personal ties with the area. While one may argue over membership of the international brand club, there is little argument that it would include Manchester United and Liverpool, and more probably Rangers and Celtic as a consequence of their historical domination of the Scottish game and knowledge of the wider social and cultural issues surrounding these two clubs.

Each of these clubs has a reputation and public profile that extends past this island. This allows them to generate revenues throughout the world by merchandising all kinds of club products ranging from replica shirts to club whisky and wine. Clubs can also take advantage of technology such as the Internet to bring them closer to their widespread marketplace. Table 4.3 sets out the proportion of revenue generated by a selection of top clubs through brand merchandising.

Table 4.3 demonstrates the significant revenue potential of the top clubs, with in the case of Manchester United almost one third of its revenue being generated by merchandising. The other clubs, although reporting smaller revenues from this source, both in absolute and percentage terms, are well aware of the potential of this source of income and along with most other top division clubs are taking steps to expand their merchandising activities. However, despite the significant revenue potential of these clubs' brands, for accounting purposes FRS 10 requires that they remain off the balance sheet. In each club's case, the brand is clearly internally generated.

Table 4.3 Branded income 1996/97

	Merchandising/ Retail income (£000s)	Merchandising as a percentage of turnover (%)
Arsenal	4479	16.5
Manchester United	28681	32.6
Newcastle United	9028	21.9
Tottenham Hotspur	3564	12.8
Celtic	2771	12.5
Rangers	3117	9.8

Source: Club accounts

As discussed previously with regard to homegrown players, an internally generated intangible asset may only be recognised as an asset if it has a readily ascertainable market value. This requires that the assets belong to a homogeneous population of assets (equivalent in all material respects) and that there is an active market, evidenced by frequent transactions for those assets. The ASB's view is that internally generated brands do not satisfy either of these criteria and hence should not be recognised as assets. The consequences of this stipulated treatment in practice could be peculiar, for instance Celtic and Rangers. Both clubs have a readily identifiable and valuable brand name. Neither club, however, can recognise this brand as an asset. But, in the face of the reality of a football brand, if Celtic were to take over Rangers, it could assign part of the cost of that acquisition to the Rangers brand and include it as an asset on the Celtic balance sheet. A true and fair view?

ACCOUNTING FOR TANGIBLE FIXED ASSETS

Other than the registrations of its players, a club's ground and facilities remain its only other major asset. The nature of football stadiums means that a substantial investment must be made in a very specialised asset, which is used infrequently. Several top clubs have substantially improved the facilities that accompany their stadiums in terms of office space, hotel facilities, restaurants and so on to attempt to improve the usage of their assets. Although there are likely to be more cost-effective ways of building and running restaurants and hotels than by attaching them to large football stadiums, these clubs are trying to use the football club's brand name and profile to market these developments. Notwithstanding alternative uses of stadium for events like rock concerts or for alternative sports such as rugby league or rugby union matches, in terms of its primary purpose a football stadium remains a limited use asset, in use for approximately 3–4 hours once every couple of weeks. Football stadiums are most akin to churches: high investment, high upkeep but in use for a very limited period of time for its primary purpose. (The widening use of stadium and their role in the community will be discussed in detail in Chapter 5.)

Accounting treatment

Accounts of UK companies are prepared under the historical cost convention. This means that assets are shown in the balance sheet at what they cost the company. The Companies Act 1985 modifies the historical cost convention to allow the revaluation of land and buildings under specified conditions. As such, football clubs can include their stadiums in the balance sheet at either cost or valuation, or indeed a mixture of both. Table 4.4 summarises the information included in the financial statements in respect of clubs' grounds and facilities.

Table 4.4 demonstrates the range that exists in the carrying value of properties on football clubs' balance sheets, with figures ranging from over £60 m for Rangers to less than £2 m for Motherwell. Differences can be explained by factors such as the size of the stadium, the date of construction (if recorded at historical cost) and the timing and basis of any revaluations that have taken place. Another factor is the components within the land and buildings asset. At many large clubs the figures do not only include the football stadium. Several clubs own their own training ground and facilities as well as properties such as club superstores. Other more diversified clubs such as Rangers and Chelsea also own properties like hotels and office accommodation.

Revaluations

Table 4.4 shows that 14 clubs have their stadium and other property assets included at revalued amounts in the financial statements. Acceptable bases of valuation are set out by the Royal Institution of Chartered Surveyors in its *Appraisal and Valuation Manual* (RICS, 1995). Much of the relevant guidance is included in the ASB's Exposure Draft FRED 17, *The Measurement of Tangible Fixed Assets* (ASB,

Table 4.4   Freehold properties/land and buildings (1997 accounting year ends)

Club	Balance sheet carrying value (£m)	Cost/valuation basis (date) for stadium	Provision for depreciation
Premier League			
Arsenal	25.2	Cost	No
Aston Villa	18.7	Cost	Yes
Blackburn Rovers	35.8	Valuation (1995)- basis not disclosed- plus cost to date	No
Caspian (Leeds Utd)	12.4	Cost	Yes
Chelsea	51.2	DRC (1997) plus cost	No
Coventry City	9.8	DRC (1988) plus cost to date	No
Derby County	0.5[1]	OMV (1996)	Yes
Everton	14.6	DRC (1996) plus cost to date	No
Leicester City	10.9	DRC (1997)	Yes
Liverpool	23.0	Cost	Yes
Manchester United	54.3	Cost	No
Middlesbrough	14.9	Cost	Yes
Newcastle United	31.5	Valuation (1993)- basis not disclosed- plus cost to date	Yes
Nottingham Forest	10.0	Cost	Yes
Sheffield Wednesday	23.9	DRC (1997)	No
Southampton	3.4[2]	Cost	Yes
Sunderland	0.4	NA[3]	No
Tottenham Hotspur	34.4	DRC (1993) plus cost to date	Yes
West Ham United	26.2	DRC (1997)	No
Wimbledon	NA[4]	NA	NA

1997b).[16] Other than the two clubs which were in the process of selling their stadium and relocating, all clubs adopted the Depreciated Replacement Cost (DRC) basis of valuation.

The ASB recommend the DRC basis for the valuation of specialised properties (1997b, para. 48). DRC is defined as 'the aggregate amount of the value of the land for the existing use or a notional replacement site in the same locality, and the gross replacement cost of the buildings or other site works, from which appropriate deduction may then be made to allow for the age, condition, economic or functional obsoles-

Table 4.4   *Continued*

Club	Balance sheet carrying value (£m)	Cost/valuation basis (date) for stadium	Provision for depreciation
Scottish Premier			
Aberdeen	4.9	Cost[6]	Yes
Celtic	27.5	Cost	No
Dundee United	7.0	Cost	Yes
Dunfermline Athletic	NA[4]	NA	NA
Heart of Midlothian	8.0	DRC (1994) plus cost to date	Yes
Hibernian	NA[5]	NA	NA
Kilmarnock	8.0	DRC (1997)	Yes
Motherwell	1.7	Cost	Yes
Raith Rovers	2.9	Cost	Yes
Rangers	67.5	Valuation (1992) – basis not disclosed – plus cost to date	No

[1] Stadium (Baseball Ground) was valued at Open Market Value prior to the club moving to its new stadium (Pride Park).

[2] Freehold land and buildings only. The company also has £697 220 of assets under development in respect of a new stadium and £5.0m in respect of investment properties. This includes the Marchwood training ground which was valued on a DRC basis.

[3] Stadium (Roker Park) transferred at directors' valuation to *assets awaiting realisation*. Tangible fixed assets includes £14.5m in respect of capital works in progress re. the new Stadium of Light.

[4] Stadium is not owned by the club, but is leased under an operating lease. This is a form of rental agreement under which the majority of risks and rewards of ownership remain with the stadium owner.

[5] Hibernian were take over by Sir Tom Farmer in 1991. At that time the club was split into two arms, with the football club being run as a separate entity from the stadium. The football club pays a lease to use the Easter Road Stadium which is owned by HFC Holdings Ltd.

[6] DRC valuation of stadium also disclosed in the notes.

DRC: Depreciated Replacement Cost.

OMV: Open Market Value.

Source: Club accounts

cence, environmental and other relevant factors; all of these might result in the existing property being worth less to the undertaking in occupation than would a new replacement' (RICS, 1995, PS 4.8.1). Specialised properties are very rarely sold on the open market to a single occupier for the continuation of their existing use, except as part of a sale of the whole company. Examples provided by the RICS include schools, universities, hospitals, oil refineries and power stations.

It would appear, therefore, that the DRC basis is the most appropriate basis upon which to revalue football stadiums, in view of the lack of comparative transactions involving such assets. Nevertheless, it is a rather unsatisfactory basis; it is represented as a valuation of property, but in circumstances where, by definition, no evidence of value can be found. Use of the DRC basis of valuation is also often likely to give a higher valuation than a valuation carried out on an open market basis. It is certainly difficult to believe that the carrying values of the property of most clubs identified in Table 4.4 could be recovered through an open market sale. (Of course, this argument also applies to property included at historical cost.)

Some evidence for this can be provided by considering the accounts of Derby County. The club's former ground, the Baseball Ground, was revalued on an open market basis taking into account the club's move to a new stadium, Pride Park. The valuation was included in the 1997 year end accounts and required a provision for loss on disposal of £2.6m. In other words, the previous carrying value of the stadium, which was included at historical cost, was some £2.6m larger than the open market value.

In that a DRC value will probably be greater than an open market value, the additional guidance provided by the RICS that the valuer, in consultation with the directors, must be satisfied that the potential profitability of the business is adequate to support the value derived on a DRC basis becomes increasingly relevant. If the valuer does not believe the profitability is adequate, then a lower figure should be adopted.

In general this consultation will be in response to economic circumstances common to the industry, rather than the business of the specific company. For all its new found wealth and income sources, in recent years football has become a less profitable business (see also Chapters 1 and 2). Table 4.5 sets out some information on the profitability of the clubs in the English Premier League.

In Scotland the position is even worse, with the clubs in the Premier Division reporting pre-tax losses in total since 1992 (Price Waterhouse, 1997). The lack of profitability demonstrated by the football industry must give rise to grave concern about the appropriateness of the DRC basis with regard to football stadium revaluations. Although the

Table 4.5   Pre-tax profit/(loss): Premier League clubs

	1996/97 (£000)	1995/96 (£000)	1994/95 (£000)	1993/94 (£000)	1992/93 (£000)
Pre-tax profit/(loss)	(9 478)	(62 358)	6 297	12 826	11 504

Source: Deloitte & Touche (1998b, 1997, 1996), Touche Ross (1995, 1994, 1993)

balance sheet is not designed to provide a current valuation of the business or indeed of individual assets, in such an unprofitable business as football it is difficult to see how including assets at figures which are likely to be greatly in excess of any open market value is meeting the objective of providing useful information to users to allow them to make meaningful economic decisions.

Depreciation

SSAP 12, *Accounting for Depreciation* (ASC, 1977a) requires that depreciation should be provided for all fixed assets which have a finite economic life. The objective of the standard is to allocate the cost less any expected residual value over the periods expected to benefit from the use of the asset being depreciated, to reflect the use of the asset each year.

Where an asset has been revalued, the subsequent depreciation charge should be based on the revaluation and the remaining useful life. As such the standard is clear: what it is concerned with is the allocation of costs to appropriate accounting periods. What it is not concerned with are changes in the value of the underlying asset.

Despite the clarity of this standard, many UK companies fail to comply with SSAP 12's requirement to depreciate all fixed assets of finite life. These companies are found in various industries, including breweries, hotels and shops.[17] Many football clubs also fail to comply by not depreciating their stadiums. Their justification is similar to that used by brewers, hotels and shops, with the clubs arguing in their Accounting Policies note that because it is company policy to maintain their properties in such a condition that the aggregate estimated residual value would be at least equal to their book values, then depreciation is not provided because it would be immaterial. Clubs which adopt this policy are set out in Table 4.4.

The growing trend towards non-depreciation of certain assets, particularly property, is considered by the ASB in its exposure draft FRED 17, *Measurement of Tangible Fixed Assets* (1997b). The exposure draft backs up SSAP 12, making it clear that although the life of a property can be extended by regular maintenance, few assets can be regarded as having a limitless life, and hence depreciation should be applied. It is worth noting that in the cases of the 11 clubs which failed to depreciate their stadium, none of the accounts was qualified by the clubs' auditors for failing to comply with SSAP 12. Given the number of companies, including football clubs who are failing to depreciate their assets, it will be interesting to watch the response of both companies and their auditors if FRED 17 is adopted as a standard in its existing form.

Grants for stadium developments

The Taylor Report coerced many clubs to invest heavily in grounds and facilities in the early 1990s. Some clubs have taken the opportunity to move to new stadiums; others have continued to upgrade an existing stadium and to increase the stadium utilisation and hence maximise revenue from the asset. These developments are often accompanied by the receipt of grants from bodies such as the Football Trust or the Sports Council.[18] The Trust has been providing support for football at every level throughout the UK since 1975. Prior to the introduction of the National Lottery the Trust's main income source were the football pools companies. However, the Trust's income declined from a pre-lottery level of £37 m to approximately £9 m per annum as the pools companies found themselves unable to continue contributing to the Trust in the way in which they had done in the past. To secure the future of the Trust and to enable it to continue to grant aid to football at all levels throughout the UK a new funding package has been put together. Under the arrangement, the Football Trust will receive:

- £5 m p.a. from the FA Premier League for each of the next four years plus £5 m p.a. from the English Sports Council for the next three years to help clubs to complete essential safety work to meet the requirements of the Taylor Report.
- The English Sports Council and the Football Association will provide £10 m each over the next four years to enable the Trust to continue its non-Taylor ground development and improvement work at all levels of the game.

The Trust will also continue to benefit from pools derived income as a result of a three per cent reduction in pool betting duty. In addition, in Scotland the Scottish Sports Council and the Football Trust have entered into a partnership which will provide Lottery Sports Fund support for the football safety work of the Football Trust.

The Trust's present priority is to help to provide grant aid for new grounds and redevelopment work at FA Premier League, Football League and Scottish Football League grounds to help clubs to implement the recommendations of the Taylor Report. Grant aid of up to £2 m per club is available for new grounds and stands, seating, cover, safety and improvement work and CCTV.

The accounting treatment for grants is covered in SSAP 4 (ASC, 1974) and in the Companies Act 1985. The basic rule is that grants should be recognised in the profit and loss account so as to match them with the expenditure towards which they are expected to contribute. This applies equally to capital grants (grants towards capital expenditure, e.g. investment in fixed assets) and revenue grants (grants towards operating expenditure, e.g. employee costs). When a company receives a capital grant the standard permits either offsetting the grant against the cost of the related asset and the setting up of a separate capital reserve which is then released or transferred to the profit and loss account over the life of the related asset. Only the latter treatment, however, is permitted under the Companies Acts 1985. But not content with the two treatments permitted under SSAP 4, clubs have adopted an extraordinary variety of accounting treatments to reflect capital grants received. These treatments shall be considered in turn.

Most clubs (Aston Villa, Blackburn Rovers, Derby County, Leicester, Liverpool, Manchester United, Middlesbrough, Newcastle United, Nottingham Forest, Southampton, Sunderland, Tottenham Hotspur, West Ham United, Aberdeen, Dundee United, Heart of Midlothian, Hibernian, Kilmarnock, Raith Rovers and Rangers) have tried to adopt the policy required by the Companies Act 1985 and recommended by SSAP 4. This involves the application of the matching concept, whereby income and the related expenses are matched in the profit and loss account of the period to which they relate. In other words, the grant income is released or credited to the profit and loss account and matched against the depreciation expense for the asset in respect of which the grant was provided.

The logic or indeed acceptability of adopting this accounting policy is not clear in the cases of Blackburn Rovers, Manchester United,

Sunderland, West Ham United and Rangers given that Table 4.4 shows that these clubs do not depreciate their stadium or similar property assets. It is thus difficult to see how the matching process is being carried out as there is no cost going through the profit and loss account in respect of the stadium against which the grant can be matched. The accounting policy notes of Manchester United and West Ham United both state quite clearly that the grants are being matched against the depreciation charged on the fixed asset purchased with the grants. On the basis of the publicly available information, one possible conclusion is that grants received by both these clubs are in respect only of fixed assets which *are* depreciated such as fixtures, fittings, floodlighting installations rather than the property assets. In West Ham's case, in view of the alleged matching in the profit and loss account of grant income against depreciation, it is somewhat surprising to find that there has been no change in the balance of the deferred grant income balance between the 1996 and 1997 year ends. This suggest one of three things: either that the club did not depreciate the related asset(s) in the 1997 accounting year, that it chose to disapply the matching process in the 1997 accounting year, or that as the assets are not depreciated, it does not have anything against which to match the grant income.

In the cases of Blackburn Rovers, Sunderland and Rangers the accounting policy states that the grants are treated as deferred income and recognised in the profit and loss account over the expected useful lives of the assets for which the grant was received. As such therefore no mention of matching against depreciation on the related assets is made. In Blackburn's case, it is clear from the accounting policy that the club has decided to disapply the matching concept in this area and simply release the grant to the profit and loss account over the assumed life of the related asset, even although no depreciation is being charged over that life. This may also be the case for Sunderland and Rangers but it is not specifically stated as such in the accounting policies. An alternative explanation, that offered previously in respect of Manchester United and West Ham, could be equally applicable to these two clubs, i.e. that grants are received in respect of assets that *are* depreciated.

Four clubs (Arsenal, Everton, Celtic and Motherwell) adopt the policy of offsetting the grants received against the cost of the related asset, resulting in the asset being recorded at a lower carrying value in the balance sheet. Because three of these clubs (Arsenal, Everton and Celtic) do not depreciate their property, then, notwithstanding the appropriateness or otherwise of the non-depreciation of property, such a treatment makes sense since it avoids the grant being included as deferred income on the balance sheet in perpetuity. The offset treatment is similar to that adopted by, for example, water companies where grants are received as a contribution towards the cost of infrastructure assets such as reservoirs. Such assets do not have to be depreciated as the companies have an obligation to maintain them indefinitely. In Motherwell's case, depreciation is, however, charged on all their assets. In their accounting policy they note that the treatment adopted fails to comply with the specific requirements of the Companies Act, but justify their treatment on the basis of the 'true and fair' override, a view apparently shared by the club's auditors. However, from an external standpoint such a view does not seem sustainable.

Two further clubs which do not depreciate their property assets (Chelsea and Sheffield Wednesday) bring capital expenditure grants, received in respect of assets which are not depreciated, into account on what they describe as an accruals basis. This means that in the first instance the grant is recorded as a liability in the financial statements. In the case of Chelsea, the accrued amount is then released or transferred to non-distributable capital reserves over the estimated useful life of the asset to which they relate. No information is provided by Sheffield Wednesday as to what happens to the grant after it is has been accrued.

The accounting treatment is not clear in the case of the remaining clubs. While the accounts of Caspian make no reference at all to grants, Coventry City state only that 'Grants received from the Football Trust and capital donations received from external organisations are carried in the balance sheet'. These are shown as part of the company's other reserves, where it has to be assumed that they remain indefinitely.

This section has demonstrated that although in general there have been improvements in the quality and quantity of disclosure of accounting information by football clubs, there is still room for improvement. The diversity of treatment adopted by clubs in respect of grants received causes concern. There would seem to be little justification for this diversity, particularly when an accounting standard exists in this area. This diversity leads to difficulties in interpreting the accounting information and a consequent lack of comparability. Furthermore the lack of clear explanation of the accounting policies adopted by some clubs also causes concern.

FOREIGN EXCHANGE RISK

Many British clubs now find themselves with a markedly international player pool. This can be risky for clubs. Language difficulties, cultural differences and club versus country conflicts are only some of the problems which have become back page news in recent years. Investment in overseas talent, however, also brings with it particular accounting and foreign exchange problems.

The problem facing clubs is that faced by all businesses which invest or do business outside the country of its home currency, namely *foreign exchange exposure*. When purchasing a player from an overseas club, in addition to the normal football and contractual decisions which the club has to take, it also has to decide how to pay for the player. If there is a time lag between the agreement of the fee and the payment of the fee, or if the fee is being paid in instalments, then assuming the fee is fixed in terms of the overseas currency, the buying club is exposed to the risk of sterling depreciating against the overseas currency. In other words, relatively small movements in exchange spot rates (the rate at which currencies can be exchanged on any particular day) could have a significant effect on the overall fee paid. Everton was one club that lost out twice on dollar denominated transfer deals because of adverse exchange rates. Equally, however, if sterling appreciates over the period then the club will be able to acquire the player for less, in terms of pounds sterling.

Example

- London City enters into an agreement on 24 November 1997 to buy player X for £5 m from Oslo FC as soon as Oslo are eliminated from the Champions League, the fee to be paid in Norwegian Krone.

- Oslo reach the knock out stage of the Champions League, being eliminated in the quarter final stage in February 1998. Player X is finally transferred on 24 February 1998.

- On 24 November 1997, the pound/Norwegian Krone spot exchange rate was 11.94 Krone to the pound. As the fee was to be fixed in Norwegian Krone, £5 m was therefore equivalent to 59.7 m Norwegian Krone.

- The fee, however, was to be settled in full on the date of transfer.

- On 24 February 1998, the pound/Norwegian Krone spot exchange rate had risen to 12.36 Krone to the pound.

- As a result the actual amount paid by London in sterling terms to extinguish the liability of 59.7 m N Kr was equal to £4 830 097 (59.7/ 12.36).

- London therefore gained £169 903 (£5 000 000 less £4 830 097) as a result of the appreciation in sterling against the Norwegian Krone.

A solution to the problem is to use risk management techniques. One such technique is the use of forward contracts. Under a forward contract the club agrees to buy a fixed amount of foreign currency at a specified future date. The exchange rate is fixed at the date of the agreement (i.e. the club is *locked into* a particular exchange rate, called the forward rate). The club is therefore not exposed to any fluctuation in the exchange rate over the period between the signing of the agreement and the payment of all or part of the transfer fee. The upside is that the exposure is fixed, the downside of course, is that any favourable exchange rate movements over the period will not benefit the buying club.

Example (continued)

- London City could have decided to reduce its exposure to movements in the sterling/Norwegian Krone exchange rate by buying Krone under a forward contract.

- The three-month rate was 11.8265 Krone to the pound sterling. Had London bought at this rate it would have cost the club £5 047 985 in order to extinguish its liability of 59.7 m N Kr.

- In this case, therefore, the club would have gained by waiting until the amount was due and then buying Norwegian Krone at the spot rate. On another transfer at another time the situation might have been reversed. The advantage of using forward contracts is that they offer certainty, in other words, London would know exactly what player X was going to cost them in terms of pounds sterling at the date the transfer was first agreed.

One club which has used forwards contracts to minimise its exchange rate exposure is Manchester United.[19] The club bought the Spanish peseta forward to help pay for the acquisition of Jordi Cruyff from Barcelona in the summer of 1996. Unfortunately for Manchester United, as in the above example, the peseta depreciated against the pound sterling, meaning that it would have been cheaper to buy the pesetas at spot prices rather than in advance.

FOOTBALL – A CASH BUSINESS?

The importance of cash to any business has long been recognised. While profit provides a measure of an entity's long term performance, it is the ability of an entity to have an adequate flow of cash that ultimately determines its survival. Historically this emphasis on cash has been of great significance to football clubs. Webb and Broadbent (1986), for example, noted that all the user decisions they identified for football clubs, in so far as they had a financial perspective, were more closely related to cash transactions than the concept of profit. (Users of football club financial statements and their information needs are discussed in Chapter 5.) The nature of the football business at that time meant that everything depended on cash flow: inflows arose primarily through gate receipts, outflows were primarily wages, transfer fees and interest charges. This dependence on cash to measure progress and survival is still prevalent at many clubs. For top clubs, however, it could be argued that changes in their financing and operation have reduced the emphasis that must be placed on cash, while of course still recognising its importance in any business.

The most significant problem faced by any cash business is the unpredictability of cash flows. For football clubs, historically the primary cash inflows would come from supporters in the form of gate receipts. As a consequence, anything which affected the attractiveness of the match (such as poor form, competing attractions, midweek matches reducing the level of away supporters, etc) or anything which affected the match actually taking place at all, such as weather conditions, would have a material impact on cash inflows. However, while cash inflows were variable and unpredictable, cash outflows were predictable, certain and unavoidable. Whether the match was played or not, the players require to be paid, albeit that additional costs such as win or stripped bonuses for players could be avoided.

Football's cash inflows

In top clubs today, it is arguable that football is no longer a cash business. This view can be supported by considering the changed nature of income and its resultant cash flows within clubs. The primary income sources in the modern club are likely to be gate receipts, commercial and sponsorship income, television income and merchandising income. The cash flows associated with each of these sources differ and will be considered in turn.

Gate receipts

Gate receipts in the old form of supporters handing over their admission fees at the turnstiles on a weekly basis, were the primary revenue source for clubs. While supporters payments for match attendance continue to be a significant source of income for most clubs,[20] a large proportion of such gate receipts are now in the advanced form of season ticket sales. Table 4.6 sets out the level of season ticket sales for the top clubs in England and Scotland compared to capacity.

As can be seen from Table 4.6, several clubs now have an exceptionally large proportion of season ticket holders. Because the majority of season ticket sales take place in the summer months leading up to the commencement of the new season, far from being reliant on uncertain and variable sources of future income, top clubs are now effectively receiving their income or sales proceeds annually in advance. Hence, there is in fact greater certainty of income for football clubs than for many other businesses. Uncertainty does, of course, continue to exist in that high season ticket sales in one year may not necessarily be repeated in the following year, if for example, the club had a poor season or was relegated. This does present a problem for clubs trying to put together budgets, given that players, whose salaries represent the major costs to clubs, are usually employed on at least three-year contracts. In other words, while costs are fixed at the start of a three (or greater) year period, revenue is variable. This problem of matching, however, arises out of the nature of the business itself, and as such is not specifically related to the issue of the timing of cash payments and receipts.

What Table 4.6 shows is that clubs with high season ticket sales such as Middlesbrough, Newcastle United and Celtic, with occupancy rates around 90 per cent are in the enviable position or receiving practically all of their revenue from gate receipts, a figure likely to exceed £10m, before a ball has been kicked. However, it must be pointed out that several clubs have introduced schemes whereby supporters are allowed to pay for their season ticket in instalments, hence spreading the cash inflows for the club. Nevertheless, other than in the event of default by the supporter, the implication of Table

Table 4.6   Gate receipts and season ticket sales

Club	Gate receipts (y.e. 1997) (£000s)	No. of season tickets sold (1997/98)	Stadium capacity (1997/98)	Percentage season ticket occupancy
Premier League				
Arsenal	10632	NA	38500	NA
Aston Villa	7346	23700	39339	60.2
Blackburn Rovers	5304	14500	31367	46.2
Chelsea	NA	NA	31791[1]	NA
Coventry City	4850	NA	23662	NA
Derby County	4425	18364	30000	61.2
Everton	NA	21500	40200	53.5
Leeds United	6562	18000	40000	45.0
Leicester City	6511	13730	22517	61.0
Liverpool	NA	25000	35000[2]	71.4
Manchester United	30111	40000	56387	70.9
Middlesbrough	NA	28524	30500	93.5
Newcastle United	25505	32124	36610	87.7
Nottingham Forest	6812	12300	30602	40.2
Sheffield Wednesday	6223	12670	39859	31.8
Southampton	NA	9000	15000	60.0
Sunderland	NA	17000	42000	40.5
Tottenham Hotspur	13641	NA	33208	NA
West Ham United	7015	13500	25985	52.0
Wimbledon	NA	4550	26309	17.3
Scottish Premier				
Aberdeen	2189	6000	21634	27.7
Celtic	10626	42500	47500	89.5
Dundee United	NA	NA	12616	NA
Dunfermline Athletic	NA	1479	12300	NA
Heart of Midlothian	2882	8636	18300	47.2
Hibernian	2039	4677	16218	28.8
Kilmarnock	NA	4600	18128	25.4
Motherwell	NA	NA	13742	NA
Raith Rovers	984	958	10721	8.9
Rangers	NA	38000	50500	76.2

[1] Rising to 41000 after ground development.
[2] Rising to 45000 February 1998.
NA: Not available.
Source: Club correspondence, club accounts, Rothmans (1997)

4.6 is that several clubs now have a significant source of certain and predictable income.

Sponsorship and commercial income

The majority of clubs are now involved in substantial sponsorship deals, with companies such as Umbro, Scottish & Newcastle, Carlsberg and JVC. The two year deal between Manchester United and the Japanese electronics firm, Sharp, which runs until the year 2000, is thought to be the largest of its kind in UK club history, with the club receiving between £2m and £3m a year (Kuper, 1998). Although the nature of sponsorship deals will vary from club to club, at least part of such sponsorship income will be received by the club as a lump sum at the beginning of the deal or more commonly annually at the beginning of each season.

Depending on the deal, other amounts may be payable in particular circumstances, for example, if the club wins the league, or gets into Europe or avoids relegation. In cash flow terms, therefore, it is likely that at least part of the amount will be paid in advance and hence will be a predictable and certain source of cash. For example, the Manchester United plc accounts for the year ended 31 July 1997 include a figure of £22.3m in respect of deferred revenue income which consists of 'season ticket, sponsorship and other elements of income which have been received prior to the year end in respect of the following football season ...'.

Television income

Television income is an important and growing source of income for top clubs. Total payments to clubs by the FA Premier League for the season 1996/97 (including parachute payments to relegated clubs) totalled £88.8m, compared to £41.3m for the previous season. The arrangements for the distribution of this money are set out in Chapter 1. Broadly 50 per cent of the money is distributed evenly among the Premier League clubs, 25 per cent is a merit payment dependent upon final league position and the final 25 per cent is a facility fee reflecting the number of times the club is featured on television.

Payments to clubs are made at not less than quarterly intervals along with a clear statement showing how each fee payment has been calculated. Therefore although the full amount clubs will receive from television is not predictable or certain, that half of the fees which is split among clubs on a pro rata basis is certain and predictable in cash flow terms.

The situation in Scotland is different, both in terms of the volume of television income and in terms of its cash flow implications for clubs. For season 1996/97 the television deal totalled only £3.3 m, with payments being divided between the home club and away clubs on a 75 per cent/25 per cent basis for live matches, while payments for highlights are split evenly between the clubs. A separate deal worth £1.3 m exists for coverage of the Scottish Cup, with payments to clubs being dependent on their progress (see the section on *Television – football's economic driver* in Chapter 1). Television monies receivable by Scottish clubs are thus far less predictable or certain than is the case for English clubs.

Merchandising

Various factors affect the merchandising cash flow. In keeping with other retail business, there is a Christmas effect, with a large part of the sales taking place at or around Christmas. There is also a seasonal effect. Sales of merchandising will normally be lower during the short (and shortening close season). The seasonal effect also exists in a more conventional sense in that sales of products like replica kits in any one season will, of course, depend to a great extent on whether or not clubs introduced a new kit during the season.

Although most top clubs now sell merchandise by catalogue and through the Internet, unsurprisingly a large part of merchandising sales still take place on home match days. Match day sales can be split into pre- and post-match sales, with one major football club financial director noting the existence of a significant identifiable relationship between match results and the level of post-match sales. While this relationship seems entirely plausible, it is not possible to provide any empirical evidence to substantiate it.

The most recent FA Premier League fan survey provided some evidence that current playing success did breed stronger merchandising sales over a season with 90 per cent of fans of clubs who finished in the top five Premier League positions buying some merchandise in 1996/97, compared to 86 per cent for the middle ten clubs and 84 per cent for the bottom five clubs (SNCCFR, 1997). However, this result also reflects the fact that big clubs which generate greater merchandising revenue tend to finish higher up the league.[21]

Paradoxically, therefore, despite merchandising being very much a key component in the new football club, for some top clubs it may be the only material source of income that is cash based, and therefore one might assume unpredictable. However, football clubs differ from many other retailers in that as discussed earlier in this chapter there is often exceptional brand loyalty (see for example Table 4.2). The most recent FA Premier League fan survey indicated that only one in eight fans in the total sample had bought absolutely no items of merchandise in the last 12 months (SNCCFR, 1997). Interestingly, the survey also found that there was an inverse relationship between supporter income and merchandising spend, with the percentage of non-spenders on merchandising increasing as supporter income increased. Taken together, the picture emerges of a very inelastic demand for merchandising products. This is good news for the clubs as it means that merchandising income has a greater degree of certainty attached to it than might otherwise be expected in a retail environment.

Conclusion

For the majority of top clubs, football is no longer a cash business. Premier League and First Division clubs in England, along with the top few clubs in Scotland such as Celtic, Heart of Midlothian and Rangers are operating in a very different business environment to that faced by clubs in earlier years, with huge increases both in the level of income and in its certainty. Outside the elite, however, nothing much has changed. These clubs, including the majority of Scottish top division clubs, remain very dependent on smaller and much less certain income sources. For these clubs, for example, the reliance on gate receipts rather than season tickets means that football still remains a cash business. The Scottish clubs will be hoping that the new break away structure will be the catalyst that will bring with it both greater income, and importantly, greater certainty of income.

DISCLOSURE: ROLE OF THE OPERATING AND
FINANCIAL REVIEW

Many companies in their annual reports disclose more information than is presented in financial statements. Whether due to social attitudes or pressures, companies may voluntarily disclose additional information intended to confirm, for example, its sense of social responsibility. Legal or regulatory provisions in some instances are eventually changed by Government or regulatory bodies to catch up with such social values, and disclosures become mandatory.

The ASB introduced the concept of an Operating and Financial Review (OFR) to UK companies in 1993. Intended to have persuasive rather than mandatory force, it is not an Accounting Standard. Rather it was designed as a formulation and development of best practice. In the interests of good financial reporting its use was commended both by the Hundred Group of Financial Directors and the London Stock Exchange. The rationale behind the OFR is that in view of the greater complexity of businesses, there was believed to be a growing need for objective discussion that analyses and explains the main feature underlying the results and financial position of a company.

Although aimed at large listed companies, the ASB does suggest that 'other listed companies, especially smaller ones or those operating in specialised or highly competitive industries, are urged to follow the spirit of the Statement and use their best endeavours to adapt the detailed guidance to their own circumstances' (ASB, 1993). It is interesting to consider whether football clubs could make more use of something like the OFR as a means of providing information themselves which is either not included in the financial statements or providing additional information on items that are included.

Very few football clubs presently include a stand alone OFR within their annual report. This is not surprising, because first, the OFR is not a standard, and secondly, it is only put forward as best practice for larger plcs, a category which does not include the majority of football clubs. A further factor is that there is no requirement that the type of information set out by the ASB is to be included in a stand alone document. Many companies prefer to incorporate some of the matters dealt with in the ASB statement within the structure of sections such as the Chief Executive or Chairman's Report. This approach has been adopted by several listed clubs. The 1997 annual reports also provide examples of Financial Reviews and Business Reviews as well as Football Reviews and Manager's Reviews. In many cases, these reports have been used to disclose some OFR-type information. Although Football Reviews may be seen as being akin to an Operating Review, in most cases, little attempt has been made to relate these activities to the results (financial) of the business as suggested by the ASB. Often, it takes the form of being a review of the football season.

Because of the flexibility of the OFR there are many issues which football clubs could legitimately address in such a document. The idea behind the OFR is that it should ensure that readers can fully understand the nature of the group and to help them to understand its future business potential. There are specifically two areas in which more informative disclosure by football clubs might meet this objective: first, with regard to player valuation information, and secondly, with regard to (revenue) investment in training and development.

Player valuation

As discussed already in this chapter, notwithstanding improvements as a result of FRS 10, it may be argued that the financial statements of football clubs provide insufficient information on a club's principal resource, namely its players, to allow an accounts user fully to understand the nature and potential of the company. In particular more information could be provided on the value of the club's players. Aston Villa, Chelsea, Coventry City, West Ham United, Celtic and Hibernian disclose an estimated market valuation for their players in their 1997 financial statements, usually either a directors' valuation or an insurance valuation. However, improvements in player valuation methodology as discussed earlier in the chapter (see also the section on *Monitoring* in Chapter 2) provide a tremendous opportunity for clubs to provide relevant information on the club's principal resource. Furthermore, the use of a player valuation model, as opposed to reliance on directors' valuations, removes the risk of bias, whether intentional or otherwise in the figures disclosed (Morrow, 1996a). The adoption of a particular valuation methodology which gained general acceptance would also allow for greater comparability amongst companies.

Other information which could usefully be provided on the club's main asset would be details of the asset life; for example, the average duration of players' contracts and the unexpired period of contracts at the club's year end. Leeds United, Manchester United and Newcastle United provide in their 1997 accounts limited information of this nature by commenting that they have taken steps to secure players on longer term contracts to protect their investment post-*Bosman*. The most detailed information is provided by Aston Villa and Tottenham Hotspur which quantify the time period to expiry of players' contacts as follows:

> ... the large majority of our first team squad have a further three seasons after this one to run on their contracts, giving us some protection against the implications of the Bosman ruling.
>
> (Tottenham Hotspur plc, Chairman's Statement,
> 1997 Annual Report)

... the strategy of the Board [is] to protect the investment by the Club in its playing squad by securing young players on long term contracts... by the year end, the Club had a first team squad with an average age of less than 25, over half of whom are secured on contracts extending beyond the year 2000.

(Aston Villa plc, Chairman's Statement, 1997 Annual Report)

Training and development

A second area where football clubs could helpfully improve their level of disclosure is information on Investment for the Future. The ASB notes that users of annual reports are interested in the extent to which the directors have sought to maintain and enhance future income or profits. One important aspect of investment for the future is capital expenditure on items such as new training facilities. Several clubs already disclose information on investment of this nature in the narrative part of their annual report, although no club quantifies it. Expenditure in other areas can also be regarded, to a greater or lesser extent, as a form of investing in the future.

Of particular relevance to football clubs is revenue investment in training and development. Such investment is, again, of the nature of an intangible fixed asset. However, it would not be recognised in the financial statements because it does not meet the general recognition criteria for recognition as an asset set out in the Statement of Principles, or the more specific criteria set out in FRS 10 or indeed the criteria set out in Statement of Standard Accounting Practice (SSAP) 13, *Accounting for Research and Development* (ASC, 1977b).

Nevertheless the fundamental importance of training and development of young players is well recognised within the football industry at all levels, by clubs, associations and players' representatives. For example, in Scotland clubs in the Premier Division are expected to replace their reserve teams with youth teams from season 1998/99. This move has been taken to reflect the importance of youth development and to increase clubs' investment in that area. Obliging clubs to disclose information on expenditure on training and development would highlight best practice within the industry and would identify those clubs which were actually looking to the future in action as well as words (see also the section on *Training and development* in Chapter 2).

Many clubs do discuss aspects of their youth development work, most commonly in the Chairman's Report. In addition to disclosure on capital investment in facilities, several clubs refer to issues such as the creation of youth academies, the importance of youth development post-*Bosman* and the performance of youth teams. The information tends to be very general in nature with little specific or quantitative disclosure which would allow an accounts users to assess the effectiveness of such training and development expenditure. Clubs such as Everton and Sunderland have identified players who have progressed through the ranks into the first team or had achieved international recognition.

The only disclosure which directly related to financial information was found in the Financial Review of Manchester United, where the club's relatively low level of transfer expenditure since its 1991 flotation (£5.4 m net) was identified as reflecting the club's key policy of investing in its own young players. Much of the training and development expenditure is of course long term, and is expenditure which by its nature provides uncertain and subjective results. Nevertheless, clubs should be able to provide some meaningful quantitative information; for example, the number of apprentices, youth players and schoolboy trainees at the club, the percentage who progress through the ranks to professional contracts, the number of coaches employed, expenditure on coaching staff and changes in the coaching structure, etc. Information of this nature would provide a much fuller picture of the organisation's position and of its future potential.

CONCLUSION

Accounting information currently presented by football clubs is now of a higher quality and a greater quantity than hitherto. However, in view of the peculiarities of football as a business, improvements are still possible, both in terms of the standardisation of accounting treatments and in terms of disclosure. Clubs also need to recognise that groups other than shareholders have a legitimate interest in their financial affairs and to structure their reporting accordingly. Issues arising out of conflicts between different stakeholder groups will be returned to in Chapter 5.

5 Accountability within the Football Industry

INTRODUCTION

Accountability has come into fashion in recent years, not just in terms of business behaviour but in wider areas such as politics. While the word itself may only have recently come into popular usage, the notion of accountability has a somewhat longer history. Accountability can be defined as the duty to provide an account (by no means necessarily a financial account) or reckoning of those actions for which one is held responsible (Gray, Owen and Adams, 1996). The requirement to report to shareholders (financial accounting) is one of the very few instances of explicit accountability being established within the law itself, and is thus a rare example of congruence between an organisation's defined responsibility and its discharged responsibility.

The 1990s has seen what can be described as the incorporation of football. This process is most clearly in evidence at clubs which have chosen to become quoted public limited companies, a process which has led to further dilemmas or conflicts of accountability. These dilemmas or conflicts arise because many groups in society beyond the club's shareholders, perceive football clubs as having a moral or natural responsibility to them, in other words of owing them a duty of accountability. These groups may include the community and, in particular the club's supporters.

Linked to accountability is the issue of corporate governance. Corporate governance can be described as the system by which companies are directed and controlled. Corporate governance in the UK has been reformed in recent years as a result of the Cadbury Report (The Committee on the Financial Aspects of Corporate Governance, 1992). The Committee was set up in 1991 by the Financial Reporting Council, the London Stock Exchange and the accountancy profession to consider the need for corporate governance reform in the light of concerns about the standard of financial reporting and accountability following a series of high profile corporate failures and collapses in the late 1980s – BCCI, Polly Peck and Maxwell Communication Corporation. The committee's recommendations were presented as a Code of Best Practice, to be monitored by the London Stock Exchange. The Exchange requires companies as a continuing obligation of listing, to state whether they are complying with the Code and to give reasons for non-compliance (see the section on *The primary market* in Chapter 3). The Code embodies underlying principles of openness, integrity and accountability. It is wide ranging, including improvements in financial reporting such as:

- effective use of the operating and financial review;
- clearer information about directors' remuneration;
- reassurance that the business is a going concern;
- a statement of the responsibilities of the auditors.

The Cadbury Code attempts to ensure high standards of governance, by placing the responsibility on maintaining good practice on the management of the firm, their financial advisers and auditors and the shareholders alike, with the emphasis being on accountability rather than regulation.

FINANCIAL ACCOUNTABILITY

Financial accountability is performed through the annual financial statements. In Chapter 4 the objective of financial statements was described as being the provision of information about the financial position, performance and adaptability of an enterprise that is useful to a wide range of users for assessing the stewardship of management and for making economic decisions (ASB, 1995). Although this objective refers to a wide range of users, it is the information needs of investors or shareholders that remain the primary focus of financial statements in the UK. Nevertheless, the ASB identified employees, lenders, suppliers and other trade creditors, customers, governments and their agencies and the public as other groups who may use financial statements to satisfy some of their different needs for information.

The objectives of financial statements and the identification of user groups and needs has been the subject of regular debate in accounting, both in academic papers and in professional reports such as *The Corporate Report* (ASSC, 1975) and *Making Corporate Reports Valuable* (ICAS, 1988). Webb and Broadbent (1986) attempted to relate this debate to football clubs, by modifying a table setting out the objectives of accounting information and the decisions to be made by users of that information (Carsberg, Hope and Scapens, 1974) for those having dealings with football clubs. In their draft Statement of Principles the ASB have revisited the issue of users groups and their information needs (ASB, 1995).[1] In the following section the ASB's work has been used as a basis for updating Webb and Broadbent's work to provide a framework within which the nature of the modern football club can be considered (Table 5.1). The differences in capital structure found in today's football clubs (see also Chapter 3) is reflected in the framework by classifying football clubs into two groups: listed clubs and traditional clubs. It should be noted that the word traditional relates only to the capital structure of a club, and in particular its relationship with the capital market place. Notwithstanding their capital structure, several listed clubs, of course, have long histories and traditions.

Table 5.1 is for the most part self-explanatory. However, the information needs of three user groups are considered in more detail in the following section. Wider issues of accountability will be considered later in the chapter, in particular the extent to which there is an equivalence between the user group of customers and supporters.

Investors

Webb and Broadbent (1986) contended that the ownership structure prevalent in football clubs – highly centralised control and restrictions on the transferability of shares and the payment of dividends – resulted in the traditional 'buy, sell or hold' decision being inappropriate to football club shareholders. Accordingly they suggested that information be provided instead about the financial support required for football ambition. As discussed in Chapter 3, ownership structures of this nature remain common in football today. Therefore, the provision of information of this nature in these clubs continues to be appropriate.

Other clubs have, however, significantly altered their ownership structure. In theory, therefore, one would expect that the information provision required by the investors in the listed clubs would be similar to that identified by the ASB. But in practice, differences continue to exist between the nature of investors in football clubs and other companies which influences the type of information appropriate. Broadly, these relate to the ownership framework and the level of trading (see Chapter 3). In many listed clubs, although ownership has been diversified, control has remained centralised. To date, therefore, despite much media comment about the City taking over football, very few clubs (Manchester United, Leeds Sporting and Tottenham Hotspur)

Table 5.1 Users and their information needs

	Companies	The traditional club	The listed club
Information provided to:			
Investors (external/ professional)	To assess the ability of the enterprise to pay dividends To determine whether to buy, sell or hold securities		To assess the ability of the enterprise to pay dividends To determine whether to buy, sell or hold securities
Investors (external/ supporters)		To inform them about financial support for football ambition so that investors may exercise any possible influence upon management	To inform them about financial support for football ambition so that investors may exercise any possible influence upon management
Employees	To assess the ability of the enterprise to provide remuneration, employment opportunities and retirement benefits	To assess the ability of the enterprise to provide remuneration and employment opportunities	To assess the ability of the enterprise to provide remuneration and employment opportunities
Lenders	To determine whether their loans will be repaid, and interest attached to them paid when due	To determine whether their loans will be repaid, and interest attached to them paid when due	To determine whether their loans will be repaid, and interest attached to them paid when due

Suppliers and other creditors	To enable them to decide whether to sell to the enterprise and to assess the likelihood of amounts owing to them being paid when due	To enable them to decide whether to sell to the enterprise and to assess the likelihood of amounts owing to them being paid when due	To enable them to decide whether to sell to the enterprise and to assess the likelihood of amounts owing to them being paid when due
Customers	To assess the extent of continuing involvement with the company	To assess the extent of continuing involvement with the company	To assess the extent of continuing involvement with the company (the new supporter)
Government and its agencies	To assist in the allocation of resources To assess taxation	To assess taxation	(To assist in the allocation of resources) To assess taxation
Regulatory bodies (football authorities)	NA	To guide in the regulation of the industry	To guide in the regulation of the industry
The public/ community	Various	Various	Various
Supporters	NA	To judge whether the club requires financial or other support	To judge whether the club requires financial or other support (the traditional supporter)

Source: Adapted from ASB (1995) and Webb and Broadbent (1986)

have substantial numbers of institutional or professional investors. Also, the level of secondary market trading reported in the shares of the majority of listed clubs is very low. In part at least, this reflects unwillingness of supporter/investors to trade their shares, which have been acquired for non-pecuniary and emotional motives. These factors continue to call into question the appropriateness of information which will assist in 'buy, sell or hold' type decisions for many football club investors.

Employees

The labour market in professional football is unique (as discussed in Chapter 2). Although professional footballers possess greater opportunity to negotiate terms of employment than most other employees, post-*Bosman* they continue to face unusual restrictions in their terms and conditions of employment. It is important, therefore, that they have sufficient information to decide whether to sign for a particular club and on what terms. For most players, unsurprisingly in the light of the brevity of their careers, the central factor is the contractual terms offered to them by clubs. While accounting information may be useful to them in terms of considering the profitability and cash position of their clubs, financial information which they can more readily interpret in terms of their contractual negotiations is likely to be of greater interest to players. In particular, recent work by economists such as Dr Bill Gerrard of Leeds University is likely to be of most relevance to them. As was discussed in Chapter 2 (see the section on *Monitoring*), Dr Gerrard has developed a model which provides an estimate of the value of players on the basis of variables such as player characteristics, time effects, selling-club characteristics and buying-club characteristics (Dobson and Gerrard, 1997).[2] To date, this model has been used as a basis for reports to several merchant banks on the value of players in quoted football clubs.

Another factor that distinguishes football players from other employees is that despite the short length of a player's career, most clubs do not provide company pension schemes for players. The majority of players in England are members of pension schemes such as the Professional Footballers' Association/Football League Limited Players Retirement Income Scheme (a defined contribution scheme) or the Football League Limited Pension and Life Assurance Scheme (a defined benefit scheme). Contributions made by clubs to these schemes are expensed in the profit and loss account as they become payable. In

Scotland several clubs operate defined contribution schemes for certain members of staff. In addition, a pension scheme was set up in 1997 by the Scottish Professional Footballers' Association, which operates under the auspices of the General, Municipal and Boilerworkers' Union, for players whose clubs do not operate company schemes.

Supporters and the community

One of the interesting differences between football clubs and other companies is the perceived relationship between a club and its supporters and local community. Although clubs are all limited companies and some are now listed companies, the question of accountability to groups such as supporters and the community remains a real issue.

Hibernian has attempted to embrace the idea of accountability to its supporters by publishing a 'Supporter Report' for season 1996/97. A 'supporter report' is recognition by management of the supporters' rights to information about the organisation in which their support, both financial and emotional, is invested. The purpose of the Hibernian report is described as being to provide key financial information on the results for the previous season in what is described as a 'straight forward manner'. The report also highlights the club's vision and seven goals, which include keeping in close touch with supporters and being responsive to their views. The document includes a Reconciliation of Profits and Cash, as well as two visual charts based on football pitches, which set out the generation and usage of cash and the components of the operating results. Other information provided in visual form includes a split of turnover by component, a comparison of the number of players between the current and previous years, information on the trends in season ticket sales, the value of player transfers and a balance sheet presented in bar chart form.

The document is similar is style to employee reports distributed by some companies to their staff. Employee reports are perceived to have certain benefits for management, employees and the organisation as a whole, some of which are also likely to be applicable to supporter reports. For management the report can be used to try to demonstrate their commitment to accountability, beyond merely financial accountability to shareholders. They can also use the report to try to build a favourable image among the supporters. For supporters it may be useful as a way of understanding the conflicts that exist in clubs between football and financial objectives and demands, and the higher level corporate strategic and operational issues which may affect them as supporters. A benefit of such reports may be to improve the climate of management-supporter relationships.

Unfortunately, at Hibernian, such benefits have not been forthcoming, with the club's serious on-field problems and what its supporters see as serious off-field problems, resulting in 'customer relations' between the support and the board being at the lowest level since 1990 when the club was the subject of an abortive takeover by the then chairman of city rivals Heart of Midlothian, Wallace Mercer. The situation at Hibernian is complicated by various factors: a prolonged period of lack of success on the field of play, what is seen by the supporters as an absentee owner who has no interest on football (a fact not disputed by Sir Tom Farmer) and what is seen by the supporters as the appointment of executive board members who have no footballing background or emotional investment in football.[3] This demonstrates that accountability needs to be about actions not just words. If one-off reporting initiatives, such as the Supporter Report are not backed up by ongoing accountability, then their benefit is very questionable.

Other problems can also arise out of this type of report. Experience of employee reports provides useful evidence in this regard. Concerns are often expressed that reports of this nature are too simplified and do not provide a full picture of company policy. Employee reports have been criticised for using patronising wording. They are perceived to be cluttered with pie charts, coloured building blocks, piles of coins and cartoon presentations (Mathews and Perera, 1996). These criticisms seem equally applicable to the Hibernian report from its stated purpose to present key information in 'a straight forward manner' through to the use of football pitches, football pie charts and other similar graphics. Nevertheless, the provision of such a report is a step forward in recognition of the legitimate information requirements of the supporter community, a point taken up later in the chapter.

STAKEHOLDER CONFLICTS

Club versus company

As for the suggestion from City analysts that [Manchester] United should give its extra money [a cash surplus of £39m reported in its 1997 accounts] back to shareholders, Mitten's response highlights the shareholder-supporter divide that runs through all stock market-quoted clubs.

He says: 'These profits have come out of the fans' pockets, in the form of gate receipts, merchandising and television revenue, yet they end up going to some anonymous, faceless investor in the City? That's not right.'

('City eyes United's cash hoard', The Financial Times,
21 November 1997)

This response came from Andy Mitten, editor of *United We Stand*, a Manchester United supporters' fanzine. It illustrates perfectly the conflict between supporters and those who have chosen to invest in football clubs. The battleground of the conflict is goal prioritisation and the objectives of a football club. In the eyes of most football club supporters the objectives of their club are expressed exclusively in football terms. Usually this will mean success (albeit relative success depending on whether we are talking about a Manchester United supporter or a Swansea City supporter), but it may also encompass more esoteric objectives such as 'entertainment', 'stylish football', 'attacking football', or 'passion'. The difficulty arises where, although supporters may still see themselves as supporting their club, in many cases professional investors (basically someone investing for a financial return) have bought into the same organisation, but see it is a commercial company. In the eyes of most investors the objectives of the company will be expressed primarily in financial terms such as 'the maximisation of shareholder wealth . . .'.[4]

The listing of football clubs exposes clubs to a form and intensity of scrutiny that many clubs and their directors are not used to. The City wants to know foremost that the money is in efficient hands. Under the rules of the Stock Exchange, directors are required to run the club on a financially prudent basis. Conflict arises for the club because while it must satisfy its City audience, it must also seek to satisfy its supporter audience.

The extent of such conflict will be affected by the ownership framework found in clubs. In clubs such as Manchester United, Leeds United (Leeds Sporting) and Tottenham Hotspur the potential for conflict is greater owing to the high level of institutional investment in the shares of that club. At most other listed clubs management still holds a controlling shareholding. Furthermore, evidence suggests that at clubs such as Aston Villa and Celtic there is a clear overlap between supporters and shareholders. In theory this overlap would reduce the chance of conflict. More importantly, however, the existence of a dominant share-holder ensures that fans and/or shareholders still have an identifiable figure to rally with or against.

While supporters have become used to the behaviour of chairmen-owners (however irrational it may have been), such individuals at least were seen as internal to the club and were also identifiable. In times of conflict, supporters had a target or outlet for their frustration or disap-pointments. Most clubs have witnessed shows of supporter displeasure and dissatisfaction with the directors, ranging from regular small scale murmurings to all out protest movements of the type seen in recent years at Brighton, Celtic and, most recently, Newcastle United. By contrast, City investors are perceived as nameless, faceless individuals, remote from the club, thus making it more difficult to rally against them. For example, at its 1997 accounting year end 124 institutional shareholders owned almost 60 per cent of the ordinary shares in Man-chester United, of whom only two had holdings in excess of three per cent. In theory, at clubs like Manchester United, in the absence of any identifiable owner, any outpouring of frustration or displeasure, would require to be directed at the ownership framework itself, or more accurately the system which allowed this framework to develop. In fact, the BSkyB bid for Manchester United has shown that in practice sup-porters' displeasure about the bid has to a large extent been directed at the club's directors, and in particular its Chairman Martin Edwards, somewhat ignoring the fact that prior to the bid the majority of shares in Manchester United were already held by groups 'external' to the club.

The ownership framework also plays a part in determining the inter-est of institutions in investing in the club, contributing to a chicken and egg situation. A fund manager interviewed in connection with this book identified his company's investment strategy as including avoidance of clubs controlled by a dominant owner. Interestingly, one concern iden-tified about such individuals was that they could use their dominant position to 'take off too much cream from the top', a concern more than a little similar to that which many supporters would probably express about institutional investors.

From fan to customer?

The conflict between supporters and shareholders in contemporary football clubs has attracted government attention. In the summer of 1997 the Sports Minister Tony Banks launched the Football Task Force under the chairmanship of the former Conservative minister, David Mellor. It was designed to represent the views of the ordinary fan with the aim of taking football back to the people.

One issue the Task force is to address is an examination of the conflict between the wishes of fans and the demands of shareholders. In a question and answer interview with stockbroker Nick Batram of Greig Middleton on the role of the Stock Exchange within football (*Financial Times*, 1 August 1997), Mr Banks asked the following question: 'When a club is floated on the stock market, where does its first duty lie – to its shareholders or supporters?'. Predictably, the answer was: 'Jointly to both'. However, according to Mr Batram, the accountability owed to supporters was owed to them as *customers* of that business, a view shared by a fund manager interviewed in connection with this book.

The traditional notion of supporters has been to view them as the club's community. The best analogy is with that of a church. A church is more than a physical building. It is a community of people who come together to worship, i.e. the worshippers become the church. Traditionally the relationship between a football stadium, the team and the supporters has been something similar. Together they become the football club. To describe a fan as a customer, therefore, becomes crucial to the debate on accountability because it envisages a quite different relationship between club and supporter.

The change in emphasis is consistent with the changing nature of football clubs, i.e. at the same time that clubs have moved towards behaviour consistent with profit maximising businesses, supporters have become customers. This view of football clubs reduces the notion of sport to free market economics: people will pay more for better services. A supporter as a customer has a choice of whether or not to buy a season ticket at the price set by the club, he or she has a choice of whether or not to buy a replica shirt at a price set by the club in consultation with the manufacturers. Under the logic of the free market the supporter in many parts of the country even has the choice of which club to 'support'. The customer gets what he or she pays for. Under such an economic model the rights of supporters are restricted to economic rights of non-purchase. This view of football is consistent with that of the fund manager interviewed who, while recognising the importance of supporters to a club, did so in the context of the importance of maintaining the value of the brand.

It may be thought that the rights of non-purchase provide little power to the supporter. For most top clubs, notwithstanding rising season and match day ticket prices, large increases in television revenues means that despite demonstrating growth in absolute terms, in future gate receipts will constitute a decreasing portion of turnover. However, there are strong arguments which suggest that the relationship between supporters and clubs cannot be adequately captured in purely economic terms. Partly this relates to the peculiarities in economic terms of the nature of the product (see the section on *Football's peculiar economics* in Chapter 1), partly to wider social and political issues.

In economic terms, the customer concept is incomplete because it fails to consider the role played by the supporters in creating the product that they are asked to buy. Unlike other goods and services, football club supporters do not just buy a product which the club present to the fans. As King (1997, p. 236) observed, 'paradoxically, at the football match, the fans are partially asked to purchase what they themselves actively and imaginatively created: the spectacle of support'. Part of the attractiveness of football on television is the atmosphere created by the supporters. Without supporters football on television would be a significantly less attractive product both as a television spectacle and consequently as a source of revenue to clubs.

The economic model also fails to capture the social and political dimension of football. In particular it fails to consider the idea of a supporter's identity with a club. Once again religion provides a useful analogy. In the same way as people may identify themselves as Catholic or Jewish or Buddhist, football supporters identify themselves with a football club. Similarly, while converting from one faith to another is not unheard of it is not a particularly common occurrence. Likewise with football clubs. While there may be a substitution choice in economic terms between club x and club y, for most supporters in social and political terms this is not a real choice. This analogy captures something of the identity of the football fan in a way that spurious comparisons between football and other service providers such as cinemas or supermarkets do not. People may prefer to visit UCI cinemas, but rarely will they go *only* to UCI cinemas and rarely will they have any sense of identity or belonging to UCI. In contrast the sense of attachment between the supporter and his or her club is strong.

Nevertheless, there is evidence to suggest that the relationship between supporters and clubs is changing and that the new fan will not be as loyal as the existing supporters. The most recent FA Premier League Fan Survey found that 40 per cent of all 'new fans' have already supported a club elsewhere, and that furthermore, more younger new fans than 'middle age range' new fans have already supported another club (SNCCFR, 1997).[5] It is ironic that one of the factors which the City likes most about football, its brand loyalty or captive market, may be being diminished in other ways by the incorporation of football, most obviously by the increasing influence of one of the major money sources, television. While televised football has a positive influence in that it ensures that people, particularly young supporters, who are prevented due to cost and capacity constraints from attending live matches, are able to maintain or develop an interest in football, its negative influence is the increased exposure of impressionable supporters to the successful clubs such as Manchester United, at the expense of other clubs, particularly home town clubs.

Admission prices at football have risen sharply in recent years. Average ticket prices in the Premier League rose from £13.25 in season 1996/97 to £15.45 in season 1997/98, an increase of 16.6 per cent, while in the Scottish Premier Division prices rose from £10.56 to £11.78, an increase of 11.5 per cent. The economic argument suggests that you must pay for quality. However, acknowledgement of the importance of wider social and political influences in understanding what makes someone 'a supporter' suggests that allowing the market to dictate prices carries with it risks.

The principal risk for clubs lies in alienating its traditional supporter community, either because they are unwilling to pay increased season or match ticket fees, or because they are unable to. As mentioned previously, there is evidence to suggest that the new breed of supporters may not be as loyal as the old breed. For example, while the most recent FA Premier League Fan Survey found that 'new fans' tend to be drawn disproportionately from higher earning brackets (more than £30 000 p.a.), it was also noted that generally speaking lower earners feel stronger about their club than higher earners and that new and returned fans are less committed to their club than long-standing fans (SNCCFR, 1997, p. 40).[6] While changes in the elasticity of demand of supporters for football may not seem much of an issue to clubs in the current boom, in the longer term this erosion of captive loyalty may become of much greater significance.

Prior to the 1997 election, the Labour Party (1996) issued *A New Framework for Football: Labour's Charter for Football*. This document, which provides the framework for the Football Task Force, discussed the risks of clubs alienating traditional supporters through pricing policies in the following terms (p. 5):

There is a danger that the traditional core of local support for many clubs is being priced out of the game. We applaud links between local authorities and clubs along the lines of leisure card schemes. Labour would like to see a more detailed investigation of ways in which pricing policies at football clubs can be geared to reflect the needs of all, on an equitable basis.

Notwithstanding the current boom, it may well be prudent for clubs to consider the possible implications of any erosion of their customer base, sooner rather than later.

Identity is also an explanatory factor in matters such as the purchase of replica strips or other merchandising. To many businessmen or city investors these issues can again be reduced to a market transaction: the supporter has the option of whether or not to purchase a replica strip costing £50. But to a supporter it may be a badge of identity. This is particularly the case at a club such as Newcastle United. Its season ticket holders are the highest spenders on merchandising within the Premier League, spending £159 per head in season 1996/97 compared to a league average of £109 (SNCCFR, 1997). This statistic makes the alleged comments of the club's directors Douglas Hall and Freddy Shepherd about the willingness of fans to spend £50 on shirts which cost only a few pounds to manufacture all the more crass. The issue of identity leaves its economic mark further when pressure is brought on parents to purchase such replica strips.

The comments on the pricing of replica kit sales in addition to other disparaging remarks allegedly made by directors of Newcastle United on issues as diverse as women in the North East of England and the club's players highlighted the issues of accountability and governance in football clubs. One interesting aspect arising out of the directors' eventual decision to resign was that even at that time of crisis there was evidence of conflict between the concept of club and company, in the form of who should take the credit for the resignations. The broadsheets provided various interpretations of the affair. Alex Brummer in *The Guardian* took the view that credit lay clearly with the non-executive directors appointed to ensure appropriate governance in accordance with the Cadbury Code (see the Introduction to this chapter):

It has been a brutal battle but the three non-executive directors at Newcastle United – Sir Terence Harrison, Dennis Cassidy and John Mayo – have struck a real blow for corporate governance with their removal of Freddy Shepherd and Douglas Hall from the board. (*The Guardian*, 25 March 1998)

Others, however, were more impressed by the notion of supporter pressure. While *The Independent* went as far as criticising the non-executive directors, the *Financial Times* saw evidence of teamwork between the two groups:

> It will probably suit the record books to show that the two men quit after running up against the defensive back line of Sir Terence Harrison, Dennis Cassidy and John Mayo. But the truth is that there was a deafening silence from the non-execs for more than a week after the allegations first appeared in the *News of the World* . . . Shareholder pressure only resulted in the departure of the two men in so far as most of the minority shareholders are also supporters. (*The Independent*, 25 March 1998)

> Rarely have a company's customers forced such a dramatic change in the boardroom in so little time . . . Their [Shepherd and Hall] decision was a triumph for Sir Terence Harrison, non-executive chairman of Newcastle United plc, the club's parent company, who applied pressure in the name of outside investors, including thousands of fans . . . Outside the realm of football, the main message is that the customer is king. (*Financial Times*, 25 March 1998)

Lessons to be learned from the Newcastle fiasco will be consider in the final section of this chapter.

Community accountability

Although widely referred to, the notion of a football club's community is not clearly defined. It can be argued that it is made up of two inter-related and often overlapping dimensions. The 'direct' or 'traditional' community is the community of supporters (discussed earlier in this chapter) who contribute directly to the resources of the club and who are thus directly affected by the behaviour of the club with regard to issues such as pricing policies, merchandising operations and player purchases. The second group is a wider notion of community encompassing people and groups who can be affected either directly or indirectly by the existence and operation of a football club within a particular community, usually geographical, but in the past also partly religious or social. As previously discussed for the narrow community, there is evidence that conflicts are arising between the role of football clubs as community resources and the same clubs acting as companies.

There exists a marked contrast between the operation of professional team sports in a country like United States and what we have grown accustomed to in the UK. In the free market economics which apply to US team sports, it is not uncommon for professional sports teams to relocate to new population centres or to relocate to attract better local government subsidies or even to change their name. For example, Cleveland lost its American football team, the Browns, to Baltimore in 1996, while the most famous relocation took place in 1958 when the New York borough of Brooklyn lost its baseball team, the Dodgers, to Los Angeles. Government officials and the public view sports organisations as mobile. Professional leagues restrict membership to ensure that demand for teams exceeds supply. As a result, negotiations take place with the threat of relocation to another community in the background, forcing the original community to find ways of enducing the sports organisation to stay put (Johnson, 1993).

In the UK, by contrast, there is a long history of local relationships between professional sporting organisations and particular towns, cities and areas. This relationship is not unique to football: for example, first class cricket in England continues to operate on a county basis. In this sense there exists a cultural difference between the UK and the US whereby clubs in the UK have a deep rooted identification with a particular city or region and hence community. Interestingly, *within* the UK this sense of identity with a football club does not appear to be geographically dependent, with Dobson and Goddard (1996) finding no evidence to support the notion that supporters in some parts of the country are more loyal than those elsewhere. Bale (1991) noted that the number of successful community initiatives to resists changes in the geography of British football contrasted dramatically with the North American situation.

In the UK there have been few examples of clubs relocating from one region to another or changing their name. Clubs which have relocated in recent years have by no means found the moves to be universally successful. In recent years two struggling Scottish lower division teams have left their traditional communities for pastures new. In both cases, the clubs (Clyde and Meadowbank Thistle) struggling in cities with dwindling populations (Glasgow and Edinburgh[7]), with an oversupply of football clubs (five in Glasgow, three in Edinburgh) and faced with both financial and physical problems of redeveloping their stadiums, took the US-style decision to relocate to new population centres, namely the new towns of Cumbernauld and Livingston. The extent to which these clubs are successfully locating themselves as part of the community is difficult to gauge. One objective measure which can be considered is attendance figures for the clubs pre- and post-relocation.

In the case of Clyde there is little evidence to suggest that the club has much chance of building a new community for itself in Cumbernauld, with the club's poor attendance continuing at its new home. In the case of Meadowbank's transformation into Livingston the position is brighter. Livingston has substantially improved upon the admittedly extremely low level of attendances inherited from Meadowbank,[8] although it could be argued that given that the club has enjoyed relative success on the field since the move, namely winning the Third Division in 1995/96, the attendance figures do not indicate a great warming by inhabitants of the new town to top class football. The club has, however, tried to forge links with its new community in West Lothian. For example, unlike Clyde, the club was quick to change its name to that of the area's biggest town. Furthermore, the club has tried to form partnerships with both the local council (one councillor sits on the board of the club) and local businesses, successfully persuading two of the region's biggest employers, Motorola and Russell Athletic, to sponsor the club. In this regard, Clyde too has been successful with the club's main sponsor being OKI the Japanese computer systems company which has a major plant in Cumbernauld. However, in the case of Livingston, it must also be noted that, rather than relocation being the promised land, in its new home the club has continued to have serious

Table 5.2   Relocated clubs: average home league attendance (division)

	1996/97	1995/96	1994/95	1993/94	1992/93
Clyde	806 (2)	1004 (2)	1134 (2)	1709[1] (1)	700 (2)
Livingston	2183 (2)	1978 (3)	NA	NA	NA
Meadowbank Thistle	NA	NA	294 (2)	312 (2)	600 (1)

[1]   Clyde's first match at their new stadium in Cumbernauld took place on 5 February 1994.
Source: The Scottish Football League

financial difficulties and was taken over in 1998 by a consortium led by the ex-Celtic director, Dominic Keane.

The case of Scotland's two newest senior teams, Inverness Caledonian Thistle (created out of a merger of two Highland League teams) and Ross County (another ex-Highland League team), is also interesting. These clubs had average home league attendances of 2495 and 1789 respectively in season 1996/97 despite being in Division 3 and being located some distance from their fellow league members.[9] In both cases, however, Highland League clubs did exist in the respective towns prior to league membership being attained. The success of Caledonian Thistle is particularly significant given that the club arose out of a particularly bitter merger between Inverness Thistle FC and Caledonian FC. The rise of Caledonian Thistle offers some hope to those who believe that clubs can find new communities, with the club's success mirroring the success of Inverness which is one of the fastest growing areas in Europe and an area with enormous potential for future growth.[10]

It has been asserted (Noll, 1997) that mobility of teams will become an issue in Europe in the near future, driven by television pressure for large successful teams to be located in large television markets. To an extent there is some evidence of this happening already. For example, UEFA under pressure from major clubs seeking to maximise revenue, has turned its blue ribbon Champions League competition into a misnomer by allowing teams finishing second in the leagues within the top ranked countries such as England, Italy and Germany entry into the competition, while genuine champions from smaller nations, such as Scotland and former Eastern and Central European countries, have been forced to take part in two qualifying rounds before reaching the League stage of the competition. Further changes are planned beginning in season 2000–01 with proposals to enlarge the Champions League to 32 teams from 24. Under the new format countries such as England could have three teams in the Champions League, with the top two teams in the Premier League qualifying automatically and the third placed side taking part in qualifying ties along with the champions of countries such as Scotland. While the ranking system is based on clubs' performance in previous European competitions, unsurprisingly this favours large countries with large television audiences and consequently lucrative television deals (see the section on *Television – football's economic driver* in Chapter 1). A further example is the attempts made by both Wimbledon and Clydebank to relocate to Dublin, the only capital city in Europe which does not boast its own full-time professional football club.

Notwithstanding the above examples, most evidence would suggest that the deeply ingrained relationship between clubs and communities will continue in the UK. One only has to consider the controversy and passion aroused among both the direct and the wider community which accompanied suggestions by a club such as Newcastle United that it was considering leaving its existing stadium to build a new stadium in Gateshead. Bale (1991) provided a classic example relating to the decision taken by Charlton Athletic in 1985 to leave its ground, The Valley, and enter into a ground-sharing scheme with Crystal Palace 7 miles away. The following comments were found in the Charlton fanzine, *Voice of the Valley*:

> It was just a football club leaving its ground, but to many, many people it was so much more. For the older fans it was the destruction of something that had run like a thread through their lives and for those of us who knew The Valley's past only at second hand it was the crushing of a dream. Charlton's moonlight flit was a cruel human tragedy that found no expression in the accountant's figures.[11]

Other differences also exist between the US and UK models of professional sport. For instance while supply in, for example the NFL (National Football League), may be limited or restricted, in countries with 92 (England) and 40 (Scotland) professional teams, respectively serving populations of 50 m and 5 m approximately there is little prospect of demand for teams exceeding supply in a purely UK context. Milton Keynes in a regularly cited example of a major English town not currently home to a senior football club.[12] However, the Scottish experience of new town relocations does not lead one to believe that any such relocation would be an unqualified success. Where excess demand may arise in the future is if moves towards a European Super League do take place.[13]

Another marked difference is that in the NFL no local competition is allowed into the league without the approval of the prior incumbent, in other words under this rule a club calling itself Newcastle City would not be able to set up a team to compete in the same league as Newcastle United without the prior approval of Newcastle United. In the UK local rivalries and derby matches have traditionally been a vital and colourful aspect of football. It is also worth bearing in mind that unlike US professional sport, football (i.e. soccer) is a global pursuit. Its top UK participants such as Manchester United, Liverpool, Celtic and Rangers have a global reach (see also the section on *Brand accounting* in Chapter 4), while international competitions attract the interest of large numbers of people who would not attend a live match (Gratton and Lisewski, 1981).[14]

Interestingly, however, in the case of Newcastle United there is some evidence that US behaviour towards sports clubs is having an influence in the UK, where the club directors apparently adopted a US-style negotiating strategy by threatening to take the club out of town in order to achieve planning permission for their preferred in town site at Leazes Park (Conn, 1997).[15] Ultimately, of course, the club decided to redevelop St James' Park.

Clubs in the community

It has long been held that football clubs are an important element within local communities. Prior to the recent influx of investment capital into the game, the importance of preserving the club as a part of the community was often used to explain the rationale behind large scale investment in football clubs (see the section on *Ownership framework in football clubs* in Chapter 3). Directors would describe their investment in terms of giving something back to the local community. Within today's football clubs some interpretations of the investments made by such as Jack Walker at Blackburn Rovers and Sir Tom Farmer at Hibernian indicate that investors of this nature are still to be found at the higher levels in football. At a lower level investors of this nature remain very important to clubs. At these clubs the reward of the investment is often measured not in financial terms, but rather through recognition and profile in the community.

The importance of football clubs to an area can be both economic and sentimental. Clubs can act as focal points for communities, something to rally round and to bring people together. Not surprisingly when the club is enjoying success, local interest and enthusiasm is higher. One only needs to think of the boost that local communities have received as a result of good cup runs. Gratton and Lisewski (1981) describe the success of the local club in a national competition as an example of a localised public good. Times of great difficulty also seem to awaken the notion of community among local people as has been witnessed by public reaction to the recent financial difficulties encountered by two of Scotland's first division clubs, Partick Thistle and Falkirk.[16] However, it is worth noting that there is little research evidence to back up these widely held and widely documented beliefs about the attitudes of people towards their team's success or survival (Bale, 1991).[17]

Johnson (1993, p. 62) in his study of the relationship between professional sports organisations and cities in the US suggested that 'the benefits that a community expects to derive from the presence of a sports organisation include enhanced economic activity such as increase in jobs and the infusion of new money into the local economy, increased tax dollars for the local government, improved image, a new recognition by others beyond local borders, improved quality of life for local residents, an added entertainment and recreational amenity, and a vehicle for community cohesion, civic identity and pride'. It is informative to consider some of these putative benefits from the point of view of football clubs.

The issue of recognition is an interesting one. In many areas the football club is one of the factors that most contributes towards knowledge of that area. One of the most commonly quoted examples is that of Borussia Mönchengladbach. There are probably very few Germans (or indeed Europeans) who do not associate the town of Mönchengladbach with football (CJEC, 1995a). Similarly, stories abound of Manchester United shirts being spotted in far flung deserts and jungles.[18]

This recognition value provides an opportunity for clubs and by extension cities and regions to promote themselves in a wider market. One such example is that of Middlesbrough. The club is 75 per cent owned by a local businessman Steve Gibson through his business Gibson O'Neill, with a further 25 per cent being owned by the region's largest employer ICI. King (1997) suggests that Gibson and ICI in particular have invested in the club not as a profit making investment in its own right, but rather to use the club as a sign or indicator of the wider regeneration of the Teesside region. In this context, the signing of high profile players such as Juninho, Ravanelli and, latterly, Gascoigne contribute not only to improving the footballing side of the operation but also to increasing the visibility of the sign.[19] This view was shared by the Head of the Teesside Development Corporation who described the rejuvenation of the football team as being like a paradigm for the whole area (*The Independent*, 23 November 1996). In the past ICI also benefited more directly in that as sponsors of the club their name was highlighted on the front of the club's jerseys. In a study into the objectives of professional football sponsorship, Thwaites (1995) found that that the three most important objectives were to 'Increase public awareness of [the] company', to 'Increase media attention' and 'Community involvement'.

A similar strategy is apparent in the way in which Sir John Hall has used Newcastle United as a sign of the identity of Tyneside in an attempt to regenerate the area and to attract international capital to the region. It is important, however, to distinguish this type of community investment from what on the face of it appears to be a more philanthropic investment made by say Sir Tom Farmer at Hibernian (see the section on *Ownership framework in football clubs* in Chapter 3). The investment made by Sir John Hall is not necessarily made simply because he believes in the importance of the football club or indeed of the region. King (1997, p. 229) argues that 'by employing Newcastle United as a symbolic representative of the economic and social vibrancy of the area, Hall intends to regenerate Tyneside through attracting international capital that will expedite his own regional business project there'. In other words, putting Newcastle on the map will increase the profit making opportunities for Sir John's other investment opportunities in the region. The relationship between football and economic regeneration is also relevant in the case of Celtic, whose 1994 Share Offer Prospectus included contributing 'to the regeneration of the East End of Glasgow' within the Directors' strategy for the club.

In terms of the sign value of football clubs, the role of the sports press is vital, given the extent of the coverage given to anything to do with football clubs. Football in the 1990s is often described as big business. However, as discussed in Chapter 3, by any conventional financial or accounting measure it is no such thing. For the most part football clubs remain small, unsophisticated businesses. Nevertheless, they are subject to an enormous degree of media interest disproportionate to their economic significance. The link between football, the media and politics is perhaps most clearly seen in Scotland, where it has been argued that the scale and most importantly the type of media coverage of sport, and in particular football, is actually used as a substitute for nationhood (Blain and Boyle, 1994).[20]

The importance of football clubs as a vehicle for community cohesion can be illustrated by recalling the attempted takeover mounted in 1990 by the then chairman of Heart of Midlothian, Wallace Mercer, for city rivals Hibernian, at that time struggling both in financial and football terms. In many ways this abortive takeover was a classic example of financial logic being inappropriately applied to football. A large part of the justification for the takeover was that the only way that Edinburgh would play a part in the expected new world of football super leagues was if the two clubs united their resources to form 'Edinburgh United'. The takeover bid was angrily rejected, with Hibernian rejecting vision in favour of tradition, and ultimately failed. Mercer repeatedly claimed that he had won the business argument but lost the social argument (Moorhouse, 1991). What was certainly clear was that he had failed to grasp the complexities of football clubs and the ways in which supporters and communities identify with clubs. In particular, he failed to grasp that a football club's community was not something which could be defined simply in terms of a city's boundaries, but rather arose out of a complex mixture of history, social issues, religion and geography.

The idea of football clubs providing an improved quality of life for local residents and an added entertainment and recreational amenity is not a view likely to be shared by all members of a local community. For example, in the case of Newcastle United's proposal to build a new stadium in Leazes Park, much of the community response to the plan came from people whose primary interest was the preservation of the park in its existing form. The park, not the football club, contributed to their quality of life and acted as a recreational activity. While to many supporters their club does provide entertainment and recreation, to other local residents football clubs provide little tangible benefit for the local community. Many football clubs are in truth remote from anything other than their direct community of supporters.

The under-utilisation of football club facilities was discussed in Chapter 4 (see the section on *Accounting for tangible fixed assets*). One of the great ironies of the idea that football clubs contribute greatly to local communities is the fact that to many, a football club is just something which causes inconvenience to their normal life at every home match, creating traffic chaos and sometime bringing uncivilised individual and group behaviour (and sometimes hooliganism) closer to them than they would wish. Much more must be done to make football clubs a more permanent part of their communities, not just a source of occasional pride if a cup is brought home. Lessons once again can be learned from the ways in which churches, despite dwindling congregations, have worked hard to ensure that if nothing else they at least have a community role to play for people if not a spiritual role. Some suggestions as to how clubs can take a more active role within local communities will be set out in the conclusion.

Preserving a community asset – the role of the banks

Despite recent improvements in the finances of football, many British clubs continue to rely heavily on their bankers to provide loan and overdraft facilities (see the section on *Role of bank funding* in Chapter

3). This is particularly true for smaller clubs, and for larger clubs who have fallen out of the elite and financially lucrative Premier League or Premier Division structure. Despite an often bleak picture of indebtedness, perhaps surprisingly there are very few examples of banks forcing clubs into liquidation to recover their loans.

The nature of security and the rationale behind banks' lending decisions was covered in detail in Chapter 3. However, one aspect of relevance in this chapter is a consideration of the extent to which banks treat football clubs differently from other customers in terms of lending decisions as a consequence of their perceived community or societal role. Through discussions with senior representatives of UK banks involved in lending to clubs Morrow (1997) investigated the extent to which the decision taken by the European Court of Justice in the *Bosman* case (the case is discussed in Chapter 2) altered the exposure of clearing banks to football clubs. One aspect which was discussed was the importance of wider social issues such as the perceived importance of a football club to a local community.

There was not universal agreement among the bankers on the importance of the community issue in lending decisions. For example, one banker stated that, looked at impassively, lending to most football clubs did not make good commercial sense. In his view, banks were involved in lending to football clubs not for commercial reasons, but because of the community profile of football clubs. He argued that the bank's involvement was a form of business development, and that banks were only involved in some clubs due to the presence of high powered individuals on the board. His view was that football clubs were treated differently to other similar sized firms. Another banker, however, felt that the importance of the community issue should not be exaggerated, commenting that while it was an issue which would perhaps influence credit decisions, community or social issues would not stop his bank putting a club into liquidation if that was what was required.

A NEW FRAMEWORK FOR TOMORROW'S CLUB?

Given the conflicts and dilemmas that they are facing, clubs may need to deal with issues of accountability and governance differently in future. In this section a framework will be put forward which will encourage clubs to recognise the importance of all its stakeholders when carrying out its business. This framework will not act as a panacea for all problems faced by clubs, but by recognising those groups that have a stake in the football club it may help to minimise unnecessary conflicts.

Acceptance of the framework is dependent on educating the stakeholders. In terms of the most fundamental conflict, supporters need to accept that the involvement of the City or the application of business practices in football is not necessarily a bad thing.[21] Equally, business people and City institutions have to understand that while football may be a business, it is a unique kind of business; a business which prioritises success on the field, rather than profits off it. Recognition already exists that the product in football is unique. Similar recognition must be provided that supporters are also unique, that they are not just customers.

Tomorrow's Company? Tomorrow's Club?

The inquiry by the Royal Society for the Encouragement of Arts, Commerce and Manufactures into *Tomorrow's Company* (RSA, 1995) brought together senior executives from 25 of the UK's top businesses including Cadbury Schweppes, Guinness and the John Lewis Partnership. Its aim was to consider how *Tomorrow's Company* will achieve sustainable success in a world which is not only increasingly competitive, but also increasingly critical and vigilant of business standards. Two key themes were identified in the report: first, the need for companies to adopt what was described as an *inclusive approach to business* and secondly, the need for companies to maintain a strong *licence to operate*.

An *inclusive approach* to business was defined as one which focused less exclusively on shareholders and on financial measures of success, instead including all stakeholder relationships and a broader range of measurements, in the way companies think and talk about performance. Specifically the report discussed an inclusive approach to business leadership, investment needs, people and society. The *licence to operate* refers to the increasing need for companies to maintain public confidence in the legitimacy of their operations and business conduct. In this section these ideas will be put forward as the basis of a new framework for accountability within football clubs.

Figure 5.1 outlines the various forces in the external environment which combine to influence a club's licence to operate. As mentioned above, a company needs to maintain confidence in the legitimacy of its operations and business conduct. A company will undermine its licence to operate by the wrong type of behaviour, thus exposing itself to the

Figure 5.1   Tomorrow's club: factors influencing its licence to operate

Source: Adapted from the RSA inquiry *Tomorrow's Company* (RSA, 1995)

risk of sanctions. Examples of companies which it could be argued have undermined their licence to operate include Ratners (in connection with Gerald Ratner's description of his company's products as 'crap'), British Gas (public, political and shareholder dissatisfaction with increases in top executives' remuneration), and Shell (in connection with the disposal of the Brent Spar oil rig). In the world of football, the behaviour of the former directors of Newcastle United, and their alleged remarks about such issues as replica kit sales, women in the

North East of England and Newcastle United players, is an example of a company undermining its licence to operate. In this case sanctions were imposed in the form of media and public (community) outcry, supporter uprising and investor pressure via the non-executive directors. As unpleasant as the story was, its resolution and the ability to interpret it in the context of this model has profound implications for football club accountability.

Regulation in the football industry

The current environment within which football operates is subject to a patchwork of regulatory influences: footballing, legal, financial and governmental, all of which constrain the way in which clubs behave and do business.

The football authorities

The primary regulators of football in England and Scotland are the respective football associations, the FA and the SFA. Their objectives include promoting the game at all levels, supporting and promoting the principle of fair play and sportsmanship and furthering football's commercial interests. The associations have a wide range of members including leagues such as the FA Premier League in England and the respective Football Leagues in both England and Scotland. The objectives of such leagues includes the provision of competitions, promoting and guarding the interests of the league's constituent members and arranging commercial contracts. The existence of the dual regulatory structure means that clubs will be operating under the jurisdiction of more than one regulatory body which can lead to problems.

The football regulatory bodies have responsibility for regulating both on-field activity, such as the disciplining of players, and also off-field activities, such as the negotiation of television deals or other commercial contracts. In recent years it has been their off-field regulatory role which has been subject to the greatest challenge, with the new breed of businessmen who are found in club boardrooms being prepared to challenge the established rules of the regulatory bodies. As was discussed in Chapter 1, the objective of top clubs has a footballing and a related financial aspect: first, the maximisation of domestic playing success thus allowing access to European competitions, and secondly, the maximisation of income subject to and arising out of the footballing objectives.

The desire of the top clubs in both England and Scotland to have a greater say in the way in which football was being run and to receive a greater share of the financial benefits being generated by the game led these clubs to break away from the Football League and the Scottish Football League and to set up new league structures. In both cases under the threat of resignation and break-away, the existing leagues were powerless to prevent the developments. Furthermore, in both cases the new league structures have received the blessing of the FA and the SFA, despite questions being asked about the extent to which the new leagues are consistent with the objectives of the associations, and about the extent to which the associations are under the control of the top clubs (see the section on *Regulatory capture* in Chapter 1).

The importance of maintaining the game's integrity was recognised by the Football Association in its commissioning of a report by Sir John Smith on *Football – Its Values, Finances and Reputation* (Smith, 1997). The Smith report followed on from the FA Premier League's report into transfer irregularities and the FA report into betting by players and others in professional football, both of which raised concerns about the effectiveness of the structure and rules that football has in place to deal with financial misconduct. Smith identifies three reasons why football must be concerned with its financial reputation:

1. all stakeholders are entitled to expect a financially responsible business;
2. television and sponsors do not want to be associated with a sport prone to allegations of financial misconduct; and
3. to avert the risk of government intervention.

The necessity for regulation within a league, including financial regulation, arises 'because it is intrinsically anti-competitive if some members of the league obey the financial rules and others break them to their own advantage' (Smith, 1997, 1.7). Among Smith's suggestions were the early introduction of rules to allow for the proper regulation of football's financial affairs, the need for an effective monitoring and compliance unit to investigate the application of such rules and the introduction of Code of Conduct applying to all aspects of the game under its jurisdiction.

It is likely, of course, that conflicts between clubs, many of whom are listed, and regulatory bodies will arise again in the future. Despite their inability or unwillingness to prevent the break-away leagues being formed, there is still an important role to be played by bodies such as the FA and the SFA. In particular, it remains their responsibility to ensure that the overall health of the game and its attractiveness to the public is considered from the point of view of the success of football as a whole, not just the success of a minority of clubs. The incorporation of football makes this an increasingly difficult role to carry out.

The law

In the past football gave the impression that it believed that it was beyond the law, both in terms of off-field activities and on-field activities, and that regulation of the football world was a matter purely for football's regulatory bodies. However, high profile legal intervention in recent years has shattered that belief. In terms of legal intervention in on-field activities, the case in which three Rangers players (Terry Butcher, Graham Roberts and Chris Woods) and one Celtic player (Frank McAvennie) were charged with conduct 'likely to provoke a breach of the peace amongst spectators' in 1987 highlighted that the police and the procurator fiscal did not accept the view that on-field misbehaviour in front of a crowd of 40 000 plus was a matter simply for the football authorities.[22] In another high profile case, the then Rangers striker Duncan Ferguson, now a Newcastle United player, became the first Scottish professional player to be sent to jail for an on-field incident, when he was convicted in 1994 of assault on a fellow professional, John McStay, in a match versus Raith Rovers.

Off-field activities have also been challenged through the courts, with the outcome having or having the potential to substantially change the operating of the game and its financing. The highest profile case to date was that of *Union Royale Belge des Sociétés de Football Association ASBL* v. *Bosman* in the European Court of Justice in 1995 in which Bosman successfully challenged the operation of the transfer system within Europe (see the section on *The Bosman case* in Chapter 2). In the light of Bosman's success, other players have resorted to the courts to challenge the accepted state of play in the transfer markets, for example, in Scotland the former Airdrieonians player Chris Honor (see the section on *The transfer market* in Chapter 2). Another ongoing case, where the implications could be as far reaching as in the Bosman case, is the referral of the broadcasting deal between the FA Premier League and BSkyB and the BBC to the Restrictive Practices Court by the Office of Fair Trading. In this case the OFT is challenging the rights of the league to enter into television and broadcasting contracts on behalf of the Premier League clubs on an exclusive basis (see Chapter 1). Off-field court intervention of a different kind arose in the allegations of match fixing which led to the trial of players John Fashanu, Bruce Grobbelar and Hans Seegers. The players and a Malaysian business-man were cleared of all charges.

These cases and others should now have left clubs and regulatory bodies in no doubt that the law will intervene as and when necessary, irrespective of the self regulatory mechanisms that are in place.

The Government

Football must put its own house into order, if for no other reason than to obviate the prospect of public authorities stepping in to regulate from the outside. Strong and effective self regulation will preserve the autonomy of football. (Smith, 1997)

The quote from Sir John Smith's Report to the Football Association indicates quite clearly that the risk of Government intervention in football is being taken seriously. The Government takes an interest in the football industry for a variety of reasons. From a negative point of view, when hooliganism was at its worst the Government was obliged to involve itself in a matter of public order. From a more positive point of view, the current enthusiasm for football, its popularity among young people and in particular a recognition of its importance within both local and national communities makes it a legitimate area for political attention. Furthermore, football is a recipient of public money: of the £250m passed to professional football by the Football Trust since 1975, some £150m has come indirectly from the state in the form of the three per cent reduction in Pool Betting Duty (Smith, 1997).

The Labour Party policy document *A New Framework for Football* (1996) considered the imbalance between top clubs and the rest and the appropriateness of unregulated free market economics to the foot-ball industry. Following the election of a Labour government in 1997, the government honoured its commitment in the policy document by launching a Football Task Force, under the chairmanship of David Mellor, designed to represent the views of the ordinary fan with the aim of taking football back to the people.

In the light of the Government's approach in other areas of the economy as not interventionist in nature, and that it is likely to be put off by the potential threat of court challenge if its intervention was seen as anti-competitive, it is not yet clear what kind of suggestions the Task Force can come up with which will see football being taken back to the people. One interesting suggestion is the creation of a regulatory body, akin to the regulatory bodies which were put in place after the utility companies were privatised, and which are now to be found in areas as diverse as the lottery and education (Perryman, 1998). Although the similarity between football clubs and privatised utility providers may seem tenuous given the differences in the services they provide and in their importance, nevertheless similarities do exist with regard to conflicts of responsibility and accountability between shareholders and consumers in the utilities, and between shareholders and supporters in football clubs. Such a body could be given a remit to protect the rights of a club's supporters and to ensure that their loyalty was not exploited by profit conscious clubs.

The City

The advent of clubs on the Stock Exchange or the Alternative Investment Market means that the City now has a role to play in the regulation of football clubs. Formally, this requires clubs to comply with the requirements of the Stock Exchange's Listing Rules or Yellow Book (discussed in Chapter 3). Once a club is listed the impact of these rules should be fairly minimal, and will normally be restricted to issues such as announcing the resignation of a manager or the signing of a player formally through the Stock Exchange before announcing it to the sports press. Informally, some clubs will find themselves obliged to communicate regularly with institutional investors and to keep them informed of the club's business performance and in particular of the relationship between what happens on the field and what happens off the field, for example on issues like player capital expenditure (see also the section on *Monitoring* in Chapter 2).

The inclusive approach in practice

The framework suggested in this chapter is an attempt to capture the nature of modern football clubs, i.e. to recognise that while it is important that clubs are run as businesses, it is equally important to recognise that they are not just businesses. The adoption of an inclusive approach to the business of football will require the focus to be on all the club's stakeholder relationships. This emphasis will ensure that the complexity of clubs is captured, that the social and political dimensions inherent in clubs are considered as well as the economic factors.

The primary conflict, as we have seen, is between club and company, between shareholders and supporters. Resolution of this conflict requires a different culture within the companies and greater industrial and corporate responsibility. In some cases it will require different behaviour from stakeholders. In all cases it will certainly require stakeholders to be better educated about the role of other stakeholders, and improved communication between those groups.

So far this chapter has focused on issues which explain *why* change is necessary? The real question is *how* can football clubs be persuaded to embrace the ideas and what practical steps can they take to begin to implement them. The report commissioned by the Football Association on *Football – Its Values, Finances and Reputation* (Smith, 1997) is a promising development. The remit of the inquiry was to consider the way in which football regulated its financial affairs and how to ensure and maintain the integrity of football and accountability in the way it operates. The report includes a Draft Code of Conduct for football, which is to form the basis for discussion and a consultation exercise among those involved in football. The introduction to the draft code states:

> Football is our national game. All those involved with football have a responsibility, above and beyond compliance with the law, to act according to the highest standards of integrity and to ensure that the reputation of football is and remains high.

It is designed to demonstrate that clubs are taking standards of conduct seriously and in many ways can be seen as an extension of the ideas discussed above with regard to *Tomorrow's Company* in terms of the *licence to operate* and the *inclusive approach*. The draft code is shown in full at the end of the book in Appendix 2. The remainder of this chapter will consider what might be meant by an inclusive approach to supporters and to the community and how this can be related to the Smith Code of Conduct.

An inclusive approach to supporters

Supporters
Football recognises the sense of ownership felt by supporters at all levels of the game and is committed to appropriate consultation of genuinely representative supporter groups.

Draft Football Association Code of Conduct (Smith, 1997)

The key to achieving this point is clearly the communication process. Clubs require to find meaningful ways of communicating with their supporter stakeholders. Earlier in this chapter the idea of supporter reports (akin to employee reports) was discussed. Such reports are a very simple way of beginning the dialogue between the club and the supporters, although use of such a report on its own offers no opportunity for the necessary two way communication process.

The issue of supporter representation on the board has been raised several times in the past. Again parallels exist with the employee stakeholder group where there has long been a demand for employee representation at board room level.[23] The supporter board member could act in a consultative role, offering advice to the directors and a supporter viewpoint to the board. It is likely that in most cases the supporter representative would be neither an executive director (i.e. a full time working decision-making role) nor a non-executive director (working in an external advisory capacity, as recommended by the Cadbury Report for plc companies). There is a risk, therefore, of the position falling between two stools and consequently being of little value, i.e. having no decision making authority and no independence. However if the club was genuine in its intention to run its business on an inclusive basis then it could provide a good mechanism for allowing representation of supporters.

From the club's point of view such an appointment would have a strong sign value, presenting a powerful image of a club which is keen to become more accountable to its various stakeholders.[24] Supporter representation on the board could also have benefits to the directors. Contrary to widely held views, directors' duties are owed to their company, not to any specific third-party group such as the company's shareholders. The fiduciary duty of directors requires them to consider and to give appropriate weight to *all* the company's key relationships, and then to reach a balanced judgement on how best to maximise the company's value on a sustainable basis in the interest of both present and future shareholders. As such 'it will do the shareholders no good if the company has dissatisfied customers, faces an antagonistic central or local government and has angry pressure groups disrupting its annual general meeting' (Davies, 1997, p. 604).

Various other suggestions for improving the communication process have been put forward which could be seen as contributing towards the adoption of an inclusive approach to supporters. In a paper written for the Fabian Society, Perryman (1998) set out various proposals for consideration by the Football Task Force. On the question of supporter representation he put forward three interesting ideas: Fan Forums, Fan Juries and an 'Investors in Supporters' scheme.

Fan Forums follow on from the idea of supporter representation on the board and envisage regular meetings between supporters and club representatives at different appropriate locations throughout the club's catchment area. In most clubs the communication or accountability infrastructure is already in place in the form of supporter clubs (McMaster, 1997), and in several clubs such forums already take place. It is often assumed that shareholders are privileged stakeholder groups when it comes to communication and decision making with companies. In practice this is often not the case.

While there is normally good and regular communication between companies and their institutional shareholders, for individual shareholders communication with the company is usually limited to receipt of the annual report and attendance at an AGM. Although in theory the AGM is a decision making forum and a mechanism through which control can be exercised over the behaviour of directors, in practice it is often little more than a social occasion. In practice only institutional shareholders have enough influence to exercise any meaningful control over boards of directors. The practical consequences of this are that the AGM has been replaced by the market for corporate control (i.e. takeovers) as a means of disciplining directors. Given the importance to supporters of identification with their club, it is to be expected that stronger bonds exist between supporters than exist for a disparate collection of individual corporate shareholders.

The difficulty of co-ordinating activity among individual shareholders was evidenced in the campaign mounted by British Gas shareholders against the rise in top executives' pay. By contrast the setting up of pressure groups such as Shareholders United Against Murdoch was achieved very quickly by Manchester United shareholders and supporters following the announcement of BSkyB's proposed takeover. The existence of supporters' clubs provides a communication forum which may offer a useful mechanism for achieving accountability. Several top European clubs are in fact run as membership organisations which effectively vests control in the hands of the supporters. The best known example is Barcelona where accountability to supporters in ensured by the fact that the club is controlled by its 102 000 official members, split into 1050 *penas* (or official supporters groups).[25]

Of course, not all supporters are members of supporters clubs. Other mechanisms may require to be introduced in parallel to avoid exclusion. Given that we are talking about 'Tomorrow's Club', one possibility is taking advantage of improvements in technology to provide a communication forum for supporters. For example, most clubs now maintain popular Internet home pages, while several, such as Celtic, Newcastle United and Sunderland, also communicate with their supporters by electronic mail.[26] Such technology can easily be used to allow two-way communication and to provide a mechanism for achieving accountability through, for example, ideas such as virtual meetings.

Another inclusive possibility is the idea of 'Fan Juries' (Perryman, 1998). Membership would be drawn from all supporter groups, with mechanisms being put in place to avoid domination by only the large supporter groups or those dominated by the more activist minded.[27] The juries would monitor the club's performance over a season and offer an annual report. Such a report taken together with a Supporter Report produced by the board may make for interesting comparative study for supporters.

Other less radical methods of achieving inclusion also exist, although often changes would be required to ensure their usefulness. For example, many top clubs have official newspapers. At present many of these papers are akin to newspapers available in the former Communist states, given their unwillingness to provide anything other than the official club viewpoint (Perryman, 1998). Allowing these organs (and by the same token match day programmes) greater editorial independence and freedom would be a step towards more genuine communication and accountability.

There may also be a greater role for fanzines. This is of particular value within the discussion on accountability if one accepts that a general role of fanzines is 'promoting and defending football, especially in helping to articulate widespread opposition to the takeover of clubs by business interests with little feel for the culture of the specific club or for football and terrace culture in general' (Jary, Horne and Bucke, 1991, p. 591).

Such a view of fanzines is not, however, universally shared. For example, Moorhouse (1994a, p. 174) takes issues with the argument that 'fanzines are said to resist the incorporation of soccer as a centrally managed commercial and commodified leisure provision and strive to maintain the subservience of full-blown commercial values to vernacular football values'. Many of the pivots of the argument, Moorhouse believes, are evoked rather than specified. In particular nowhere is information provided as to what 'full blown' commercial values applied to sport might involve; and the values of terrace culture are assumed (and assumed to be good), rather than detailed.

In many ways this argument is symptomatic of the difficulties and conflicts facing clubs in the new football world. Nevertheless, although the value of fanzines would be diminished by any kind of official recognition, encouraging their sale in club shops and allowing cross advertising in programmes and official club newspapers could perhaps contribute to the feeling of a more inclusive club.

Parallels between demonstrating accountability within football clubs to supporters and the demands and needs for accountability to employees within companies more generally have been alluded to throughout this chapter. Perryman (1998) takes the parallel further by suggesting the introduction of *'Investors in Supporters'* award akin to the *'Investors in People'* award. Investors in People has been developed to provide a benchmark against which organisations, which may not seem comparable in any other aspect, can measure their achievements and performance in placing the development of their employees at the heart of their organisational strategy. Clubs would be required to set standards and targets they were aiming for as regards their relationships with their supporters and to provide quantification of the extent to which those targets have been achieved. Give that any of the ideas discussed previously in this section could be included within this type of award, an Investors in Supporters award may provide an all-inclusive route to demonstrating an inclusive approach to supporters.

An inclusive approach to the community

The Community
Football recognises that its constituent clubs – at all levels – are a vital part of their communities, and it will take into account community feeling when making decisions which affect those clubs.
     Draft Football Association Code of Conduct (Smith, 1997)

The draft report identifies two challenges for clubs: first, to demonstrate that they are vital parts of their communities, and secondly to remember that community role when making decisions. Many suggestions have been put forward as to how clubs can overcome their remoteness from the wider community. One of the easiest to achieve would be turning under-utilised grounds and facilities into a genuine community resource. The model for this can be seen in the way in which churches have found an important role to play in communities, seven days a week. This is particularly significant given that most churches, unlike football clubs at present, are having to deal with a dwindling direct community in terms of falling congregations. Similarly, the way in which schools have turned themselves into community schools provides a model for football clubs.

Much more could be done. Interestingly, Perryman (1998) suggests that one problem is that clubs think that identification has become synonymous with merchandising. What is required is to break out of that mind set and to open out the club and its facilities, to allow links to be forged between clubs and their communities at an affordable level. Many clubs already host weddings and have restaurant and bar facilities which are available to the public. How many, however, act as sports centres during the week? How many use their hospitality suites during the week for anything other than conferences? How many after-school clubs or mother and toddler groups or unemployed groups use facilities available at football grounds? Night classes? Community council meetings? The list of possibilities is considerable.

One club which has taken up the challenge of demonstrating that it is a part of the community is Leeds United, through its Community United programme.[28] Its publicity document states:

> Football clubs do not recognise the strength of their brand in the local community and the attraction that the community has to the Club. We have a responsibility in the community and a major opportunity to benefit from it.

The programme has six themes (Education, Football in the Community, Pre-school Playgroup and Crèche, Senior Citizens Club, Welfare to Work and the Leeds United Family Club) which put into practice some of the ideas discussed above and others. The club is also actively engaged in trying to involve other local companies in the community project:

> Through our pivotal role in the community, Leeds United have established a programme of investment requiring partnerships with business and the commercial community in the region . . . Together we can provide a range of community activities which not only encompass social recreation for the community but also offer skills and learning opportunities, creating positive benefits to Leeds as a business and commercial centre.

Other clubs such as Leicester City and Newcastle United also refer to community involvement in their annual reports.

The Community Department acts as a networking arm reaching out to the community at large and encourages the increasingly important development of the younger generation . . .

(Leicester City Football Club plc, Annual Report and Accounts 1997)

It is important for the Club to remain a focal point of the Community . . . This will help the club to sustain revenues and encourage the youth development programme but it is also important in its own right.

(Newcastle United plc, Annual Report and Accounts 1997)

The most recent FA Premier League Fan Survey identified Wimbledon as the most successful club at attracting in fans through its community scheme, with 22 per cent of the club's current season ticket holders having been attracted to the club by its Football and the Community Scheme, compared to an average of seven per cent for the Premier League (SNCCFR, 1997). The Survey notes these schemes can provide considerable commercial gains to clubs by assisting the recruitment of new fans to their clubs, estimating that attracting approximately seven per cent of the home fans each week is worth about £400 000–£500 000 per club per season on average.

The survey found that 64.3 per cent of all fans thought that their clubs' community activities were either good or excellent. The fact that there was little distinction between local fans and those who live at a distance, however, suggests an element of club loyalty rather than more tangible awareness of community activities (SNCCFR, 1997). These surveys also only take the opinion of the direct supporters, not members of the wider community. Furthermore, if clubs genuinely consider that they have a role to play within communities, then it is to be hoped that they will involve themselves because of the importance of such initiatives in their own right rather than because it may be a way of improving the company's profit in the longer term.

The issue of supporters being priced out of their local club has been discussed earlier in this chapter (see the section *From fan to consumer?*). In that regard ideas put forward by the Labour Party (1996) such as the community-based leisure card schemes are to be applauded. Existing schemes in, for example, local authority leisure centres offer differential pricing for groups such as the young, the aged and the unemployed. A particular issue that clubs require to address in this context is to ensure that the next generation of supporters will not feel disenfranchised by their inability to see top class football. Capacity constraints and increased prices, which along with safety issues mean that the traditional method of introducing young supporters to matches (i.e. being lifted over the turnstiles) is no longer an option, have resulted in an ageing spectator population. Even from a purely business and profit point of view clubs urgently need to address where the future direct community is going to come from.

The majority of clubs do operate family stands and parent and child areas, although such areas are often quite small and can quickly be oversubscribed. However, even with the price reduction which accompanies such tickets, the costs of introducing a child or children to regular top class football can be prohibitive. The most recent FA Premier League Fan Survey found that more than half the sample, and seven out of ten of those fans who had school-age children, were put off bringing school-age children to matches because of ticket prices (SNCCFR, 1997). Clubs require to find more imaginative ways of ensuring the succession. One club which has taken the initiative is Sheffield Wednesday, introducing what it describes as 'perhaps the most radical ticket policy **ever seen** in Premiership Football' (Wednesday Supporter, 1997/98). The unique pricing structure allows children ('the supporters of tomorrow') to watch teams such as Chelsea, Aston Villa, Barnsley, Everton and Tottenham Hotspur for free if they are accompanied by two paying adults, or half price if accompanied by one adult. Wimbledon was identified in the most recent FA Premier League Fan Survey as the club where season ticket holders were most satisfied with ticket pricing for children (SNCCFR, 1997).

Other approaches include clubs using reserve team matches as a way of attracting young supporters to the club. Both Leicester City and Blackburn Rovers have turned reserve matches into Family Nights, offering low price or free tickets in a bid to build up the supporter base of the future (*Soccer Analyst*, 1997). Similarly the Scottish Football Association's policy of distributing free tickets to schools for international matches which are not sold out could easily be replicated by top clubs. The approaches which will be adopted will depend on which club and which matches, but what is important is that more clubs need to start adopting these types of inclusive approach to young supporters.

The charitable aspect of their community relationships is also something which more clubs could focus attention on. Many players do actively engage in charity work such as visiting hospitals and schools, which is of course entirely commendable. Given the pivotal role of a club in its community and the high profile of the club and of its star players, greater emphasis could be placed on charitable activities both as important activities in their own right and as a sign to the community. Evidence from the most recent FA Premier League Fan Survey suggests growing disquiet about the level of players wages, with 42 per cent of clubs' season ticket holders being of the opinion that players wages were currently too high (SNCCFR, 1997). Improving the community work carried out by players and its visibility may be one way of countering this negative feeling about players and what they take out of the game (see also the section on *The future* in Chapter 2).

Two clubs which do involve themselves in charitable activities, and which also highlight this involvement, are Arsenal and Celtic. In his statement in the Statement of Accounts and Annual Report 1996/97, the Chairman of Arsenal refers to the Gunners Community Fund which was set up to support charities and self-help groups within 1000 metres of the stadium. The amount distributed by the fund over the last five years is in excess of £100000. In the case of Celtic, given that the club was established in the late nineteenth century by a Marist Brother known as Brother Walfrid principally as a means of using the game of football to raise money to provide food for the poor in the East End of Glasgow, its charitable involvement is perhaps not surprising. The Annual Report and Accounts distributed to shareholders contains a page on the Celtic Charity fund. Information is provided on amounts raised and the beneficiaries. In the 1997 annual report the three main beneficiaries were charities in support of children's needs, community action on drugs and projects that develop and promote religious and ethnic harmony. The relationship between Celtic as a business and Celtic's role in the community is specifically commented on:

> It is important for a club of Celtic's traditions to remember that although the club must be a highly professional and successful international business to meet the aspiration of shareholders and supporters there are several groups in our society to whom leisure activities such as professional football are very important but are not readily available.

The amount raised by the fund during 1996/97 was over £100000, being raised by supporters, staff, directors, players, club funds, corporate clients and the general public. There is, however, no indication in the annual report or the charity report as to how much was provided by the club and how much by the other groups. Although the initiative is laudable and although there is clearly more to charity than simply raising cash (e.g. the benefits of a hospital visits to a sick child are often enormous but not quantifiable), the amount raised in total by all the contributing groups identified represents less than 0.5 per cent of the club's turnover. Nevertheless, the position is much worse at other clubs. The total amount donated to charity by Premier League and Scottish Premier Division clubs as disclosed in the clubs' 1997 accounts amounts to the shockingly low total of £190 288 split between 12 clubs, with the amounts ranging from £50 000 by Sunderland to £210 by Sheffield Wednesday.[29] Eighteen clubs disclosed no charitable donations. Once again there would seem to be much more that clubs could do in terms of charitable works within their communities.

CONCLUSION

Perhaps the biggest challenge facing today's football clubs is how they are to address issues of governance and accountability. This chapter has advocated an inclusive approach to accountability. Such an approach requires a recognition of the objectives of the organisation and an awareness of the legitimate interests of different stakeholder groups. Central to the notion of improved accountability is improved communication between all stakeholders. The ideas in this chapter should not be interpreted as prescriptive or legislative. Rather they are an encouragement to clubs to seek out and adopt best practice in all aspects of their corporate behaviour thus ensuring improved governance.

Conclusion

Football off the field has changed beyond all recognition in the last decade. Satellite television, freedom of contract, super leagues, the Stock Exchange: all have contributed to turmoil in the football industry. Whether change has benefited football on the field is open to debate. What is certain is that there is no going back. In fact, it seems more likely that the pace of change in the football industry will continue to accelerate in the coming years.

Further changes in football's broadcasting arrangements seem likely. There are two aspects to this: first, the possibility that in the near future clubs will individually be able to negotiate the sale of television rights to their own matches as opposed to collectively on a league basis, and secondly, the possible introduction of Pay-Per-View television (PPV). As was discussed in Chapter 3, much of the early growth in football club share prices was influenced by forecasts of the expected revenues which would be generated for clubs by PPV. Similarly, much of the subsequent downward correction in prices was influenced by doubts about when PPV would come on line, and revised forecasts as to the income it would generate for clubs. It is unclear what the true worth of PPV to clubs will be with forecasts varying enormously.

Perhaps the most realistic figure is the estimate provided by Fletcher Research (1997) that PPV will generate £450m in revenue by the year 2003 with 2.5m people paying to watch individual matches. This estimate was based on an authoritative study of the number of fans each club has, and was less than 25 per cent of some earlier forecasts. While the amount may not be clear, one thing that seems certain, however, is that when PPV is introduced, as discussed in Chapter 1, its introduction will be accompanied by pressure from the big clubs for the largest share of the revenues that are to be generated. This pressure, along with the possibility of clubs already being able to sell television rights to their matches on an individual basis, means that clubs will move further still from the concepts of income distribution and competitive balance that historically have been common in the economics of sports industries.

Interestingly, the current state of play is that the introduction of PPV in season 1998/99 was rejected by the chairmen of the Premier League clubs at their annual meeting on 29 May 1998. One reason for this may be that clubs were unhappy with the financial terms of the deal, particularly with regard to the split between BSkyB and the clubs; another reason may be that the clubs are holding out on PPV until they are in a position to launch a digital television channel of their own.

Perhaps also the decision is a recognition by club chairmen that football is indeed more than just a business, that supporters are more than simply consumers. It would be reassuring to think that club chairmen are concerned about maintaining their *licence to operate* (as discussed in Chapter 5) and have recognised that moving to PPV would be a step too far for supporters who have already tolerated major changes in their relationship with their clubs, both financial vis-à-vis substantial increases in season ticket and match ticket prices and social vis-à-vis changes to match days and times and so on.

Asking them to pay £8–£10 per match on top of approximately £200 for a digital decoder box, as well as agreeing to a package which would have led further to the demise of traditional Saturday afternoon football with initially five fixtures per week being moved to Sundays may well have led to supporters losing confidence in the legitimacy of their club's operations and business conduct. The ultimate risk for clubs in such a scenario is that they impose sanctions in the form of withdrawing their support, both direct and indirect.

Although the introduction of PPV seems inevitable, it is hoped that rejection of the BSkyB package by the Premiership clubs in May 1998 is a recognition by them that PPV must be introduced in a manner which benefits not just the clubs, their shareholders and the television companies, but also the supporters.

Financial developments in the future will not, however, be confined to the introduction of PPV television. While doubts continue about whether or when a European Super League will take to the field, movement towards a European financial Super League is already advanced. While British clubs (along with four Danish clubs) have taken the lead in terms of raising capital through the Stock Exchange, major continental clubs, despite declining share prices have viewed the British flotations as successes, and as a result have started to follow the path to the market.

The first continental European club to come to the market was the Italian club Lazio which was floated on the Milan Bourse in May 1998, closely followed by the Dutch club Ajax which listed its shares on the Amsterdam Stock Exchange later the same month. Others are set to follow, with a large number of major clubs like Borussia Dortmund, Bayern Munich, AC Milan, Porto and Athletico Madrid already making moves to go public.

Other top clubs, like Real Madrid, AS Roma and nearer to home Arsenal and Rangers, however, have so far resisted the advances of the Stock Exchange. Whether that position will be sustainable is debatable. By the time a European Super League comes into being, it may not be fantasy to suggest that one condition for entry will be that shares in the participating clubs must be publicly traded on a national stock market.

However, globalisation of football also brings problems. One of football's most pressing sport/business conflicts is the question of cross ownership of football clubs. Rules have long existed with regard to the conditions in which individuals can play a role in the affairs or ownership of more than one club (see section on *The football sector in perspective* in Chapter 3). While some modification of these rules has been necessary since clubs began to float to take on board the recognised financial logic of diversification by investors, a larger problem exists where companies have taken the decision to invest substantially in more than one European club. The risks that arise out of such joint ownership in a European context are exactly the same as those which caused the domestic authorities to put rules in place to prevent domestic cross ownership – namely that competition may be, or may be seen to be, compromised if two clubs with common ownership play against each other.

At present the most prominent examples are the English National Investment Company (ENIC), a sports and entertainment group which has majority holdings in AEK Athens, Slavia Prague, Vicenza and FC Basel, as well as a 25 per cent stake in Rangers, and the French media group Canal Plus which has control of Paris St Germain and Servette of Geneva. The objective of companies like ENIC has been to build up a portfolio of high value football companies. The problem for UEFA is that such portfolios carry the possibility of conflict between desired investment and the integrity of the sporting competition. As a result in May 1998 UEFA ruled that where two or more clubs are under common control then only one may participate in the same European club competition.

UEFA's view is that it has the right to intervene and take appropriate action where one company is in a position to influence the management, administration and/or sporting performance of more than one team. This view was subsequently backed by the world governing body FIFA which approved a motion calling on national associations to make sure that no more than one club belongs to the same company. The ruling meant that one of ENIC's clubs, AEK Athens, would have been prevented from taking part in the UEFA Cup on the grounds that another of ENIC's clubs, Slavia Prague, had already qualified for that competition. Unsurprisingly the ruling was rejected by ENIC which was of the opinion that UEFA would be in breach of European law if it were to block clubs with common ownership from playing each other in European competitions.

Once again it was left to the courts to resolve an apparent conflict between business and sport, and once again UEFA was the loser, when on 17 July 1998 the Court of Arbitration for Sport in Lausanne upheld ENIC's appeal for one season only. The reported response of both parties emphasises the nature of the conflict: while ENIC said it was keen to find a solution which would ensure the protection of sporting integrity while not restricting much needed investment in clubs, UEFA's view was that the economic interests of major investors had been given precedence over the protection of sporting integrity (Harverson, 1998).

What these ongoing developments in the football industry highlight is the issue of identity which has been apparent throughout this book. Football clubs need to find a way of embracing both their business identity and their sporting identity, a way of facing up to issues of governance and accountability. Chapter 5 advocated an inclusive approach to accountability. Such an approach requires a recognition of the objectives of the organisation and an awareness of the legitimate interests of different stakeholder groups. Central to the notion of improved accountability is improved communication between all stakeholders. To a great extent the future prosperity of a football business which will be recognisable to today's supporters in a decade's time requires clubs to adopt an inclusive approach to their identity and to their stakeholders.

Appendix 1

[1] Celtic moved from AIM to the Official List in September 1998.
[2] Leeds United was originally taken over by Caspian plc. The company changed its name to Leeds Sporting plc on 16 January 1998.

Appendix 2

Draft Football Association Code of Conduct
Football is our national game. All those involved with football have a responsibility, above and beyond compliance with the law, to act according to the highest standards of integrity and to ensure that the reputation of football is and remains high.

The Community
Football recognises that its constituent clubs – at all levels – are a vital part of their communities, and it will take into account community feeling when making decisions which affect those clubs.

Equality
Football is opposed to discrimination on any grounds and will actively cooperate with measures to prevent it, in whatever forms, from being expressed in football.

Supporters
Football recognises the sense of ownership felt by supporters at all levels of the game and is committed to appropriate consultation of genuinely representative supporter groups.

Young people
Football acknowledges the extent of its influence over young people and pledges itself to set a positive example to its young supporters.

Propriety
Football acknowledges that public confidence demands the highest standards of financial and administrative behaviour within the game and will not tolerate corruption or improper practices.

Competition
Football will uphold a relationship of trust and respect between clubs to ensure that competition at all levels is fair and differences are resolved within football.

Violence
Football rejects the use of violence by players or spectators and will, in co-operation with the public authorities, punish those involved.

Discipline
Football will investigate and punish breaches of its rules, on and off the field, with a clear and fair system of hearings and penalties, operating as openly as possible and conforming to the principles of natural justice.

Source: Smith, Sir John (1998), *Football – Its Values, Finances and Reputation.* Report to the Football Association by Sir John Smith.

Notes

1 The New Economics of Football

1. There is no entitlement to facility or merit fees (FAPL, 1997, Section D, Rule 11.1).
2. Manchester United also have separate revenue streams in respect of their European involvement with regard to sponsorship and replica kit sales.
3. In addition to this deal, a highlights package has been negotiated with the BBC and separate deals are being negotiated for the Scottish Cup and the League Cup. As a result a sum of between £60m and £70m is likely to be received by the Premier League, quadrupling the previous total.
4. The specialised economics within the football industry is questioned by Cairns, Jennet and Sloane (1986) who note that many aspects of club and league behaviour are in fact found elsewhere in the economy. Examples of cross-subsidisation in both the government and the private sector are also provided in Arnold and Beneviste (1987a).
5. For example, when BBC Scotland first televised the Scottish Cup Final in 1955, transmission was dependent on 80 per cent of the tickets having been sold (Boyle and Haynes, 1996).
6. In the United States there is no history of a formal transfer market in professional sports.
7. In the United States, federal broadcasting rights are equally distributed among all teams in American football.
8. UEFA draw up a ranking list in which the calculated total co-efficient of each national association is taken into account. The calculation is made on the basis of the performance achieved by the clubs over the previous five seasons (Regulations of the UEFA Champions League 1998/99, Article 5).
9. This is an ongoing process. Continued pressure from top clubs seeking improved financial rewards from European competition has forced UEFA into making proposals to further alter its competitions. Under the proposals agreed by its executive committee in October 1998, from season 2000–01 the Champions League would be enlarged to 32 teams from 24. Prize money available is expected to be in excess of £300m, with over £30m going to the winners. Under the new format England could have three teams in the Champions League, with the top two teams in the Premier League qualifying automatically and the third placed side taking part in qualifying ties along with the champions of the Scottish Premier League. The proposals are a direct response to the threatened European Super League breakaway being spearheaded by the Italian firm, Media Partners International.

2 Rich Man, Poor Man – Players in the New Business of Football

1. For example, at the time of the 'Big Bang' deregulation within the London Stock Exchange (October 1986) there was some evidence of a transfer

market for highly regarded brokers and dealers, with fees being paid to buy out contracts. Similarly, in industries such as advertising in boom periods there have been a limited number of transfers of highly regarded account executives. In universities, prior to the last Research Assessment Exercise in 1996 there was evidence of a transfer market for research active staff. More recently, it was reported that 'a transfer market has now taken root as Scottish Universities throw off past restrictions and embrace the free market philosophy of major corporations' ('Superbrains for sale', *Scotland on Sunday*, 31 May 1998). However, the operation of most of these markets is more similar to the post-Bosman situation, in which the rewards or economic rents are earned by the transferring staff, not their former employer.

2. *Eastham* v *Newcastle United Football Club Ltd*. [1964] Ch 413, [1963] 3 All ER 139, [1963] 3 WLR 574.

3. Griffith-Jones (1997, p. 42) notes that, interestingly, many of the arguments rejected by the judge in the Eastham case were deployed thirty years later in the Bosman case. For example, the judge did not accept that the transfer rules were necessary to prevent the richest clubs acquiring the best players, nor did he accept that abolition of the rules would deter clubs from investing in the training and development of their players.

4. Rule 60(A) of the Scottish Football League Rules applies to the expiry of contracts prior to 1 October 1996 (SFL, 1997). These rules have been changed for contracts expiring after 1 October 1996 (Rule 60(B)). The basic difference is that if at the end of the 31-day period the club wishes to protect its right to receive compensation in respect of the player, it must offer the player Continuing Monthly Contracts on terms no less favourable in all monetary respects than the previous contract. Such contracts can only be terminated when either (i) the player's registration is transferred to another club, or (ii) termination in agreed by mutual consent, or (iii) formal written notice in given by either party. Where the player does not accept the offer of Continuing Monthly Contracts as set out above, or where he terminated the contract in terms of point (iii) above then he loses all rights to wages at the end of the 31-day period but the club is still entitled to receive a compensation fee (SFL, 1997, Rule 60(B)(7)(2)).

5. This description is most applicable to the pre-Eastham transfer market, less so after the introduction of freedom of contract. Nevertheless, even under so-called freedom of contract, clubs retained an element of retention over players, a fact which, of course, led to the Bosman case.

6. For example the *Radio 5 Live Sports Yearbook* (Nichols, 1997) identifies Britain's top sporting earners. The top British earner for the year to November 1997 was identified as the boxer Lennox Lewis, with earnings of £6.4m, of which all but £150 000 was earned in the boxing ring. The highest paid football player was Alan Shearer with earnings of £3.5m, much of which comes through off-field endorsements and sponsorship activity. In the 1996/97 season, the average salary for a regular first team player in the Premier League was estimated at £350 000. Although large, these earnings are dwarfed by those earned by top American sports people, according to *Forbes Magazine*, which identified the world's 40 best paid sports people. Top of the league was the basketball star Michael

Jordan with earnings estimated at \$78.3m (*Forbes Magazine*, 15 December 1997). Lennox Lewis was ranked a lowly 35th in the world list.

7. Spending on players included wages and transfers. However, it was noted that the majority of this spending was on wages as for most clubs net transfer spending was close to zero (Szymanski, 1993).

8. Deloitte & Touche (1997, p. 30) also noted that in general terms a higher wage bill leads to on the field success. The top three clubs in the Premier League also had the highest wage bills, although Newcastle United which had the highest wages bill did not win the title. Furthermore, seven of the top eight clubs in the league were among the eight clubs with the highest wage bills, while the bottom club also had the lowest wage bill.

9. Entry to football leagues in the UK is, however, restricted by rules. For example the rules of the new Scottish Premier League require clubs to have an all-seated stadium with a capacity of at least 10000, under-soil heating, a full time playing staff and an accredited youth development scheme. Gaining membership also, of course, means entering the league structure via the lowest league. Furthermore, entry can also thought of as being restricted in practical terms by the difficulties faced by clubs which are trying to build themselves up, through factors such as supporter loyalty, geography and wider community issues.

10. *The Financial Times* Lex column noted that the costs of relegation from the Premier League exceed even a 25 per cent increase in the largest club's wage bill and therefore clubs will spend on wages in order to ensure a continued presence in the top flight (*The Financial Times*, 14 February 1998). (See also section on *Redistribution and Competition – Implications of Change* in Chapter 1.)

11. Several chairmen including Doug Ellis at Aston Villa, Alan Sugar at Tottenham Hotspur and Fergus McCann at Celtic have commented to this effect in their annual reports and in the press.

12. This issue was raised most vociferously at the company's AGM on 1 June 1995. See for example, 'Pressure on British Gas', *The Financial Times*, 31 May 1995, or 'Investors see British Gas row as the watershed in corporate governance', *The Financial Times*, 2 June 1995.

13. Evidence from newspaper reports, however, suggests that while language itself may not be a footballing problem wider cultural differences can result in some players (and/or their families) quickly becoming unsettled in other countries. For example the reported difficulties of the Brazilian Emerson fitting into life on Teesside are well documented, as was the reluctance of Jorge Cadete's family to join him in Glasgow while playing for Celtic. In terms of exports, it was reported that Paul Lambert's decision to leave the then European Champions Dortmund to return to Celtic was partly due to difficulties his family had settling in Germany. Closer to home it has not been unknown for Scottish players to claim homesickness as a reason for seeking to return to Scotland from England (e.g. Chris Hay at Swindon Town).

14. For example, see 'Spurs accused of poor buying', *The Financial Times*, 5 November 1997.

15. For example, press reports indicated that the Italian Fabrizio Ravanelli was astounded at the lack of training (and training facilities) that he found

at Middlesborough, with the result that he spent large periods of time training alone. See for example, 'Points deduction adds to pressure on Middlesbrough', *The Times*, 15 January 1997, or 'Ravanelli poised to quit', *The Times*, 18 January 1997.

16. Although the number of international players is low, these are the players who have reached the peak of their achievement within the current framework of Scottish football and hence consultation was thought to be important (Moorhouse, 1997, para. 18).

3   The Capital Structure of Football Clubs

1. In strict terms, the Exchange is itself a secondary market, but its existence makes the issue of new securities, which can subsequently be traded, a more attractive proposition.

2. The London Stock Exchange is the third largest in the world in terms of market capitalisation after the New York and Tokyo Stock Exchanges.

3. In the five years since the publication of the Taylor Report, English clubs have spent £417m on their stadia (Deloitte & Touche, 1997).

4. There are exceptions to this rule, such as scientific research-based companies.

5. Deloitte & Touche (1998c) found that only seven of the 18 Italian Serie A clubs made a profit in the 1996/97 season. Taken together Serie A made an overall post tax loss of £30.7m for the 1996/97 season (1995/96 – £18.9m). All Italian clubs capitalise player transfer fees in the balance sheet and then write them off over the contract period (see Chapter 4). Eliminating this write off would result in Serie A reporting an overall operating profit of £5.5m.

6. The Spanish Securities Commission can however waive this requirement.

7. In his autobiography, the former manager of Newcastle United, Kevin Keegan, blamed the decision to float for his departure from the club. He claims that although he informed the Newcastle chief executive of his intention to resign at the end of the 1996/97 season, his immediate resignation was sought to meet the needs of the flotation (Keegan, 1998).

8. Loftus Road, owners of Queens Park Rangers, also own Wasps Rugby Union club, while Rugby League is represented on the Stock Exchange by AIM listed Eagles plc, owner of the Rugby League Challenge Cup winners Sheffield Eagles. Eagles plc also has a 40 per cent stake in Sheffield Sharks basketball team.

9. The Club shares were subsequently converted into ordinary shares in May 1997 when shares were floated on the Stock Exchange Official List.

10. Restrictions placed on the transferability of shares were another example of the unequal treatment of shareholders. In many clubs, existing shareholders could only sell or otherwise transfer their shares with the approval of the club's directors. Often the shares had to be offered in the first instance to the directors. Furthermore, it was often the right of the directors to determine the transfer price.

11. The ability of football to assume a position beyond that which its status would seem to deserve is not limited to finance and the Stock Exchange.

For example, it has been argued that the extent and more importantly the nature of football coverage in Scotland has in fact been used as a substitute for nationhood (Blain and Boyle, 1994).

12. No rules exist to prevent companies diversifying and expanding through the acquisition of non-footballing companies.

13. The tradition of football clubs paying little to their shareholders has a long history. *The Athletic News* in 1909 [6 September] thought 'no one who is out for a business return would look at football shares . . . not one club in fifty has paid interest on shares, year in and year out', and informed its readers [27 September] that only six of the leading 62 clubs had paid a dividend that year. In England at that time there was a 5 per cent dividend ceiling. However, Vamplew (1982) found that in Scotland (where there were no dividend restrictions) few League clubs paid dividends in the period 1906–1914 (quoted in Arnold, 1991).

14. Such restrictions exist in other countries also. For example, French clubs are prohibited from paying dividends under current legislation.

15. Some economists (e.g. Cairns, Jennet and Sloane, 1986, p. 71) argue that from a competition perspective such supporter benefactors who seek playing success are potentially more damaging to the interests of the League than pure profit maximisers because they may create greater inequality in playing performance among the member clubs and hence raise the degree of instability in the League as a whole.

16. Many Western European football clubs are integrated within larger capitalist interests, and hence footballing losses may be tolerated if the club provides the parent company with international profile and assists in easing relations between capital and labour (King, 1997).

17. While Fergus McCann points to membership of the Croy Celtic Supporters Club in the 1960s as evidence of his supporter credibility, Alan Sugar's memories of supporting the club as a boy are more vague, being unable to remember the names of his side's famous FA Cup and League winning team of the 1960s (Cameron, 1994). Before deciding to invest in Queens Park Rangers, Chris Wright looked at investing in both Leeds United and Portsmouth.

18. David Murray was quoted as saying: 'If you think only about the bottom line then, yes, Brian Laudrup could have been sold for four to five million over the summer. But we are not only dealing with money, we are dealing with dreams of a football club' (*The Scotsman*, 12 January 1998).

19. It is worth noting, however, that while Sir Tom Farmer was initially hailed by Hibernian supporters as a 'local hero', the club's recent footballing difficulties, culminating in its relegation from the Premier Division in May 1998, has seen the club's supporters deference towards him dissipate.

20. There have been recent examples of hostile takeovers of football clubs, most noticeably at Leeds United where the club was taken over by Caspian. However, this takeover was different in nature to the idea of a disciplinary takeover being discussed. Essentially, the takeover involved the directors of Leeds United selling their substantial majority shareholdings to Caspian. Other recent takeovers of football clubs have similarly involved the directors reducing their shareholding in the clubs. The highest profile takeover of a football club to date, BSkyB's bid for Man-

chester United, was not a hostile bid as it was supported by the board of Manchester United.

21. Although the share price has halved since flotation, the paper worth of the original directors holdings remains approximately £3.5 m.

22. For example, the announcement by Manchester United in February 1996 of a six-year sponsorship deal with Umbro estimated to be worth at least £50m caused the share price to rise 13p to a high of 242p.

23. No secondary market figures have been provided for Millwall due to the fact that the club was put into administration on 30 January 1997, resulting in the suspension of trading in its shares.

24. Statistics on trading volume in Heart of Midlothian were not available on Datastream. However, in the week immediately following the club's placing on the Stock Exchange, the flotation sponsors Williams de Broe were quoted as being unable to find buyers for stock in Hearts (*The Herald*, 22 May 1997).

25. 59% of the club's turnover in 1997 was made up of gate receipts (1996–58%).

26. The publicly stated desire of the Celtic chairman and majority shareholder, Fergus McCann, is that he wishes to find a way of selling his shares to the Celtic supporters, when he relinquishes control in 1999. In anticipation of this sale, the share structure was altered in September 1998 when the company's shareholders voted in favour of sub-dividing each Ordinary Share of £1 each into 100 Ordinary Shares of 1p each, thus increasing the number of shares in issue from 290 000 to 29 million.

27. This is not to say that there will be no financial returns to the investors. For example, investors in Manchester United, Newcastle United, Southampton, Sunderland and Tottenham Hotspur all received dividends on their ordinary shares in respect of the year 1996/97.

28. A fund manager interviewed in connection with this book identified quality of management as being the most important factor in deciding whether or not to invest in a club. He also indicated that he would not choose to invest in a club in which there would remain a dominant shareholder post-flotation.

29. The RSA inquiry *Tomorrow's Company* (RSA, 1995) noted that in fact few funds act capriciously: the average length of a client manager relationship, reported to be around eight years, is similar to the typical period for which a fund manager holds an investment. Even so the perceived lack of security in these relationships may cause damaging behaviour.

30. Such loan schemes may also be viewed as an extension (or indeed, increasingly perhaps a replacement (Morrow, 1997)) of the historical recognition by banks of the importance of football clubs as community assets, whereby banks have continued to provide financial support to loss making football clubs, beyond that which might have been expected by similar companies in lower profile industries (see Chapter 5).

31. It would also have been useful to have calculated an interest cover ratio in terms of operating cash flow, given that ultimately interest payments require to be made in cash terms. However, differences in the treatment of transfer fees and differences in disclosure prevented a meaningful table being presented.

32. In the event of liquidation, Company Law puts in place a procedure for the ranking of creditors. Only preferential creditors (such as debts due to the Inland Revenue and certain remuneration of employees) have priority over secured lenders such as the banks. Hence if the loan or overdraft was secured by a floating charge on the club's stadium, then any proceeds on the sale of the stadium would be due to the bank after payment of any preferential debts (s. 175, Insolvency Act 1986).

33. Most football clubs which have revalued their land and buildings have done so on a depreciated replacement cost basis (see Chapter 4). Such a basis therefore has no relationship to the realisable or market value of such an asset. Given this, it is surprising that one football club banker interviewed about the impact of the Bosman case on bank lending policies, stressed the importance and reliance that banks placed on valuations provided by external, expert valuers in respect of assets such as stadium (Morrow, 1997).

4 Accounting in the Football Industry

1. The Review is available from Deloitte & Touche, 201 Deansgate, Manchester, and is free to clubs, football organisations and students.

2. Despite being based on publicly available information, the Price Waterhouse Review is *not* publicly available. Summaries of the Report are, however, published extensively by the Scottish press usually in August.

3. Clubs may also publish an additional performance statement, a Statement of Total Recognised Gains and Losses (STRGL). In the STRGL the profit for the period is added to other items which may have increased or decreased the value of the business to its owners such as increases in the value of assets held by the company. If a football club has revalued its stadium then any gain or loss on the revaluation would be reported in the STRGL.

4. The idea of financial statements as a *visible illusion* is common in discussions of new or knowledge industries.

5. The residual value is basically an estimate of the value of the player at the end of his contract. In most cases the estimate was based on the application of a UEFA multiplier dependent on a player's age being applied to his earnings.

6. Northampton Town, Preston North End, Tottenham Hotspur, Aberdeen, Celtic, Heart of Midlothian and Rangers.

7. Derby County and Newcastle United.

8. West Bromwich Albion.

9. Portsmouth, Sunderland and Swansea.

10. Bournemouth, Bristol Rovers, Darlington and Sheffield United.

11. Dundee.

12. A new domestic transfer system was introduced in the UK in the summer of 1998. Under the new system any player aged 24 or more, who is out of contract on or after 1 July 1998 in England or on or after 16 May 1998 in Scotland, is free to transfer his registration to another club without that club requiring to pay a transfer fee to the club which previously held his registration.

13. In Italy, clubs are required to capitalise players' contracts bought from other clubs, writing off the transfer fee over the contract life (Deloitte & Touche, 1998c).
14. The survey consists of the 20 Premier League clubs in season 1996/97 plus Glasgow Rangers.
15. Replica kit sales in any one season will, of course, depend to a great extent on whether or not clubs introduced a new kit during the season.
16. Prior to the issuance of a Financial Reporting Standard, the ASB will normally issue an exposure draft as part of a consultation process.
17. In addition, certain companies such as the privatised water companies do not depreciate their infrastructure assets, because they are legally obliged to maintain them to a high standard.
18. A recent example of a club receiving a grant is Dunfermline Athletic. The club has received funding of £1.55 m towards the first phase of the redevelopment of East End Park. The Scottish Sports Council has committed £1 m, while the Football Trust is providing £350 000, plus an interest free loan of £200 000. This if the first example of an award made jointly by the two organisations in Scotland ('East End race against time', *The Scotsman*, 6 May 1998).
19. In their 1997 accounts West Ham United also disclose the use of forward contracts.
20. According to Deloitte & Touche (1997, p. 36), gate receipts/season ticket income represented 42 per cent of the turnover of English football for season 1995/96, compared to 43 per cent for commercial and other income and 15 per cent for television.
21. The demand for replica kits can be subject to wider social and political factors also. For example, during the 1998 World Cup sports shops across Scotland reported a surge in demand for Argentina strip in anticipation of their clash with England. Perhaps economic factors were influencing the demand as the kits were manufactured in Scotland! ('Argentina strips in demand', *The Scotsman*, 30 June 1998).

5 Accountability within the Football Industry

1. The Statement of Principles is the conceptual framework upon which financial reporting is based in the UK. At present, the document is an Exposure Draft (i.e. in a consultative stage) but is expected to become a standard in due course.
2. See also Carmichael, Forrest and Simmons (1996) and Carmichael and Thomas (1993).
3. The club's relegation from the Scottish Premier Division at the end of season 1997/98 was followed by the resignation of the club's chairman, Lex Gold, a former chairman of the Scottish CBI.
4. Interviews were requested with eight non-specialist fund management companies (i.e. non-football funds) identified as having holdings in UK clubs. Unfortunately, only two positive responses were received, out of which one interview took place.
5. A *new fan* is defined by the researchers as a supporter who has started watching within the last five years (SNCCFR, 1997).

6. In this regard, however, is noted that new fans may require time to build up loyalty and depth of feeling for a club.
7. The population of Glasgow fell from 1 144 342 in the 1971 census to 680 000 in 1994. Over the same period the population of Edinburgh fell less dramatically from 476 600 to 443 600 (*Scottish Abstract of Statistics*).
8. Such attendances are not uncommon in the lower reaches of Scottish professional football. The Royal Commission on Gambling (1978) suggested that one lower division Scottish club actually budgeted for the coming season on the assumption that no spectators would attend their matches. As such every spectator who came through the turnstiles was effectively pure profit to the club.
9. In a study of English Football League teams, Walker (1986) found that that teams from large conurbations tend to be more successful and that this has a positive effect on attendance. Furthermore he found that road mile distance between clubs involved in the same fixture had a predictable, negative exponential effect on attendances in general.
10. The population of Inverness has risen from 58 341 in 1984 to 64 290 in 1994, a rise of over 10 per cent (*Scottish Abstract of Statistics*).
11. Everitt, R. (1989), 'Battle for the Valley', *Voice of the Valley*, 11, 22–28, quoted in Bale (1991).
12. In 1984 Luton Town did consider moving to Milton Keynes but abandoned the plan as a result of supporter pressure (Bale, 1991).
13. The question of whether or not a European Super League will be formed is currently the subject of much debate among regulators and football club owners. The overwhelming majority of respondents to a survey carried out by the accountants KPMG in conjunction with the publication *Soccer Investor* felt that a European Super League was likely by the season 2002/ 2003 (KPMG, 1998). It should be noted, however, that this survey was based upon a small number of interviews (35), drawn from a limited 'universe' of potential respondents. Those sampled were chosen 'because they had the potential to provide an authoritative and informed opinion on likely developments in European club football'. Furthermore, within the sample of clubs all those targeted 'were seen to be most likely to be included in any European Super League'. Consequently the results of this 'survey' must be treated with caution as the sampling techniques clearly introduces the risk of bias and indeed circularity.
14. More recently this has been demonstrated in the 1998 World Cup. Viewing figures for the World Cup Final were 22.31 m, while 23.78 m watched the England v Argentina match. The record UK viewing figures for a sports programme was the 25.1 m who watched the West Germany v England World Cup Semi Final in 1990. The French viewing audience for the 1998 World Cup Final was 20.58 m, while the Brazilian audience was estimated at 51.0 m (*The Financial Times*, 17 July 1998).
15. A similar strategy is apparently being followed by the president of Real Madrid who believes that he can solve the club's financial problems by selling the Bernabeu Stadium, located in a prime city site, to developers and persuading the city council to build a new out-of-town super stadium ('Spanish temperatures rising as Real's recent results cause blame fever', *Scotland on Sunday*, 29 March 1998).

16. In both cases, local communities have rallied around their clubs, including the formation of fund raising campaigns such as 'Save the Jags' and 'Back the Bairns'.
17. One of the few studies which has investigated the relationship between sporting success and economic benefits in the community was that of Derrick and McRory (1973) into the effects on the people of Sunderland of Sunderland FC's victory in the 1973 FA Cup Final. Their study identified wide ranging benefits to the local community including increased pride in the city, decreased vandalism in the city, increased productivity and enthusiasm in the workplace and decreased absenteeism.
18. My own experience occurred while running a course in a remote college on the Hungarian/Slovakian border. In a tiny family restaurant one evening, the owner asked me in faltering English where I was from, to which I responded 'Scotland'. This brought the lightning response of 'football'. Admittedly this was then followed up by 'Liverpool'! I assisted by offering the words 'Celtic' and 'Rangers', to which I received the extraordinary response 'ah yes – Rangers Catholic, Celtic Protestant!' Despite the minor errors of detail, this demonstrates the extent of recognition which football brings.
19. ICI has indicated an intention to dispose of its investment in the club (*The Financial Times*, 16 February 1998). Following the logic of the importance of investing in a club as a sign value, it is to be hoped for the people of Middlesbrough's sake that the divestment is not a negative sign for the region and ICI's involvement therein.
20. This disproportionate media emphasis on football is also evidenced by the amount of coverage received by the government's very modestly funded Football Taskforce, in comparison to other government initiatives.
21. Interestingly, the most recent FA Premier League Fan Survey found that 59.7 per cent of season ticket holders believed that their club had struck the right balance between football and 'business' activities. However, within the Premier League clubs a league table emerged. Supporters of clubs which have maintained a traditional capital structure (see Chapter 3) like Wimbledon, Derby County and Arsenal were most satisfied, followed by supporters of clubs which had floated with reasonable success like Chelsea, followed by floated clubs which have recently had difficulties of one sort or another like Tottenham Hotspur and Sunderland (SNCCFR, 1997).
22. Butcher and Woods were convicted and fined, McAvennie was discharged while the case against Roberts was adjudged 'not proven'.
23. The Germans system of corporate governance for companies of substantial size is based on a 'two-tier' principle. A supervisory board is appointed by the company's stakeholders (i.e. the shareholders and the employees), which in turn appoints an executive board.
24. It is important that any supporter appointed to the board is seen to be and to act as the supporters' representative on the board, not as the board's mouthpiece to the supporters. Parallels exist in politics. The former Secretary of State for Scotland, Malcolm Rifkind recently contrasted his view of that role with the view of the former Primer Minister, Lady Thatcher. While her view was the Secretary of State was there to repre-

sent the Cabinet in Scotland, Mr Rifkind's view was that his job was to represent Scotland in the Cabinet ('Parcel of Rogues', Channel 4, 4 April 1998).

25. Interestingly, however, other prominent clubs run as membership organisations such as Borussia Dortmund are attempting to change their structure to that of a limited company to allow them to access funds available through the Stock Exchange.

26. For example, Sunderland's web site was voted the number one football web site in England in 1996 and was runner up in the UK Internet site of the year awards in 1997. The club estimates that the web site is visited by approximately 5–6 m people per annum. The club also maintains a voluntary e-mail database which allows it to communicate with approximately 2000 of its supporters. The club uses this regularly to inform interested parties about fixtures, results, ticket availability and so on.

27. Similar rules would require to be implemented in electing a supporter representative to the board.

28. Leeds United is also acting as a pilot club for the Premier League Study Support Centre initiative, 'Playing for Success', part of the Government's drive announced in its White Paper, 'Excellence in Schools', to expand study support and out-of-hours education provision.

29. The league table of donations is as follows: Sunderland, £50000; Newcastle United, £31252; Rangers, £28757; West Ham United, £20000; Arsenal, £19176; Liverpool, £15000; Middlesbrough, £11500; Manchester United, £8476; Chelsea, £2730; Heart of Midlothian, £2392; Coventry City, £795 and Sheffield Wednesday, £210.

References

Alberstat, P. and Johnstone, C. (1997), 'Competition Law and Sports: The Way Forward', *Soccer Analyst*, No. 8, 2–6.

Arnold, A.J. (1991), 'An Industry in Decline? The Trend in Football League Gate Receipts', *The Service Industries Journal*, Vol. 11, No. 2, 43–52.

Arnold, A. and Beneviste, I. (1987a), 'Producer Cartels in English League Football', *Economic Affairs*, Vol. 8, Pt. 1, 18–23.

Arnold, A. and Beneviste, I. (1987b), 'Wealth and Poverty in the English Football League', *Accounting and Business Research*, Vol. 17, No. 67, 195–203.

Arnold, A. and Beneviste, I. (1988), 'Cross Subsidisation and Competition Policy in English Professional Football', *Journal of Industrial Affairs*, Vol. 15, No. 1, 2–14.

Arnold, A. and Webb, B.J. (1986), 'Aston Villa and Wolverhampton Wanderers 1971/2 to 1981/2: A Study of Finance Policies in the Football Industry', *Managerial Finance*, Vol. 12, No. 1, 11–19.

ASB (1993), *Operating and Financial Review*. (London: The Accounting Standards Board).

ASB (1995), *Statement of Principles for Financial Reporting Exposure Draft*. (London: The Accounting Standards Board).

ASB (1997a), FRS 10, *Goodwill and Intangible Assets*. (London: The Accounting Standards Board).

ASB (1997b), FRED 17, *Measurement of Tangible Fixed Assets*. (London: The Accounting Standards Board).

ASC (1974), SSAP 4, *Accounting for Government Grants*. (London: ICAEW).

ASC (1977a), SSAP 12, *Accounting for Depreciation*. (London: ICAEW).

ASC (1977b), SSAP 13, *Accounting for Research and Development*. (London: ICAEW).

ASSC (1975), *The Corporate Report*. (London: The Accounting Standards Steering Committee).

Baimbridge, M., Cameron, S. and Dawson, P. (1996), 'Satellite Television and the Demand for Football: A Whole New Ball Game?', *Scottish Journal of Political Economy*, Vol. 43, No. 3, 317–333.

Bale, J. (1991), 'Playing at Home: British Football and a Sense of Place' in *British Football and Social Change*, eds Williams, J. and Wagg, S. (London: Leicester University Press).

Betts, P. and Harverson, P. (1998), 'Wealth polarity grows in Italian football', *The Financial Times*, 3 September.

Blain, N. and Boyle, R. (1994), 'Battling Along the Boundaries: The Making of Scottish Identity in Sports Journalism' in *Scottish Sport in the Making of the Nation*, eds Jarvie, G. and Walker, G. (London: Leicester University Press).

Boyle, R. and Haynes, R. (1996), '"The Grand Old Game": Football, Media and Identity in Scotland', *Media, Culture and Society*, Vol. 18, 549–564.

216

Brummans, R.J.J. and Langendijk, H.P.A.J. (1995), 'Human Resource Accounting in Football Clubs: A Comparative Study of the Accounting Practices in the Netherlands and the UK', *University of Amsterdam Working Paper*.

Cairns, J.A. (1987), 'Evaluating Changes in League Structure: The Reorganisation of the Scottish Football League', *Applied Economics*, Vol. 19, 259–275.

Cairns, J. (1990), 'The Demand for Professional Team Sports', *British Review of Economic Issues*, Vol. 12, No. 28, 1–20.

Cairns, J., Jennet, N. and Sloane, P.J. (1986), 'The Economics of Professional Team Sports: A Survey of Theory and Evidence', *Journal of Economic Studies*, Vol. 13, No. 1, 1–80.

Cameron, C. (1994), 'Net Loss', *Management Today*, October, 86–88.

Cameron, S. (1997), 'Regulation of the Broadcasting of Sporting Events', *Economic Affairs*, Vol. 10, No. 3, 37–41.

Carmichael, F., Forrest, D. and Simmons, R. (1996), 'The Labour Market in Professional Football: Who Gets Transferred and for How Much?', mimeo, Department of Economics, University of Salford.

Carmichael, F. and Thomas, D. (1993), 'Bargaining in the Transfer Market: Theory and Evidence', *Applied Economics*, Vol. 25, 1467–1476.

Carsberg, B., Hope, A. and Scapens, R.W. (1974), 'The Objectives of Published Accounting Reports', *Accounting and Business Research*, Vol. 5, No. 15, 162–173.

CJEC (1995a), *Opinion of Advocate General Lenz – Union Royale Belge des Sociétés de Football Association ASBL v Bosman.* Case C-415/93. 20 September. (Court of Justice of the European Communities).

CJEC (1995b), *Judgement of the Court – Union Royale Belge des Sociétés de Football Association ASBL v Bosman.* Case C-415/93. 15 December. (Court of Justice of the European Communities).

Committee on the Financial Aspects of Corporate Governance (1992), *The Financial Aspects of Corporate Governance.* (The Cadbury Report).

Conn, D. (1997), *The Football Business – Fair Game in the '90s?* (Edinburgh: Mainstream).

Corry, D., Williamson, P. and Moore, S. (1993), *A Game Without Vision: The Crisis in English Football.* (London: Institute of Public Policy Research).

Cowie, C. and Williams, M. (1997), 'The Economics of Sports Rights', *Telecommunications Policy*, Vol. 21, No. 7, 619–634.

Crampsey, R.A. (1986), *The Economics of Scottish Professional Football.* (Glasgow: Scottish Curriculum Development Service).

Davies, P.L. (1997), *Gower's Principles of Modern Company Law.* (London: Sweet and Maxwell).

Deloitte & Touche (1996), *Annual Review of Football Finance.* (Manchester: Deloitte & Touche).

Deloitte & Touche (1997), *Annual Review of Football Finance.* (Manchester: Deloitte & Touche).

Deloitte & Touche (1998a), *Opinion – Capitalisation of Purchased Football Player Registrations.* (Manchester: Deloitte & Touche).

Deloitte & Touche (1998b), *England's Premier Clubs.* (Manchester: Deloitte & Touche).

Deloitte & Touche (1998c), *Italian Serie A: Deloitte & Touche Financial Review.* (Milan: Deloitte & Touche)

Department of Education and Science (1968), *Report of the Committee on Football (The Chester Report)*. (London: HMSO).

Derrick, E. and McRory, J. (1973), 'Cup in Hand: Sunderland's Self Image after the Cup', University of Birmingham Centre for Urban and Regional Studies Working Paper No. 8.

Dobson, S. and Gerrard, B. (1997), '*Testing for Rent Sharing in Football Transfer Fees: Evidence from the English Football League*', Leeds University Business School Discussion Paper E97/03.

Dobson, S.M. and Goddard, J.A. (1992), 'The Demand for Standing and Seated Viewing Accommodation in the English Football League', *Applied Economics*, Vol. 24, 1155–1163.

Dobson, S.M. and Goddard, J.A. (1996), 'The Demand for Football in the Regions of England and Wales', *Regional Studies*, Vol. 30, No. 5, 443–453.

Fama, E.F., Fisher, L., Jensen, M.C. and Roll, R. (1969), 'The Adjustment of Stock Prices to New Information', *International Economic Review*, Vol. 10, No. 1, February, 1–21.

FAPL (1997), *The FA Premier League Handbook 1997–98*. (London: The Football Association Premier League Limited).

Finn, G.P.T. (1991a), 'Racism, Religion and Sectarianism: Irish Catholic Clubs, Soccer and Scottish Society – I The Historical Roots of Prejudice', *International Journal of Sports History*, Vol. 8, 1, 72–95.

Finn, G.P.T. (1991b), 'Racism, Religion and Sectarianism: Irish Catholic Clubs, Soccer and Scottish Society – II Social Identities and Conspiracy Theories', *International Journal of Sports History*, Vol. 8, 3, 370–397.

FIR (1982), *English Football League Clubs – Financial Status and Performance.* (London: Financial Intelligence and Research).

Fletcher Research (1997), *Net profits.* (London: Fletcher Research).

The Football League (1983), *Report of the Committee of Enquiry into Structure and Finance* under the Chairmanship of Sir Norman Chester. (Lytham St Annes: The Football League Limited).

Forsyth, R. (1992), 'Sport' in *Anatomy of Scotland: How Scotland Works*, eds Linklater, M. and Denniston, R. (Edinburgh: W&R Chambers).

Franks, J. and Mayer, C. (1994), 'Ownership and Control in Germany', *London Business School Working Paper*.

Franks, J. and Mayer, C. (1996), 'Hostile take-overs and the correction of managerial failure', *Journal of Financial Economics*, Vol. 40, No. 1, 163–181.

Gratton, C. and Lisewski, B. (1981), 'The Economics of Sport in Britain: A Case of Market Failure', *British Review of Economic Issues*, Vol. 3, No. 8, 63–75.

Gray, R., Owen, D. and Adams, C. (1996), *Accounting and Auditability.* (London: Prentice Hall).

Griffith-Jones, D. (1997), *Law and the Business of Sport.* (London: Butterworths).

Harding, J. (1991), *For the Good of the Game: The Official History of the Professional Footballers' Association*. (London: Robson Books).

Harverson, P. (1997a), 'Investors tackle the ups and downs of success', *The Financial Times*, 3 May.

Harverson, P. (1997b), 'Rivals switch to the English style', *The Financial Times*, 28 November.

Harverson, P. (1998), 'Same-owner football clubs have ban lifted', *The Financial Times*, Weekend 18/19 July.

Holmström, B. and Tirole, J. (1993), 'Market Liquidity and Performance Monitoring', *Journal of Political Economy*, Vol. 101, No. 4, 678–709.

Home Office (1990), *The Hillsborough Stadium Disaster: Inquiry by the Rt. Hon. Lord Justice Taylor, Final Report*, Cmd. 962. (London: HMSO).

Hopwood, A. and Page, M. (1987), 'The future of accounting standards', *Accountancy*, September, 114–116.

Horne, J. (1995), 'Racism, Sectarianism and Football in Scotland', *Scottish Affairs*, No. 12, 27–51.

ICAS (1988), *Making Corporate Reports Valuable*. Institute of Chartered Accountants of Scotland. (Edinburgh: Kogan Page).

Jary, D., Horne, J. and Bucke, T. (1991), 'Football "Fanzines" and Football Culture: A Case of Successful Cultural Contestation', *Sociological Review*, Vol. 39 , No. 3, 581–597.

Jennet, N. (1984), 'Attendance, Uncertainty of Outcome and Policy in Scottish Football League', *Scottish Journal of Political Economy*, Vol. 31, No. 2, 176–198.

Johnson, A.T. (1993), 'Rethinking the Sport-City Relationship: In Search of Partnership', *Journal of Sport Management*, Vol. 7, 61–70.

Keegan, K. (1998), *Kevin Keegan*. (London: Little, Brown).

King, A. (1997), 'New Directors, Customers, and Fans: The Transformation of English Football in the 1990s', *Sociology of Sport Journal*, Vol. 14, 224–240.

KPMG (1998), *European Super League. Results of a survey carried out by MORI on behalf of the KPMG European Football Unit*, March. (KPMG/Soccer Investor Ltd)

Kuper, S. (1998), 'Manchester United renews deal with Sharp', *The Financial Times*, 28 March.

Kuyper, T. (1997), 'Football on the Box', *New Economy*, Vol. 4, No. 4, 207–211.

Labour Party (1996), *A New Framework for Football: Labour's Charter for Football*.

McMaster, R. (1997), 'The Market for Corporate Control in Professional Football: Is there an Agency Problem?', *Economic Affairs*, Vol. 17, No. 3, September, 25–29.

Mathews, M.R. and Perera, M.H.B. (1996), *Accounting Theory and Development*. (South Melbourne: Thomas Nelson).

Miller, F. (1993), *Free Market Football: The Effects of the EC Law on the Professional Football Industry in Europe with specific reference to the Restraint of Trade*, M.Phil Thesis. (University of Coventry).

Moorhouse, H.F. (1991), 'On the Periphery: Scotland, Scottish Football and the New Europe' in *British Football and Social Change*, eds Williams, J. and Wagg, S. (London: Leicester University Press).

Moorhouse, H.F. (1994a), 'From Zines Like These? Fanzines, Tradition and Identity in Scottish Football' in *Scottish Sport in the Making of the Nation*, eds Jarvie, G. and Walker, G. (London: Leicester University Press).

Moorhouse, H.F. (1994b), 'The Economic Effects of the Transfer System in Professional Football in Scotland 1982–1991', *University of Glasgow Training and Research Unit Working Paper.*

Moorhouse, H.F. (1997), *Professional Players in Scotland Including the International Squad.* (University of Glasgow: Scottish Football Independent Review Commission).

Morris, P.E., Morrow, S. and Spink, P.M. (1996), 'EC Law and Professional Football: Bosman and its Implications', *Modern Law Review*, Vol. 59, No. 6, 893–902.

Morrow, S. (1987), *The Capital Structure of Scottish Football*, unpublished dissertation. (Heriot-Watt University, Edinburgh).

Morrow, S. (1996a), 'Football Players as Human Assets. Measurement as the Critical Factor in Asset Recognition: A Case Study Investigation', *Journal of Human Resource Costing and Accounting*, Vol. 1, No. 1, 75–97.

Morrow, S. (1996b), 'What Price Freedom? Implications for Scottish football of the Potential Abolition of the Transfer System', *Scottish Affairs*, No. 15, Spring, 83–100.

Morrow, S. (1997), 'Accounting for Football Players. Financial and Accounting Implications of *"Royal Club Liégois and Others versus Bosman"* for Football in the United Kingdom', *Journal of Human Resource Costing and Accounting*, Vol. 2, No. 1, 55–71.

Morrow, S. (1998), 'FRS 10 – Is it Time to Put Players Back on the Balance Sheet', *Soccer Analyst*, No. 9, 2–5.

Murray, B. (1984), *The Old Firm: Sectarianism, Sport and Society in Scotland.* (London: John Donald Publishers).

Murray, B. (1998), *The Old Firm in the New Age.* (Edinburgh: Mainstream).

Neale, W.C. (1964), 'The Peculiar Economics of Professional Sports', *Quarterly Journal of Economics*, Vol. 78, No. 1, 1–14.

Nichols, P. (1997), ed. *Radio Five Live Sports Yearbook 1997.* (Brighton: Oddball Publishing).

Noll, R. (1997), 'Competition Policy and Professional Sports: Beyond Labor Markets', *Paper presented at CIES conference on The Economic and Financial Consequences of the Transfer System, University of Neuchâtel, Switzerland,* October.

Peel, D.A. and Thomas, D.A. (1992), 'The Demand for Football: Some Evidence on Outcome Uncertainty', *Empirical Economics*, Vol. 17, 323–331.

Peel, D. and Thomas, D. (1996), 'Attendance Demand: An Investigation of Repeat Fixtures', *Applied Economics Letters*, Vol. 3, 391–394.

Perryman, M. (1998), *Football United: New Labour, The Task Force & The Future of the Game.* (London: Fabian Society).

Price Waterhouse (1997), *The Eighth Price Waterhouse Review of Scottish Football.* (Edinburgh: Price Waterhouse).

Quirk, J. and Fort, R.D. (1992), *Pay Dirt: The Business of Professional Team Sports.* (Princeton, New Jersey: Princeton University Press).

RICS (1995), *Appraisal and Valuation Manual.* (London: The Royal Institution of Chartered Surveyors).

Robinson, J. (1969), *The Accumulation of Capital.* (London: Macmillan St. Martin's Press).

Rothmans (1997), *Rothmans Football Yearbook 1997–98*, ed. Rollin, G. (London: Headline).

Rottenberg, S. (1956), 'The Baseball Player's Labour Market', *Journal of Political Economy*, Vol. 64, No. 3, 242–258.

Royal Commission on Gambling (1978), *Final Report – Cmd. 7200*. Chairman The Lord Rothschild. (London: HMSO).

Rowe, D. (1996), 'The Global Love Match: Sport and Television', *Media, Culture & Society*, Vol. 18, 565–582.

RSA (1995), *Tomorrow's Company: The Role of Business in a Changing World*. (London: The Royal Society for the Encouragement of Arts, Commerce and Manufactures).

Sadler, M. (1998), 'Rugby league puts a cap on pay', *The Financial Times*, 9 January.

SFL (1997), *The Scottish Football League Handbook 1997/98*. (Glasgow: The Scottish Football League Limited).

Simmons, R. (1996), 'The Demand for English League Football: A Club-Level Analysis', *Applied Economics*, Vol. 28, 139–155.

Simmons, R. (1997), 'Implications of the Bosman Ruling for Football Transfer Markets', *Economic Affairs*, Vol. 17, No. 5, 13–18.

Sloane, P. (1969), 'The Labour Market in Professional Football', *British Journal of Industrial Relations*, Vol. VIII, No. 2, 181–199.

Sloane, P. (1971), 'The Economics of Professional Football: The Football Club as a Utility Maximiser', *Scottish Journal of Political Economy*, June, 121–146.

Sloane, P. (1980), *Sport in the Market*, Hobart Paper Number 85. (London: Institute of Economic Affairs).

Smart, R.A. and Goddard, J.A. (1991), 'The Determinants of Standing and Seated Football Attendances: Evidence from Three Scottish League Clubs', *Quarterly Economic Commentary*, Vol. 16, No. 4, 61–64.

Smith, Sir John (1997), *Football – Its Values, Finances and Reputation*, Report to the Football Association by Sir John Smith.

SNCCFR (1997), *FA Premier League Fan Surveys 1996/97 General Sample Report*. (University of Leicester: Sir Norman Chester Centre for Football Research).

Soccer Analyst (1997), 'Making Money from Reserve Team Football', *Soccer Analyst*, No. 8, 10–11.

Soccer Investor (1997a), 'TV Rights', *Soccer Investor*, No. 2, 8.

Soccer Investor (1997b), 'Italy', *Soccer Investor*, No. 2, 8.

Soccer Investor (1997c), 'Scottish League Breakaway', *Soccer Investor*, No. 3, 7.

Stewart, G. (1986), 'The Retain and Transfer System: An Alternative Perspective', *Managerial Finance*, Vol. 12, No. 1, 25–29.

Sutherland, R.J. and Haworth, M. (1986), 'The Economics of the Industry', *Managerial Finance*, Vol. 12, No. 1, 1–5.

Szymanski, S. (1993), 'The Economics of Footballing Success', *Economic Review*, Vol. 10, No. 4, 14–18.

Szymanski, S. (1997), 'The Market for Soccer Players in England after Bosman: Winners and Losers', *Paper presented at CIES conference on The Economic and Financial Consequences of the Transfer System, University of Neuchâtel, Switzerland*, October.

Szymanski, S. (1998), 'April is the Cruellest Month', *Soccer Analyst*, No. 9, 5–8.

Szymanski, S. and Smith, R. (1997), 'The English Football Industry: Profit, Performance and Industrial Structure', *International Review of Applied Economics*, Vol. 11, No. 1, 135–153.

Thomas, D. (1996), 'Recent Developments in Sporting Labour Markets: Free Agency and New Slavery', *Review of Policy Issues*, Vol. 2, Pt. 2, 19–28.

Thwaites, D. (1995), 'Professional Football Sponsorship – Profitable or Profligate?', *International Journal of Advertising*, Vol. 14, 149–164.

Touche Ross (1993), *Survey of Football Club Accounts*. (Manchester: Touche Ross & Co).

Touche Ross (1994), *Survey of Football Club Accounts*. (Manchester: Touche Ross & Co).

Touche Ross (1995), *Survey of Football Club Accounts*. (Manchester: Touche Ross & Co).

Vamplew, W. (1982), 'The Economics of a Sports Industry: Scottish Gate-Money Football 1890–1914', *Economic History Review*, Vol. xxxv, No. 4, 549–567.

Walker, B. (1986), 'The Demand for Professional League Football and the Success of Football League Teams: Some City Size Effects', *Urban Studies*, Vol. 23, 209–219.

Webb, B.J. and Broadbent, J.M. (1986), 'Finance and Football Clubs: What Cash Flow Analysis Reveals', *Managerial Finance*, Vol. 12, No. 11, 6–10.

Williams, J. (1994), 'The Local and the Global in English Soccer and the Rise of Satellite Television', *Sociology of Sport Journal*, Vol. 11, 376–397.

Yadav, P.K. (1992), 'Event Studies Based on Volatility of Returns and Trading Volume: A Review', *British Accounting Review*, Vol. 24, No. 2, 157–184.

Zhang, J.J., Pease, D.G. and Smith, D.W. (1998), 'The Relationship Between Broadcasting Media and Minor League Hockey Game Attendance', *Journal of Sport Management*, Vol. 12, 103–122.

Index